CUBA

FROM REVOLUTION TO DEVELOPMENT

KEN COLE

PINTER

London and Washington

PINTER
A Cassell Imprint
Wellington House, 125 Strand, London WC2R 0BB, England
PO Box 605, Herndon, Virginia 20172, USA

First published 1998

British Library Cataloguing in Publication Data
A catalogue record for this book is available from the British Library.

ISBN 1 85567 502 1 (hardback)
     1 85567 554 4 (paperback)

Library of Congress Cataloging-in-Publication Data
Cole, Ken.
    Cuba : From revolution to development / Ken Cole.
        p.   cm.
    Includes bibliographical references (p.   ) and index.
    ISBN 1-85567-502-1 (hardcover). ISBN 1-85567-554-4 (pbk).
    1. Cuba—Economic policy. 2. Cuba—Economic conditions—1959–
I. Title
HC152.5.C64   1998
338.97291–dc21   97-30478
                                                                             CIP

Typeset by York House Typographic Ltd, London
Printed and bound in Great Britain by Biddles Ltd, Guildford and King's Lynn

CUBA

CONTENTS

PREFACE

The opportunity to write this book was an unforeseen consequence of a book I published in 1995, an economics textbook entitled *Understanding Economics* (Cole 1995). The argument of the book sought to understand the ideological implications of alternative economic analyses. Economic theory only has relevance in so far as it informs policy strategies, and therefore how it affects people's lives. Clearly the political pretensions of policy-makers influence the choice of economic perspective upon which policy is based. And it seems fairly obvious that to understand the relevance of economic (and therefore development) policy prescriptions, the student of economic and development theory has to be conscious of the political dimension of economic argument.

However, the economic 'mind' rarely acknowledges political bias. Economists prefer to see themselves above the political fray, as neutral, scientific observers of economic activity. As a consequence, 'orthodox' approaches to teaching economics as a 'science' are incapable of explaining why different political parties and movements, rationalizing priorities through a particular theoretical perspective, can coherently analyse essentially the *same* issue or problem, differently, arriving at distinct conclusions, which are compatible with the moral bases of their particular political programmes. Differences in economic policy are inexplicable, and often students are frustrated that after up to three years spent studying economics they still can't explain reports on policy initiatives in the press or on television! But many academic and professional economists are similarly at a loss to explain and understand debates between theorists working within the intellectual parameters of different theoretical perspectives: knowing without understanding.

Understanding Economics was a development of the analysis in *Why Economists Disagree* (Cole *et al.* 1983, 1991), and both John Cameron and Chris Edwards played an important part in my intellectual development in the late 1970s and early 1980s. Jointly, after debates among ourselves, trying to make sense of how we were taught economics and how we might teach economics to avoid the confusions we faced when experience did not match with theory, we developed an intellectual framework for making sense of economists' disagreements: theories of value. This has been extremely successful in our own teaching practice.

Understanding Economics went beyond *Why Economists Disagree*, and tried to ask: *why* do people find different intellectual perspectives (and therefore theories of value) more or less plausible? And I concluded that *all* intellectuals and scientists come to their work with a set of intuitive preconceptions: a set of beliefs, beliefs which define the assumptions upon which the theoretical analysis is based. Applying this approach to the understanding of development theory and strategy has been extremely productive in making explicit the implicit political and ideological bias in development programmes, and hence identifying who are likely to be the beneficiaries of apparently 'neutral' development strategies. This is the approach applied to the analysis of the Cuban development experience in this book.

With the collapse in trade with the Soviet bloc (1989–91), Cuba has had to adapt to the trade in the world market, and economists within Cuba have had to become more familiar with the theoretical justification of markets. In this regard, George Lambie of De Montfort University, Leicester, has been closely involved with the reform of the Cuban financial system, in particular with the development of a new tax regime and the introduction of European budgeting techniques. As part of this project he was looking for someone to deliver a course on the practical implications of different theoretical approaches to budgeting and economic management. My book *Understanding Economics* is deliberately written in such a comparative and contrasting style. Hence, through George the book became known in Cuba and its application to economic issues was highlighted.

Almost invariably, in one form or another, economic textbooks take as axiomatic the benign effect of free or managed markets, and my book argued that such opinions, while coherent, implied a political and ideological bias. The argument seemed relevant to the Cuban context, given the pressure on the Cuban authorities to embrace the 'market' and abandon such naïve and idealistic notions as justice and equality, and let the market be the arbiter of 'fairness'.

As a consequence, I was invited to give a short course at the Ministry of Finance and Prices in Havana, entitled Cuba, the Market, and Economic Theory. The course was given in February 1996, and the participants included senior economists from the National Bank, the Ministry of the Economy and Planning, and the Ministry of Finance and Prices.

While I have long had an interest in Cuba, until preparing this course I had not had the opportunity to study seriously the Cuban experience. Almost without exception, analyses of the Cuban economy conclude with the need for a liberalized market regime to achieve economic efficiency and development, but my 'intuitions' saw something more valuable in the Cuban experience than the achievement of a restricted definition of economic 'efficiency'. I decided to use Cuba as a 'case study' of the theoretical themes of *Understanding Economics*.

On return to the United Kingdom, in April 1996 I wrote a paper based on the research for the course offered in Havana, plus my conversations with Cubans, some of whom have become good friends, and my impressions of Havana, entitled 'Cuba: the options'. This paper was submitted to Pinter Publishers, and Petra Recter, one of the editors, after advice offered me a contract to write this book. So really, had *Understanding Economics* been published, say, six months later, George might never have seen that book, and I might never have had the chance to write this one. And my intellectual life would have been the poorer.

I would not have had the opportunity to study the Cuban enigma, or to meet so many committed, sincere and passionate Cubans, who showed me that a society based upon principles of social responsibility and human decency is not a fanciful illusion, but can be a viable basis for social and economic policy and development.

But apart from George Lambie, I owe a debt to all those people who have helped me to progress intellectually over the past 20 years, through teaching, writing and talking and arguing, with students, friends, colleagues and some enemies. More recently, new friends Max Azicri, Felix Masud and Jose Moreno have read the whole book in draft form, and their detailed knowledge of the Cuban experience has been invaluable to a new recruit to 'Cubanology'. And my conversations with my friends Gilberto Valdés and Humberto Miranda at the Instituto de Filosofia (Institute of Philosophy) in Havana have been crucial in helping me to get a 'feeling' for the reality of development for the majority of Cubans.

Ian Yaxley has also read the whole draft, and many people have expressed interest in the themes of particular chapters, all of whom have made constructive suggestions as to how to improve the argument. To all those who have read all, or part, of the work in progress, or argued with me about the significance of the Cuban development process, I gratefully acknowledge their help, advice and comments.

All remaining deficiencies are entirely my fault.

Ken Cole

ABBREVIATIONS

ANAP	Asociación Nacional de Agricultores Pequeños (Association of Small Farmers)
CAI	Complejos agro-industriales (agro-industrial complexes)
CAME	Consejo de Ayuda Mutua Económica (see CMEA)
CDR	Comité de Defensa de la Revolución (Committee for the Defence of the Revolution)
CIA	Central Intelligence Agency
CMEA	Council for Mutual Economic Assistance
COMECON	Council for Mutual Economic Aid
CPA	Cooperativas de producción agropecuaria (agricultural production cooperatives)
CTC	Confederación de Trabajadores de Cuba (Confederation of Cuban Workers)
EU	European Union
FAO	Food and Agricultural Organization of the United Nations
FAR	Fuerzas Armadas Revolutionarías (Revolutionary Armed Forces)
FEEM	Federación de Estudiantes de la Enseñanza Media (Federation of Secondary School Students)
FEU	Federación de Estudiantil Universitaria (Federation of University Students)
FMC	Federación de Mujeres Cubanas (Federation of Cuban Women)
GATT	General Agreement on Tariffs and Trade
GdelP	Granjas del pueblo (people's farms)
IBRD	International Bank for Reconstruction and Development (World Bank)
IEAPA	International Economic Association Partnership Agreements
IMF	International Monetary Fund
ITT	International Telephone and Telegraph Corporation
JUCEI	Juntas de Coordinación, Ejecución y Inspección (Local Government Council)
JUCEPLAN	Junta Central de Planificación (Central Planning Board)
LISAP	Low Input Sustainable Agriculture Programme
OECD	Organization for Economic Cooperation and Development
ONAT	Oficina Nacional de Adminstración Tributaria (National Tax Administration Office)

OPP	Organs of Popular Power
ORI	Organizaciones Revolutionarias Integrada (integrated revolutionary organizations)
PCC	Partido Comunista de Cuba (Communist Party of Cuba)
SDPE	Sistema de Dirección y Planificación de la Economía (System of Economic Direction and Planning)
UBPC	Unidades Básicas de Producción Cooperativa (Basic Units of Cooperative Production)
UJC	Unión de Jóvenes Comunistas (Union of Young Communists)
UN	United Nations
UNICEF	United Nations Children's Fund
UPC	Unión de Pioneros de Cuba (Pioneers Union)
WB	World Bank (IBRD)
WTO	World Trade Organization

FOR
ALEX AND JENNY

And for all my Cuban friends whom
they haven't been able to meet yet.

CHAPTER 1

THE CUBAN PREDICAMENT

ECONOMIC CRISIS AND ITS EFFECTS

When the Soviet Union still existed and the problems that have arisen in the Soviet Union hadn't appeared, we had solid bulwarks on which to depend and on which we have depended for the past 30 years. Now these solid bulwarks no longer exist. We are our own bulwark, together with all the people throughout the world who support our cause, admire our cause and admire our people's heroism and determination.
(Fidel Castro's opening address to the Fourth Congress of the Cuban Communist Party, 10 October 1991; Castro 1991a: 33)

In the 1990s, the policy challenges facing the Cuban government in the attempt to further the process of socialist development are unprecedented since Fulgencio Batista Zaldívar was deposed by the military forces of the 26th July Movement on 1 January 1959.

The collapse of the Eastern bloc of centrally planned communist states in 1989–91 (the economies of the Consejo de Ayuda Mutua Económica, CAME, or the English equivalent, the Council for Mutual Economic Assistance, CMEA, or COMECON, the Council for Mutual Economic Aid) seriously reduced economic links between Cuba and the CAME. Since trade was first constrained with the beginning of the US economic blockade on 6 July 1960, when the US Congress gave President Eisenhower authority to reduce the import quota for Cuban sugar by 700,000 tons, these links have been an economic lifeline. The demise of the CAME deprived Cuba of markets for exports, sources of imports and a trading relationship which, compared to the world market, was advantageous to Cuba: some 85 per cent of Cuba's trade had been within the CAME, 'under reasonable conditions, which contrasted with the unequal terms of trade between the developed and underdeveloped countries [in the world market]' (Fourth Party Congress 1991a: 132). Cuba was further deprived of overt development aid, and political and ideological support.

[The collapse of the Soviet-bloc] adversely affected us terribly in material terms, for ever since the triumph of our revolution we have received co-operation and solidarity from the Soviet Union and the rest of the socialist camp.
(Castro 1991a: 35)

Economic dependency on the CAME was the consequence of the US trade embargo, first formalized in 1963, although initiated earlier, when the

1917 Trading with the Enemy Act was applied to Cuba. The embargo has recently been exacerbated by the Cuban Democracy Act (Torricelli Bill) of 1992 and the Cuban Liberty and Solidarity Act (Helms–Burton Act) of 1996. According to Cuban statistics, the trade embargo has cost the island some US $450 million a year, a total of at least $15 billion in the thirty years since 1961 (see Ministry for Foreign Relations 1991: 1).

Within the CAME, international trade was based on a world technical division of labour within the communist bloc, with member states specializing in particular lines of production. The Cuban economy was essentially a sugar and nickel producer. The terms of trade were defined as a sophisticated form of 'barter', and 'goods essentially were compensated bilaterally by other goods' (Brunner 1977: 113). The prices of commodities, such as Soviet oil and Cuban sugar, were indexed, though increasingly towards the end of the 1980s trade was denominated in 'hard currency', at world market prices. The changed trading relationship cost Cuba dear. The slashing of sugar prices by $300 per ton in 1990, and the reduction in the quantity traded with the CAME from 469,000 tons to 55,000 tons (1990–1), cost Cuba more than $1 billion in purchasing power within the ex-CAME.

Cuba consistently ran a trading deficit within the CAME, which from 1980 to 1985 was the equivalent of $6 billion (see Pérez-López 1986: 21), which effectively became long-term debt. Up until the late 1980s, the Cuban economy did not have the impetus within the CAME to develop high-technology, high-productivity industries, essentially being a 'primary' goods producer (nickel and sugar). However, Cuba was protected from the vagaries of world market forces, which were increasingly operating to the detriment of poorer, 'primary goods' producing, developing economies.

From the beginning of 1987 in the Soviet press (*Moscow News*, *New Times*, *Sputnik*, *Literaturnaya Gazeta*, *Pravda*, *Izvestia*, *Komsomolskaya Pravda*) and on television news broadcasts (*Vremy*), there was increasing criticism of Cuba in general, and Fidel Castro in particular (see Mesa-Lago 1993a: 7). The economic effect of the political upheavals in Eastern Europe began to be apparent in 1989, and trade with Eastern Europe (not including the Soviet Union) was cut approximately in half. In January 1990, imports of grain and other animal feed stuffs began to lag. In the second half of 1990, deliveries of fuel oil were some 3.3 billion tons in deficit, forcing a drastic cutback in fuel consumption. This rapidly affected trade in general. During 1990 the crisis unfolded. Planned imports of a range of products never arrived: rice, split peas, edible fats, butter, canned meat, powdered milk, fertilizer (only 5 per cent of the 1.1 million tons of fertilizer were delivered), lumber, sulphur, caustic soda, wood pulp for paper, laminated steel for engineering, tin, detergents, soap, etc. (for a full list, see Castro 1991a: 40–53).

The effect was dramatic:

> Hospital equipment, without spare parts goes unrepaired. Medical doctors, lacking medicines, anxiously seek herbal cures. Newspapers and magazines are

in short supply: no paper. Lack of gas, batteries, and tires cripples buses, trucks, and cars. Stores, offices, and homes darken as electrical output falters. Cooking gas is available for only a few hours each morning and evening.

(Fitzgerald 1994: 1)

Between 1988 and 1993, the *Financial Times* (27 September 1994) reported there had been a total fall in imports from $8 billion to $1.7 billion – a decline of over 80 per cent. Crop yields fell for lack of imported fertilizers and weed killers. Shortages of fuel affected harvesting and closed factories. Food was in short supply, and children over seven years old were no longer guaranteed a litre of milk a day. Over 50,000 cases were diagnosed of nerve damage and vision loss, attributed to vitamin deficiencies. Television transmissions were limited to save energy and operating costs. Bus and train schedules were cut in half, and to relieve the burden on public transport, hundreds of thousands of bicycles were imported from China and distributed. Agriculture converted from tractor power to animal power in 'the largest scale conversion from conventional agriculture to organic or semi-organic farming in history' (Rosset and Benjamin 1994a: 34). The global social product of the Cuban economy (referring exclusively to 'productive' output, and therefore excluding private and public services such as education, health, culture, housing, passenger transportation, government administration and defence) declined by 3.1 per cent in 1990, then nose-dived to minus 25 per cent in 1991, and minus 14 per cent in 1992 (EIU 1993: 10).

Where Cuba had, in the past, negotiated with the Soviet state on trade, now, after *perestroika*, relations had to be with the separate republics, and contracts had to be made with over 25,000 separate enterprises (see Eckstein 1994). 'All told, the Cubans assessed the cost of the collapse of Soviet-bloc relations as $5.7bn in 1992. They lost 70% of their purchasing power in three years' (Eckstein 1994: 93). The privations resulting from the collapse of the CAME and Cuban trade led to the calling of a Special Period in Time of Peace in 1990 (discussed in Chapter 3), which included a 'zero option' contingency plan for the possible total isolation of the economy, with no imports being received.

The USA tried to capitalize on Cuba's economic dilemma and frustrate economic adjustment. The trade embargo initiated nearly 30 years earlier was tightened in 1991 by the Bush administration, when the US Treasury Department denied licences for trade to US subsidiaries in third countries, or firms trading products containing US components. German, Swedish, Japanese, Argentinian and French firms were affected. And the threat of exclusion from the US market by the US Treasury and the Department of Commerce affected Cuba's links with enterprizes in Brazil, Spain and Canada. In September 1991, the US Treasury Department announced tighter restrictions on remittances and travel to Cuba.

In November 1992, the economic 'blockade' became even tighter, with the passing of the Cuban Democracy Act (Torricelli Bill). The Bill included:

tightening the restrictions of travel to Cuba by US citizens; an authorization to finance dissident groups in Cuba; the seizure of any ship entering US waters within 180 days of docking in Cuba; the making illegal of foreign subsidiaries of US corporations trading with Cuba. Just before the collapse of the Soviet Union, Cuba was importing some $350 million worth of food from US corporations' foreign subsidiaries, and the last section of the Torricelli Bill was intended to stop the shortfall in food imports from the defunct CAME being made up by imports from US subsidiaries. In this regard the Bill was largely successful. In 1992, trade with US corporation subsidiaries was about $760 million, and in 1994 such trade was down to less than $10 million (see Pérez Villanueva and Marquetti Nodarse 1995: 35). This came to be known in Cuba as the 'double' blockade, between a one-time friend and an implacable foe: Moscow's betrayal and Washington's obsession.

> Not until 1993 ... did Cuba face the full and combined force of the collapse of Soviet-Bloc Communism and of the US economic blockade, newly strengthened by the malicious Cuban Democracy Act. In 1993, primarily because of this 'double blockade' and particularly destructive weather conditions, Cuban sugar production, which had averaged 7.5 million tons per year in the period from 1987 to 1991, dropped to a low 4.2 million tons. The country braced to earn hard currency sufficient to pay for little more than its planned imports of food and fuel; and the value of Cuba's total imports fell another 24 percent. By 1993, the Cuban revolution had entered the full depths of the crisis.
>
> (Fitzgerald 1994: 174)

However, the crisis deepened. In March 1996, the harshest ever package of measures against Cuba was approved by President Clinton: the Helms–Burton Cuban Liberty and Solidarity Act (which coincided with the Republican presidential primary elections in Florida, a state where the political influence of some 700,000 Cuban-Americans is pivotal). Originally presented to the US Senate by Senator Jesse Helms on 8 February 1995, a virtually identical bill was introduced into the House of Representatives by Congressman Dan Burton. The Act was drawn up in consultation with leading figures in the anti-Castro, conservative faction of the Cuban-American community. 'Indeed, one such individual has boasted to colleagues that his organization "wrote the bill" and handed it to Helms in virtually finished form' (Gunn Clissold 1997: 80).

The European Union, Canada, Russia, Mexico, Brazil and the CARICOM group of Caribbean countries protested that this bill was an illegal extension of US sovereignty beyond its own borders. Sir Leon Brittan, the European Union Trade Commissioner, described the legislation as a threat to Europe's legitimate trading relations with Cuba, and 'unacceptable, unjustified and unproductive' (reported in the *Guardian*, 19 February 1997). Apart from the Act cementing into law existing US restrictions on trade with and travel to Cuba, there were restrictions preventing any US President from relaxing sanctions as long as Fidel Castro remains in power.

Under Title 3 of the Act, the way was cleared for law suits in US courts against foreign firms dealing in Cuba. The Act allowed for Cuban-Americans to sue foreign companies accused of doing business on, with or through property confiscated by Castro's regime. This covered virtually all economic activity on the island.

There has been intense international opposition to this Act (see Brenner and Kornbluh 1995).

> Stuart Eizenstat, a former US ambassador to the EU and deputy commerce secretary, was dispatched to Europe and the Americas to calm the outrage of US allies at the prospect their business executives being excluded from the US or hauled into courts because their companies traded with Cuba.
>
> (*Guardian* 4 January 1997)

Mr Eizenstat was pelted with eggs when he arrived in Mexico on his first diplomatic shuttle mission, but it seems the US was unrepentant *vis-à-vis* Cuba. In November 1996, a newly created court established under the World Trade Organization (WTO) in Geneva, established specifically to resolve such trade disputes, agreed to hear a legal challenge from the European Union. The United States threatened to disregard any ruling from the WTO, the US ambassador, Booth Gardner, pointing out that the US did not 'believe that recourse to a WTO panel will lead to a resolution of this dispute ... [and] that proceeding further with this matter would pose serious risks for this new and invaluable organisation' (quoted in the *Guardian* 4 January 1997). However, because of the level and intensity of international criticism and opposition to the Act signed into law by President Clinton in March 1996, the clause allowing for legal action in the US was initially 'suspended' for six months in the following July. This temporary waiver was extended for a further six months in January 1997, well after the electoral victory in which President Clinton carried the state of Florida. On how the Helms–Burton Act has paradoxically worked against US economic interests, see Gunn Clissold (1997: 78–82).

The Cuban economy had to be rapidly reoriented towards trading on the world market, and a 'Special Period in Time of Peace' (Special Period) was announced in the daily newspaper *Granma* on 29 August 1990. The Special Period was based on contingency plans drawn up for the possibility of an embargo that cut off all imports when Ronald Reagan was US President. Carlos Lage, executive secretary of the Council of Ministers, took charge of economic policy, the Special Period being intended to put Cuba on to a stable economic footing in the light of the collapse of the CAME and the continuing American blockade (see Zimbalist 1992a).

Consumption was restricted overall, with a reversion to near-total food rationing to 'equalize sacrifice', and with restrictions on the use of oil and petroleum; there has been a concerted effort to achieve greater food self-sufficiency, with an emphasis on *agroponicas*, or community gardens, often on waste ground (by 1992 there were more than a million such gardens tended by families, neighbourhood groups, workers and students). To facilitate the reinsertion of Cuba into the world economy the state's monopoly of foreign trade was ended, and incentives were offered to attract foreign investment, with a guarantee on property rights and profit repatriation.

> We are analyzing all the forms of co-operation with foreign capital in many fields. They should be governed by one principle: if we have factories and a workforce but we don't have raw materials, we must put that factory into production ... There are variants of all kinds ... Naturally we have to make concessions, such as [in the tourist industry] exemption from profit tax for 10 years, but we share the profits ... both they and we recover our investment in three years ... We are very well aware of what we should reserve for our country.
>
> (Castro 1991a: 69–70)

This market opening, or *aperatura*, has not been confined to the external sector. Enterprise price subsidies have been reduced. Firms pay the 'real' price of goods purchased from abroad, although retail prices are still subsidized, again to 'equalize sacrifice'. And there are fewer restrictions on domestically organized private economic activity. Private, family-based, service work has been legalized, and the government has authorized private pig breeding in Havana province, although for consumption rather than sale.

The tightening of the US blockade under the 1992 Torricelli Bill and the 1996 Helms–Burton Act was intended, by making people's lives increasingly intolerable with reduced levels of consumption, to lead to hardship, unrest and, ultimately, open revolt. Attempts by the state to 'restore order' would lead to repression, costing the government its legitimacy and leading to the inevitable collapse of the Cuban 'totalitarian' state.

INTERPRETATIONS OF ECONOMIC CRISIS

The expected demise of Cuban socialism rested on an interpretation of human behaviour, based on the assumption that individuals are motivated to increase their own happiness selfishly, what economists call 'maximizing utility'. In the absence of free exchange, and when individuals' welfare cannot be guaranteed by the state, the implied social contract between the state and the populace breaks down, and 'so does the view that Cuban socialism has any future' (del Aguila 1994: 105). Consequently, 'The 1990–93 macroeconomic crisis in Cuba has arisen essentially as a result of the elimination of the subsidization of the Cuban economy' by the Soviet Union. (Ritter 1994: 69).

It was the trade and aid relationship within the CAME that allowed Fidel Castro to give the illusion of socialist 'development' and rising living standards, and to buy the political acquiescence of the Cuban people to satisfy his obsession with personal power. For orthodox, 'neo-liberal', free-market theorists, essentially the issue is one of maximizing utility. People's action is directed to fulfilling their own potentials and happiness through consumption, and is motivated by individuals' interests. The only rationale for seeking power is self-aggrandizement, a motivation held in check in 'advanced' societies by periodic, one-person-one-vote elections, in a mechanism of 'representative' democracy. This approach to development is discussed in detail in Chapter 5.

However, rather than understanding individuals to be selfishly motivated by 'hedonistic expediency', potentially being free to realize individual potentials, competing to satisfy their own preferences, we can understand individuals behaviour as being constrained by the need to cooperate to produce.

With economic development, and higher standards of living and greater efficiency in production, goes an extended technical division of labour. Individuals specialize in their economic activity, and do not produce what they consume. People depend on the economic 'system' as producers to earn an income, to buy products as consumers. Economic activity and development no longer reflect consumer satisfaction: the maximization of utility. Free consumer choice and demand in competitive markets is no longer the economic dynamic. Specialized productive activity, reflecting a technically defined division of labour, has to be coordinated. Free competitive markets are potentially disruptive of technical efficiency, periodically generating unemployed resources. Markets have to be managed to ensure full employment in the general interest, and not organized to fulfil individuals' private interests. The economic dynamic is now conceived of as the exigencies of technical cooperation between producers, to be managed by economists and planners.

Economic efficiency and rising standards of living reflect increasing economic specialization, an expansion of the technical division of labour in production, which concomitantly leads to an expansion of trading relations, as exchange between producers and consumers widens. Hence,

> The proximate cause of Cuba's present predicament is not hard to identify. Cuba has a small and heavily trade-dependent economy. In the presence of the US embargo, Cuba came to depend on the former Soviet trade bloc (CMEA) for over four-fifths of its imports. Without access to the US market, with access to other markets restricted and with imports from the former CMEA countries reduced by roughly two-thirds, Cuba's economy and its people are struggling to survive.
>
> (Zimbalist 1992a: 407)

The economic problem is not, fundamentally, limited to the sphere of consumption, but involves 'structural' obstacles to trade, and the efficient use and management of economic resources in production. A perspective on development is discussed in detail in Chapter 6.

Paradoxically, the neo-liberal emphasis on individuals' consumption and the 'structuralist' concern with technical dependence in production conclude in the need for the pricing mechanism in Cuba to be fundamentally reformed if there is to be economic growth and, potentially, social stability. But the emphasis is distinct.

The neo-liberal interpretation of economic activity is fundamentally concerned with the freedom of individuals to maximize utility (pleasure) in consumption. Since individuals' preferences for utility are subjective, they themselves must choose their consumption package. Economies can only be organized to satisfy the desires of millions of independent individuals if markets are 'free', and prices reflect the ebb and flow of consumer demand and producers' supply. The prices of commodities reflect the pleasure (utility) of individual consumers.

The economic performance of whole economies, the macroeconomy, is only a reflection of the economic choices made by individuals, the micro economy. Where 'free', individual, consumer choice, with market prices reflecting consumers' subjective preferences, does not obtain, individuals will be frustrated from maximizing utility, and the result will be unemployment, inflation and a slide into economic 'disequilibrium', evoking increased repression to maintain the political status quo.

Economic policy formulation is based on an ideal state known to economists as 'general equilibrium', where each individual simultaneously 'maximizes utility', reflecting conditions of 'perfect competition'. This theoretical potential is not meant to 'describe' any actual economy. Individuals are assumed to be 'endowed' with a unique set of tastes and talents, and 'perfect competition' is the image of utopia, where each individual would be free to fulfil his or her own potentials, subject only to subjective preferences. Economic policy is then determined by comparing this ideal, abstract model of utopia with actual society, with policy being intended to make the 'real' world more like the 'ideal'.

Alternatively, the structuralist interpretation of economic activity understands economies to be *systems* through which people cooperate to produce (not *mechanisms* in which individuals compete to consume and maximize utility). Individuals are not independent consumers, 'free' to choose, but dependent producers, who have to cooperate to produce. There is still a role for competition between producers as an incentive to be as efficient as possible, but only in so far as competition does not prejudice the wider, technical objective of the full employment of economic resources, an objective achieved through appropriate economic management.

Neo-liberal and structuralist theories offer alternative, intellectually coherent interpretations of the *same* economic experience. The resulting different theoretical explanations of the Cuban economic predicament are, potentially, equally coherent: both being based on logical analyses from assumptions to conclusions; both citing evidence to substantiate the analysis, and therefore claiming to represent the Cuban 'experience'. Yet the two perspectives arrive at distinct policy conclusions for addressing essentially the same problem (see Cole *et al.* 1991: Chapter 3; Cole 1995: Chapters 1, 2, 6 and 7).

THE BIAS OF ECONOMIC ANALYSIS

It is the intellectual project of this book to explain how the assumptions that underlie economic analyses define the understanding of the economic 'real world'. *Relations* of exchange between producers and consumers are *abstractions*, based on experience. We can see *what* people exchange, we can't see *why* people exchange: what is the *dynamic* of economic activity. It is this abstract reality of individuals motivation and the causation of economic phenomena, the intellectual parameters of the economic real world, which we have to try to understand if appropriate policies, intended to change people's economic activity and 'develop' society, are to be formulated.

We have to interpret theoretically why and how people respond to economic policy, in such a way as to 'make sense' of their economic experience. And there are potentially different rationales to economic activity, different intellectual real worlds, offering different policy options, generating different responses within people's economic activity. The process of economic development has 'intellectual parameters'. In the case of Cuba, I will show how this leads to particular strategies for, based on distinct analytical interpretations of, the central development issue that has dominated Cuban policy initiatives from 1959 to the present day (1998), almost 40 years: the reconciliation of the socialist ethics of national policy with the inexorable demands of international economic specialization.

Development, connoting higher standards of living, and/or more predictable and secure livelihoods, implies greater efficiency in production, which necessitates expanded international economic specialization: an expanding world division of labour.

Economic, productive specialization to achieve economic development is only possible within the context of expanded international exchange. And the concentration of economic resources into particular lines of production is crucial in determining the terms of exchange, and the standard of living of the population.

> With the exception of a few food, lumber and textile industries, Cuba continues to be a producer of raw materials. We export sugar to import candy, we export hides to import shoes, we export iron to import ploughs. Everybody agrees that the need to industrialize the country is urgent, that we need steel industries, paper and chemical industries, that we must improve cattle and grain production.
>
> (Castro 1967: 47)

These words, from his famous 1953 speech 'History Will Absolve Me', were delivered in his defence at his trial after the failed attempt by 125 armed militants to attack the Moncada garrison in Santiago de Cuba. Castro had thought that the taking of Santiago would presage a spontaneous rising throughout Cuba against the corrupt Batista regime. Although the need to industrialize to develop is baldly stated, there is no hint of the complex national and international economic and political implications that have dominated Cuban socialist politics ever since.

Investment resources intended for industrial (secondary) development come, at least initially, from agricultural and raw material (primary) production. These competing uses for economic resources are, at the same time, complementary, mutually dependent activities. But each requires the administrative, labour and other resources that are in short supply. This conflict is as much social and political as economic. The contradiction is between industry and agriculture, town and country, and the national economy and the international market, as well as socialist ethical principles and international economic vicissitudes.

The assumptions upon which any economic analysis is based, the intellectual parameters of the economy, imply a distinct rationale to economic activity, and a bias in the explanation of economic activity, directing the analysis towards specific conclusions and policy prescriptions, prescriptions which have moral, ideological and political implications.

Consequently, if we are to understand Cuban economic priorities and development strategies, it is necessary to situate policy initiatives in a theoretical context, highlighting the moral imperatives that give meaning and significance to explanations: that is, the policy debate and the parameters within which the 'real world' is defined and interpreted. Failure to define these theoretical terms of reference means that the logic and implications of policy initiatives cannot be understood.

For instance, Susan Eckstein (1994) believes that there are economic imperatives that are independent of political interest. Economic analysis is potentially ideologically neutral: theoretical analysis is not contingent upon underlying assumptions. The real world is obvious. Essentially the economic dynamic is assumed to be independent individuals' drive to maximize utility (i.e. be 'happy'). This is an economic imperative contingent upon 'free' markets. Consequently, when the political objectives of Fidel Castro have conflicted with this economic 'reality', the resultant policy prescriptions have had to be ideologically disguised, to hide and justify ulterior political motives, denying individual Cubans freedom of choice in order to maintain Fidel Castro in power. In this interpretation, Cuba is essentially an anachronistic, repressive, Caribbean outpost of the now-defunct Soviet totalitarian empire. And the march of history will inevitably be towards individual freedom and economic liberalization.

Referring to the policy change after 1986, the Rectification of Errors and Negative Tendencies (the 'Rectification Campaign', discussed in detail in Chapter 3), Eckstein writes: 'there were "underlying" economic reasons for reforms rooted in the domestically orientated economy that the state justified *ideologically*, in the name of "rectification"' (Eckstein 1994: 77, emphasis added). In such a scenario Cuba is held together only by Fidel Castro's belligerence and charisma, which he uses to manipulate the Cuban population in order to hold on to personal power. 'He understands the need for change, but his heart is with the hard-liners' (Wayne Smith, former head of the US Interests Section, quoted in *Time* 19 September 1994).

However, within a structuralist theoretical perspective, Cuba is not inevitably destined to be 'liberalized' as economic 'reality' constrains policy alternatives. Instead, the future will be determined by the coordination of different economic interests, including foreign capital, in the reconciliation of the Cuban economy to the vicissitudes of the world market. These are the international economic priorities which have shaped the Special Period.

For yet other theorists, Cuban economic policy has a logic which defies the 'inevitable' move towards a free enterprise, capitalist economy; or an economy managed in response to international economic pressures. The economy cannot be understood distinct from the political imperatives of economic organization. In a different interpretation of the Rectification Campaign from that of Susan Eckstein, the Campaign was (and is) a political reaction to the social trends engendered by the system of economic planning prevalent in the late 1970s and early 1980s.

> From 1976 on, a system of economic management was introduced whose basic elements were copied from other socialist countries ... which involved an excessive appeal to personal income and to financial gain ... [leading to] an alienation of consciousness and a considerable deterioration of ideology ... The active and conscious participation of the masses and their enormous potential for developing the country was practically ignored.
>
> (Fourth Party Congress 1991d: 102)

Fundamental to the Rectification Campaign is the reassertion of ideology, the articulation of economic activity and political participation, and the conscious organization of economic activity to fulfil social objectives.

In this theoretical context the problem is not seen as the absence of 'free exchange' or 'inappropriate economic management', but not 'enough participation' and socialist democracy.

> Decisive as the revolution has been ... it has not produced an effective system of participation ... With respect to the deficiencies of the existing regime, the debates and the preoccupations with it reflect a need not to replace the regime but to improve it by deepening its ideals and its socialist project.
>
> (Heredia 1993: 75–6)

Development, economic policy and institutional change in Cuba have evolved as a process in the attempt to build a more 'just' social order. Cuban socialist development can only be explained, and prospective policy initiatives understood, if the moral convictions and principles that propelled the 1959 victory over Batista are placed in the context of unabated US hostility and the economic blockade, the period of economic dependency on the CAME, the 1986 Rectification Campaign, the collapse of the Soviet bloc, the tightening of the US economic blockade and the post-1990 Special Period.

Economic exigencies may 'constrain' policy initiatives, but they do not *determine* development priorities. As an interpretation of development, this perspective will be addressed in detail in Chapter 7.

Alternative theoretical interpretations of economic development rationalize and legitimize alternative policy strategies. This book, while seeking to understand the policy options for development in Cuba, also addresses the potential for reconciling the ethics of socialist development with the economic imperatives of doing business on the world market, according to capitalist criteria and priorities.

CHAPTER 2

THE REVOLUTIONARY IMPERATIVE

THE ACHIEVEMENT

The Cuban revolution declared, from the outset, that no one should go malnourished. No disappointment in food production, no failed economic take-off, no shock wave from the world economic crisis has deterred Cuba from freeing itself from the suffering and shame of a single wasted child or an elderly person ignominiously subsisting on petfood. No other country in this hemisphere, including the United States, can make this claim.

(Benjamin *et al.*, 1994: 189)

Such is the ethical basis of Cuban development policy since 1959. Moral principles have explicitly informed policy choices, and the ebb and flow of development strategy has reflected the reconciliation of these principles to the exigencies of the world economy. The 'umbilical cord' of international exchange, based on the sugar industry, redefined national economic priorities.

Fulfilling Cuban's social potentials has been a priority, with particular attention to health care and education provision: 'they have been spectacularly successful and astonishingly innovative in the . . . areas of health and education' (MacDonald 1995: 3). For revolutionary Cuba, health welfare is a basic human right. The year 1962 saw the first mass vaccination campaign; the last vestiges of private health care were incorporated into the Ministry of Public Health in 1967; 'Health in the Community' policy initiatives were in train in 1975; and the 'Family Doctor Programme', where a doctor and nurse team live in the middle of a community and serve about 140 families (700 people), was initiated in 1984 (see Waller 1993: 6). By 1989 the population per physician ratio had improved from 1038 in 1960 to 303, the population per nurse ratio had improved from 1199 in 1960 to 183 and the population per hospital bed had improved from 216 in 1960 to 136 (see Eckstein 1994: 225). There is an extensive network of health care in both rural and urban areas. Concomitantly, life expectancy increased from 64 years in 1960 to 75 years in 1990, and infant mortality per 1000 live births in the first year of life improved from 35 in 1960 to 11 in 1990 (see Eckstein 1994: 226), falling to 7.9 in 1996. 'Cuba now finds itself among the 20 countries with the lowest infant mortality' (de la Osa 1997: 3). This is to be compared to an average life expectancy in the late 1950s of between 55 and 62 years, with infant mortality of 70 per 1000 live births. Conditions in rural areas were often worse: in 1957 up to 14 per cent of the rural population suffered from tuberculosis, 13 per cent from typhoid, 31 per cent malaria and 36 per cent from intestinal parasites (see Guevara 1996: 155).

However, health welfare is achieved by more than just the provision of a health service infrastructure. More generally, it is a consequence of policies aimed at fulfilling each person's potential: full employment, decent housing, the provision of running water and adequate sewage facilities and minimum nutritional standards. In Cuba, hunger and homelessness have been abolished, albeit that, in the Special Period (since 1991), almost universal rationing has been necessary to equalize dietary consumption. However, even after the economic crisis and austerity measures of the Rectification Campaign of 1986 and the Special Period, allocation of resources to social services has actually increased.

> On the launching of the Rectification Campaign Castro proudly asserted ' ... we do not take such measures as leaving senior citizens without help, reducing pensions for retired people, giving less medical care to the sick, or less resources to hospitals or schools; we do not sacrifice our social programmes.'
>
> (Azicri 1988: 153)

Investment in the health service continued apace. By the end of the 1980s, Cuba manufactured over 200 biomedical products, 900 drugs, medical equipment and software. Vaccines and treatments, including micro surgery, were offered that few other countries could match. By the end of 1996 over 90 heart transplants had been carried out, with three of the recipients celebrating the tenth anniversary of their operations in 1996. 'Cuba is the only country in the Third World that has a heart transplant program ... An operation of this kind can cost 300,000 dollars in other countries, but in Cuba it is free of charge' (Valencia Almeida 1997: 2).

In the Special Period, with the reduction in medical imports, emphasis has shifted towards herbal medicines. However, in the midst of the Special Period, in 1992, Fidel Castro could still confidently assert that:

> I am certain ... there will be no product in the universal pharmacopoeia that we won't be able to produce, nor will there be any international medical equipment that we will not be able to produce besides the new products we'll be able to create.
>
> (Castro 1992)

However, more generally since 1959, there have been spectacular improvements in the standard of living for the majority of Cubans. The average daily calorific intake between 1970 and 1984 increased from 2565 to 2963; from 1970 to 1984, agricultural production rose by 27 per cent and industrial production by 80 per cent; the GDP rate of growth between 1972 and 1981 was 7.8 per cent per annum, and GDP/capita growth was 6.5 per cent (see Fitzgerald 1994: 125). A United Nations Economic Commission for Latin America report (cited by G. Reed 1992: 11) estimates that GDP in Cuba grew by 33.5 per cent between 1980 and 1988, while for the Latin American region as a whole there was a decline of 8.3 per cent.

With regard to social policy, before the revolution of 1959, only

63 per cent of the labour force were insured for old age and disability pension, and there was no health insurance or unemployment compensation. By 1963, old age and disability pensions applied to all in a non-contributory scheme, and the 1979 law tied pensions to up to 90 per cent of salary (see Eckstein 1994: 141). Health care and unemployment provision became universal, with unemployment benefit up to 70 per cent of salary (see Mesa-Lago 1981a: 169–70). The massive literacy campaign of 1961 increased the number of literates by 707,000, and illiteracy was reduced to 4 to 5 per cent. Between 1960 and 1988, the student : teacher ratio in primary schools fell from 36 to 12, at a time when the number of pupils doubled, and in secondary schools from 19 to 11 (see del Aguila 1994: 77). In 1991 there were 300,000 teachers in the country, the 'highest per capita rate of teachers in the world' (Castro 1991a: 78).

> 20 percent of all workers are in education and public health. The educational level attained by the average Cuban worker is tenth grade ... One in every fifteen employees has a university degree and one in every eight is a technician.
>
> (Figueros and Vidal 1994: 110)

Education is not a privilege, and all private education has been abolished, the state assuming responsibility from kindergarten to university.

The greatest social need has been in rural areas, and to address rural/ urban inequality, there has been substantial investment in rural education and health needs. With the first Land Reform Act of 17 May 1959, the first Act of the revolution, individual land holdings were limited to 30 *caballerías* (approximately 1000 acres), and share-croppers, tenant farmers and squatters were granted legal title to the land they tilled. Rural unemployment was effectively ended. Land ownership was further restricted in 1963 to about 165 acres. Although, subsequently, there was an emphasis on large state farms, small farmers were not coerced to collectivize, although many did, to benefit from the schools, houses and guaranteed income provided by the state (see Benjamin *et al.*, 1994: 65).

While Cuba, compared to the rest of Latin America, does not have the highest GNP per capita, it has almost the highest level of adult literacy (only surpassed by Argentina), the highest 'mean years of schooling', the highest life expectancy, the lowest level of child (under-5) mortality, the lowest ratio of population per doctor, etc. (see UNDP 1994; cited in NACLA 1995: xx).

Pre-1959, Cuba was considered to have one of the higher per capita incomes of Latin America, with, in 1950, GDP per capita standing at US$450, 60 per cent of that of Argentina and Uruguay, slightly lower than Chile and Venezuela, and higher than Mexico, Panama and Costa Rica (see Bulmer-Thomas 1996a). However, the poorest 40 per cent of the population received only some 0.066 per cent of income. By the mid-1970s this had improved to 25 per cent (see Barraclough 1996: 15).

In Mexico in 1992, the poorest 40 per cent of the population shared only

4.16 per cent of national income (see Scott 1996: 151), and between 1980 and 1992 the urban real minimum wage has declined by over 50 per cent in Argentina, Ecuador, El Salvador, Guatemala, Mexico and Peru (see Thomas 1996: 90). In Cuba, 'the income of those with the highest earnings is around four times higher than those with the lowest earnings' (Lage 1996: 5). People with access to US dollars and/or active in the comparatively small free market may earn substantially more. As Francisco León points out, the shortages and austerity of the Special Period have meant limited state coordination of economic activity, and on 8 September 1993 the government authorized self-employment in more than a hundred occupations, 'where the opportunity existed to earn ten, fifteen or even twenty times more than a university educated state employee' (León 1997: 44). Presently there exist in excess of 200,000 licences for self-employment, with earnings being curbed by new income tax regulations. In comparison, in 1990 in Brazil the difference was 62 times (see Ferreira and Litchfield 1996: 254).

While Cuba is addressing the exigencies of the international economic order without sacrificing the socialist, collective principles of the revolution, the norm in the rest of Latin America is a move towards individual responsibility and market rationality. Although it is theorized as the 'new economic model in Latin America' (see Bulmer-Thomas 1996a), there is in fact nothing 'new' about it. It is a return to nineteenth-century, economic liberalism, the moral expediency for which is 'individual freedom' (see Lal 1983: 1–5). The 'liberating' effect of this has been increased poverty, inequality, unemployment and falling real wages (see Weeks 1996: 300), and all this from an appalling base line: 'in 1980 an estimated 41 per cent of the population [of Latin America] lived in poverty, with nearly half (19 per cent of the total) living in extreme poverty' (Bulmer-Thomas 1996b: 7).

In the rest of the developing world, the international debt crisis has precluded the expansion, and even maintenance, of social provision and expenditure, and measures to offset the falling rate of profit in the developed market economies have included cutting the welfare state and privatizing social services. Invariably the effect is worsening inequality. On the trend towards spiralling inequality, both within nation states and internationally, see Robinson (1996: 339–46) and Braun (1991). Cuba, in contrast, has increased social service expenditure, and even during the austerity of the Special Period, exacerbated by an ever tightening US-sponsored economic blockade, public health expenditure has increased. Cuba ranks among the top nations in the world in terms of per capita health, education, social security, employment and daily consumption of calories, and income equality.

The ethically based responsibilities of the Cuban state extend beyond the shores of the island: 'Unresolved social, economic, and political problems at home never kept Castro from extending aid to other Third World countries ... Cuban internationalism ... [is] *morally inspired* by the revolution' (Eckstein 1994: 171, emphasis added). According to Che Guevara:

There can be no socialism without a transformation of consciousness leading to a growth in fraternal feeling, not only among socialist societies moving into socialism, but also internationally, toward all people suffering from imperialist oppression.

(Quoted in Karol 1970: 334)

Edith Felipe, a Cuban economist, estimates that by 1989 the US dollar value of Cuban aid donations to other developing nations was $1537.2 million (see Felipe 1992: 16). Civilian aid workers have constructed roads, schools, hospitals, agricultural complexes (especially for sugar, chicken and beef production), transport infrastructure, irrigation and industry, as well as planning expertise and communications know-how in radio and television, education and medical aid. In the medical field alone, by 1990, 30,000 medical personnel (doctors, nurses, etc.) had worked in over 20 countries and treated over 60,000,000 people (see Eckstein 1994: Chapter 7). At its peak, 'Cuba came to have more doctors abroad than the World Health Organization' (Eckstein 1994: 176).

Aid has never been restricted to politically sympathetic countries, having been provided to Ecuador and Venezuela, and to Nicaragua *after* the Sandinistas were voted out of office. To put Cuba's commitment to international aid in context, between 1982 and 1985, for every 625 Cubans there was one civilian aid worker overseas; in the United States the ratio was one worker per 34,704 inhabitants (see Eckstein 1994: 175). During the Special Period, Cuba has not only maintained the international aid programme but expanded it.

Fulfilling our internationalists duties, Cuban scientists, doctors, engineers, agronomists, teachers and researchers now work in 32 countries, bringing Cuba's technology and experience to our brothers and sisters in Africa, Asia and Latin America. More than 2000 doctors and medical workers share the responsibility of improving health standards in the underdeveloped world. At the same time, tens of thousands of students from Africa, Asia, the Middle East and Latin America have either graduated from or are presently studying in schools on the Isle of Youth and in Cuban technological schools and universities. For Cuba their training is a revolutionary duty of solidarity and a genuine source of satisfaction.

(Fourth Party Congress 1991b: 145)

Which prompts Fidel Castro to ask how socialism in Cuba can be portrayed as a failure, a society with no future (see Castro 1989).

THE AFTERMATH OF THE REVOLUTION

Capitalism sacrifices the human being, communism with its totalitarian conceptions sacrifices human rights. We agree neither with one nor the other ... Our revolution is not red but olive green. It bears the colour of the rebel army from the Sierra Maestra.

(Castro 21 May 1959, quoted in Binns and González 1980: 13)

The armed struggle culminated in the revolutionary overthrow of Fulgencio Batista on 1 January 1959, when Batista fled, handing over power to General Eulogio Cantillo. 'His grisly tenure of corruption, torture and disappearances ended – 20,000 lives later – when he hopped on a private plane to Santo Domingo (and later Miami) on New Year's Eve, 1958' (G. Reed 1992: 13). Next day, Fidel Castro, in a radio broadcast from near Santiago de Cuba, called for a general strike, which paralysed the island. The main rebel army entered Havana on 8 January, and Castro was appointed prime minister on 13 February (for a detailed account of this period, see Castro 1989b: 39–58; Franklin 1992: 24–5).

The struggle began on 26 July 1953, when Castro led a group of fewer than 200 in an attack on the Moncada army barracks in Santiago de Cuba. The operation was a failure, with half the rebels killed and the rest imprisoned, most of whom were tortured. The movement, subsequently victorious five and a half years later, came to be known as the '26th July Movement' (for details of the 1953–9 period see, Guevara 1996: 54–9).

New Year's Day 1959 marked more than just the victory of the 26th July Movement. Henceforth, the ethical basis of development policy was directed towards the fulfilment of everyone's potential, not just the rich and powerful's (on the immediate precursors to the revolutionary victory, see Eckstein 1994: 14–19). Peasants, the critical base of Castro's support, were not motivated by ideology, but by the prospect of improving their life situation. Support was not *for* national liberation or socialism, but *against* the injustice, exploitation, uncertainties and rigours of rural life. Before 1959, in the nine months between sugar harvests, 600,000 of one and a half million workers were unemployed; fewer than 0.1 per cent of landowners held 20 per cent of the land, and 8 per cent controlled 70 per cent; over 40 per cent of the rural population were illiterate; fewer than 10 per cent of rural homes had electricity, and only 3 per cent running water and sewage; malnutrition was widespread and there were only three general hospitals in the countryside (see Nelson 1950; MacGaffey and Barnett 1965; Eckstein 1994: Chapter 1).

But Cuba was in America's 'backyard'. In pre-revolutionary Cuba, over 90 per cent of the telephone and electricity supplies, half the public service railways, a quarter of all bank deposits, about 40 per cent of sugar production and 23 per cent of non-sugar economic activity, including mining, oil production and cattle-ranching, was in the hands of United States businessmen (see Blackburn 1963; Cannon 1981: 55).

The United States had had a history of intervening in Cuban politics to ensure that its interests were protected and served. 'America likes its neighbours biddable and quiet; Cuba, with wars, coups and corrupt governments, has always made a nuisance of itself' (*Economist* 1996). In the nineteenth century, as the Cuban nationalist struggle for independence from Spain neared victory, and after decades of United States–Spanish rivalry over the future of Cuba, on the destruction of the battleship

USS *Maine* in Havana harbour on 14 February 1898 the US militarily intervened – although not until Spain had offered to sell Cuba to the USA for $300 million. War was declared on 25 April, and ended in August, after a few skirmishes in Oriente Province and the destruction of the Spanish fleet. On 10 December, Spain and the United States signed the Paris Peace Treaty, whereby Spain renounced sovereignty over Cuba, Puerto Rico and the Philippines. The island was officially occupied on 1 January 1899, the Americans only leaving on 20 May 1902, after the Platt Amendment, drafted in Washington and approved by the US Congress in 1901, was incorporated into the Cuban constitution, giving the United States the 'right' to intervene to preserve 'individual liberty' in Cuba, and the Cuban government the obligation to 'sell or lease to the United States land necessary for coaling or naval stations at certain specified points, to be agreed with the President of the United States' (Article VII of the Platt Amendment, cited by Ricardo 1994: 48).

Consequently, in 1903, 'independent' Cuba *had* to grant Guantánamo Bay to the USA to build a naval base, which to this day is still under US control; 47 square miles of Cuban territory, sealed behind a chain-link fence and a double set of minefields. This is despite Article I of the Amendment, which precluded 'any foreign power or powers to obtain ... for military or naval purposes ... control over any portion of the said island [Cuba]' (Ricardo 1994: 47). Since 1959, the $4000 yearly rental cheques have never been cashed, as a point of principle. On Cuban nationalism see Montaner (1985: Chapter 2).

Until 1959, Cuban politics was characterized by massive corruption and fraudulent elections, associated with authoritarian and repressive political administrations, and successive military occupations by the USA. The overwhelming predominance of US economic interests, in alliance with Cuban politicians, stifled the emergence of a domestic bourgeoisie and the development of an independent Cuban nation state.

Given this historical dependency relationship, when on 3 March 1959 the Cuban Telephone Company, a subsidiary of the American corporation the International Telephone and Telegraph Corporation (ITT), was nationalized, and rates were cut, US reaction was swift. On 10 March the US National Security Council met to consider how to put another government in power in Cuba.

In March 1959 housing rents were reduced by up to 50 per cent and the prices of medicines were reduced; and in April gambling casinos, many of which were owned by US interests, were confiscated, and private beaches made public. The 17 May 1959 Agrarian Reform Law (mentioned above) went into effect on 11 June, and inevitably exacerbated conflict with the US government, with the confiscation of vast estates, mainly owned by US companies, five of which owned more than two million acres (see Franklin 1992: 26). The nationalization of foreign property was in line with the 1940 constitution, reinstated on 6 February 1959 after it had been suspended by

Batista's coup in 1952, and 'included the indemnification of those lands [confiscated]; it was not intended to be a nationalization without compensation' (Blanco and Benjamin 1994: 14). Indeed, compensation agreements for nationalized properties were subsequently negotiated at government level with Switzerland, France, Great Britain, Italy, Canada, Mexico and Spain (see Lage 1996: 7).

Compensation to US interests was to have been in 20-year government bonds at 4.5 per cent per annum interest, a higher rate than that paid by US corporate bonds, with valuation based on the value of the land as declared for tax purposes to the Cuban government. However, these values, and the tax liability, had not been adjusted for 30 or 40 years. The US government rejected these terms in June 1959 (on the offer of compensation for nationalization, see Molina 1996). The nationalization of US assets 'without compensation' became the rationale for US hostility, which began with the bombing of sugar mills in Pinar del Rió and Camagüey provinces in October 1959. On 17 March 1960 President Eisenhower ordered the CIA director Allen Dulles to organize and train Cuban exiles for an invasion, ending in the Bay of Pigs (Playa Girón) fiasco of 16 April 1961, when US backed forces were routed by the Cuban army and popular militias within 72 hours. President Eisenhower said he began planning the invasion of Cuba just three months after the revolutionaries came to power in 1959.

It was not until the Bay of Pigs invasion that the Cuban revolution declared itself to be 'socialist'. 'The problem of the Cuban revolution is not so much that it became a communist revolution but that it proclaimed from the very beginning that it was going to take an independent path from that of the United States' (Blanco and Benjamin 1994: 14). It was the United States that rejected the terms of compensation, even though the nationalizations were in line with international law and practice, and in accordance with the provisions of the 1940 Constitution in force at that time. That US owners of property were never compensated has been used to justify the trade embargo, formalized under the 1917 Trading with the Enemy Act, which was applied to Cuba in 1963, and escalating to an economic blockade with the Torricelli Bill of 1992 and the Helms–Burton Cuban Democracy Act of 1996.

On the confiscation of the first 70,000 acres of land owned by US sugar companies in January 1960, President Eisenhower sought authority to cut Cuba's sugar quota to the United States, which went into effect in July. Four days later the Soviet Union agreed to buy 700,000 tons of sugar that the US refused to purchase. And later in July, China agreed to buy 500,000 tons of sugar for five years at world market prices.

In May 1960, US owned oil refineries in Cuba were asked to refine a consignment of oil from the Soviet Union, the result of a trade agreement with Soviet Foreign Minister Anastas Mikoyan, who visited Cuba in February 1960. This trade agreement, exchanging Soviet oil, petroleum, wheat, fertilizer and machinery for Cuban sugar, included $100 million credit at

2.5 per cent interest. On the refusal of the refineries to handle Soviet oil, they were nationalized on 5 July 1960. The Soviet trade deal, by itself, 'did not determine the shift to socialism [formal Soviet–Cuban diplomatic relations were not restored until May 1960] but it was a major economic and political turning point for the revolution' (Domínguez 1978: 146).

The ethics of the Cuban revolution were intended to broaden the fulfilment of Cuba's potentials. They were based as much on the nationalism of José Martí, a nineteenth-century anti-Spanish colonial revolutionary, as on Marx's class-based analysis of capitalism, and geared towards a just society free of racism, foreign domination and the political dominance of propertied interests.

> What would remain of the dignity and honor of every man and woman in this country [without socialism]? . . . the first thing Martí talked about was the dignity of human beings . . . the specific nature of the Cuban Revolution . . . consists of the fusion of José Martí's radical thinking and a singular tradition of struggle for national and social liberation . . . We must ensure the principles of Marx and Martí endure.
>
> (Castro, quoted in G. Reed 1992: 78, 89, 158)

The Cuban revolution has been characterized by voluntarism, rather than determinate, authoritarian control; egalitarianism, rather than privilege for the powerful; ruralism, rather than the urban bias of industrial development; and humanist principles emphasizing the subjective fulfilment of individuals' potentials, rather than the dogmatic assertion of 'objective' class interest.

For the leadership,

> social, cultural, organizational and ethnic schisms are in some sense 'unnatural', the product of an imperfect past and a still imperfect revolutionary experience. This egalitarianism and ruralism . . . blur class lines without ever coming to grips theoretically with the 'class problem'.
>
> (Fagen 1989: 56)

The emphasis is upon *Cubanidad* (Cubanness). 'The Cuban people . . . have achieved . . . national independence . . . They enjoy a personal dignity that has always been denied them. For the first time, Cubans are masters of their own country' (Castro, quoted in Taber 1985: 132). On the influence of Martí on Castro's thinking and the course of the Cuban revolution, see Liss (1994: Chapters 3 and 4).

For Castro, the Cuban revolution contradicts the Marxist-Leninist dogma that revolutions only succeed if the appropriate 'objective' conditions prevail. Rather, the task of the revolution is subjectively to 'create' these conditions, in particular through education, ideology and the development of social and political consciousness. Eliminating 'individualism' is not to deny the rights of the 'individual'. The revolutionary 'spirit' is not denied, which is the antithesis of the authoritarian central control, of the ex-Soviet Union (see Antonio Mella 1975: 35).

Following Gramsci, 'revolution' is the process of constructing the 'objective' and 'subjective' conditions for the transformation of society: the 'subjects' (people) produce the 'objective'. The revolutionary process is *more than* the overthrow of Batista, and in creating the conditions for change a degree of benign paternalism is implied. It is Castro's stated objective that 'the present generation of Cubans must consolidate the revolution and make it depend less on him' (Liss 1994: 62).

The 26th July Movement came to power with an army of only about 3000, without a party structure, without a coherent development policy or articulated ideology, and 'shared with the rest of Cuba a general antipathy toward communism' (Bengelsdorf 1994: 77). But as a consequence of US hostility to government policy, the revolution became explicitly anti-capitalist. Even so, progress and prosperity in Cuba was seen to depend crucially upon the capitalist nature of the world economy, which had to be addressed. Cuba's move towards the Soviet camp was reluctant. Documents released in the United States in April 1996 indicate that on 17 August 1961, four months after the failed US-sponsored Bay of Pigs invasion, Che Guevara, in Uruguay, told Richard Goodwin, US President Kennedy's Assistant Special Council, that Cuba would forgo an alliance with the Soviet Union, compensate US owners of confiscated properties and curb Cuban support for left-wing insurgents in third countries if the United States would cease hostile actions (see the *Guardian*, 30 April 1996).

The USA continued to sponsor armed counter-revolutionary movements, air-attacks, attempts to assassinate Fidel Castro and the sabotage of economic installations, enforced a near total embargo on commerce and trade between the USA and Cuba, and interfered with Cuba's diplomatic and commercial relations with the rest of the world. Ties with Eastern Europe and Soviet Union became progressively closer.

US policy was based on the apparent belief that 'economic pressures and external and internal discontent' (Sigmund 1980: 106) would overwhelm the regime. But in Cuba, with a strongly anti-communist society in 1958/9, socialism came to be seen as the only alternative to the kind of relations with the USA that it had been subjected to before the revolution. Free enterprise was synonymous with corruption, unemployment, slums and impoverishment. 'So thanks to the United States, the Cuban people entered into a very quick and dialectical process of education' (Blanco and Benjamin 1994: 15).

Pre-revolutionary economic dependency on the USA was all pervading. In 1959, US investment in Cuba totalled more than $1 billion, and the USA provided more than 65 per cent of Cuban imports and purchased some 75 per cent of Cuban exports, mainly sugar (see del Aguila 1994: 55). Subsequently, as a consequence of US hostility, economic dependence on the United States was effectively replaced by dependence on the Soviet Union. In the 1980s, sugar still accounted for between 74 per cent and 85 per cent of exports, the export structure being as much dependent on sugar as ever, with some 65 per cent of imports being supplied by the Soviet Union.

Even though Soviet–Cuban relations were not as exploitative and rapacious as US–Cuban relations, as we will see below, the Cuban economy was still in an association which effectively precluded the national direction of economic strategy and an industrial development strategy. The contradiction between socialist ethics and international exchange reappeared in a new guise. Of the 1970s, Mesa-Lago could argue:

> it can reasonably be maintained that in terms of trade-partner concentration [trade with the USSR], Cuba today is as vulnerable to external economic and political influence as it was before the revolution.
>
> (Mesa-Lago 1981a: 94)

Technical development, and the resultant higher standard of living, were to be stymied by Cuba being, again, locked into an international division of labour which preserved the sugar monoculture (see Mesa-Lago 1981a: 8).

As we will see in Chapter 3, Cuban development strategy since 1959 has reflected the need to balance the egalitarian ideals of the Revolution with the need to address the exigencies of international trading relations.

> Cuban development strategy since the Revolution has always been in the context of a dependent external sector which has been a major obstacle.
>
> (Rodríguez 1990b: 209, my translation)

CUBAN DEVELOPMENT: EVOLVING STRATEGY

1959 to 1963: IDEALISTIC SPONTANEITY

After January 1959, the development strategy implied by the ethics of the revolution quickly led to the nationalization of economic activity, the expansion of welfare provision and the delivery of health services and education as of right by the state, which meant an enormously enlarged public sector. But economic control and organization was, in this early period *ad hoc*, guided by ideas and principles about what *should* happen. The few economists who occupied government posts were soon dismissed, and their jobs passed to inexperienced, but enthusiastic, revolutionaries. The leadership were not economists; most of them were lawyers (see Mesa-Lago 1981a: 11).

There was no comprehensive development strategy, though there was a realization that continued dependence on sugar for export revenue precluded a growth strategy under Cuban control, and economic diversification and industrialization were a development priority for the government. 'When it took control of the national means of production, the Castro government introduced a development policy which emphasized above all decreased dependence on foreign trade as a prerequisite to economic growth' (Brunner 1977: 31). The production of sugar pervades the history of Cuba, which can be read as a process of struggle against the vested interests and institutional constraints generated by the exigencies of international specialization: from the *encomienda* system of the sixteenth century to the Rectification Campaign of 1986.

The history of Cuba is a chronicle of resistance:

> against slavery and racism, against inequality and injustice, against uncertainty and insecurity. Against, above all, the conditions that make Cuba particularly vulnerable to the dictates of the market and the metropolis and out of which was forged Cuban nationality. These elements have served as fixed correlates of the Cuban national experience past and present.
>
> (Pérez 1988: ix–x)

The initial post-revolutionary strategy was one of 'import substitution'. The agricultural sector had to be orientated to domestic demand and food crops, such as grain, rice and tropical fruit, although the sugar economy as a source of foreign exchange could not be neglected, and had to become more intensive. However, harvests suffered as a consequence of land being 'set aside' for new agricultural crops. The dynamic of economic development was to have been industry, with Cuba to be eventually a significant producer of steel, cement, electrical power, oil refining, tractors, textiles, etc.

The requisite capital goods were to be supplied by the Soviet bloc, and the import of consumer goods consequently curtailed. However, it was soon discovered that Soviet-built plant was obsolete, there was a problem obtaining spare parts and after 1961 some factories had to be cannibalized to keep the others working.

The relatively buoyant economic performance of 1959–61, reflecting the government's redistribution policy and stimulating an upswing in domestic consumption, was based upon the full utilization of equipment, and accumulated stocks and inventories, as well as foreign exchange reserves and reasonable sugar harvests. In this atmosphere of optimism and growth, the disorganization of economic affairs and low productivity were not recognized as significant problems. However, the drive to overcome dependence on sugar and import substitution industrialization foundered, as the production of agricultural and manufactured consumer goods decreased, the import of capital goods and raw materials escalated and Cuban exports declined with the drastic reduction in sugar production. In 1962, there was a $200 million trade deficit with the Soviet bloc (see Brunner 1977: 34).

In 1961, with the defeat of US backed mercenaries at the Bay of Pigs, diplomatic relations were broken with the United States, and the Soviet Union became an economic lifeline. Cuba was drawn ever more into the Soviet economic orbit. Market regulation of the economy was clearly not compatible with the egalitarian ideals of the revolution, and the organization of economic activity, following technical advice from the Soviet Union and Czechoslovakia, was centralized.

> The Cubans tried rapidly to convert an economy in chaos into a command economy, through highly centralized physical planning for which the island lacked the necessary infrastructure.
>
> (Mesa-Lago 1981a: 15)

JUCEPLAN (Junta Central de Planificación), the Central Planning Board, was created to plan and coordinate economic activity. Different sectors, such as foreign trade, mining, agriculture, labour and banking, fell under the jurisdiction of the relevant ministry, and investment and financing were carried out through state budget allocation, prices were centrally fixed and consumer goods were allocated through rationing.

However, the lack of an accurate statistical base, the inappropriateness of Soviet and East European planning techniques to the Cuban economic context, the lack of experience and of trained planners and the tendency for the political leadership to make economic decisions without consulting JUCEPLAN led to serious inconsistencies. Further, the early plans were not based on an overall investment or development strategy, production norms and prices were arbitrary and there was no mechanism to ensure the coherence and efficiency of plans.

There was a severe economic downturn in 1962/3. In 1963, agricultural output was 23 per cent below that of 1959, and overall output in most important industries was below the 1961 level.

> Contributing to this economic failure were the lack of spare parts – most Cuban factories were still US made – the exodus of US and Cuban industrial managers and technicians, and the poor planning for the instalment and integration of newly bought [Soviet] factories.
>
> (Mesa-Lago 1981a: 17)

The decline in production in 1962/3 produced a significant trade deficit, creating a bottleneck in the ambitious plans for industrial development. In particular, the decline in export revenues, reflecting reduced sugar production, provoked a serious economic crisis, which threatened social service expansion, especially housing. 'At that point, the Cuban leadership ... had to recognize that the course followed hitherto had to be abandoned. In 1963 a reformulation of the development strategy of the Cuban economy began' (Brunner 1977: 35). Consequently, the industrialization drive was suspended, and sugar was once again emphasized as the development dynamic.

1963 to 1970: CENTRALIZED PRAGMATISM

Although the economic chaos of the early 1960s, if the principles and the priorities of the revolution were to be honoured, implied a planned rather than a market economy, the Soviet model was not seen as a model to be emulated. The Soviet authorities were judged to be obsessed with production, ignoring the moral and ethical dimensions of socialism:

> for both Che [Guevara] and Fidel [Castro], socialism was not simply a matter of developing a new way of distribution, it was a question of freeing people from alienation at the same time.
>
> (Valdéz Gutierrez 1996: 20)

Socialism was not merely an issue of economic organization:

> Our task is to enlarge democracy within the revolution as much as possible ... to assure channels for the expression of the popular will.
>
> (Guevara 1961, quoted in Zeitlin 1970: 78)

How to reconcile these ideals, the ethics of the revolution, with the regulation of the economy in general, and the need to produce export surpluses in particular, became the subject of a wide ranging debate.

Any programme of economic modernization and industrialization had to be based on the costly import of machinery, fuel and other basic commodities, to be paid for out of export revenue. While the objective was to diversify out of sugar as the development dynamic, the sugar industry was the only viable source of substantial foreign exchange earnings. Sugar production, at least initially, had to be expanded. In 1961, 6.8 million tons of sugar were produced, the second biggest sugar harvest. This dropped in

1964 to 4.5 million tons, and thereafter the planned targets were: 6 million tons in 1965; 6.5 million tons in 1966; 7.5 million tons in 1967; steadily rising to 10 million tons in 1970 (see MacEwan 1981: 98).

But how were these targets to be achieved?

The post-revolutionary rise in incomes of the rural poor, the increased job security and opportunities for urban employment had led to a labour shortage in the sugar industry, much of the labour being seasonal. Labour requirements were to be met by the sugar harvest being transformed into 'a national activity in which everyone would be encouraged to participate for the good of the nation' (MacEwan 1981: 105). This was but one aspect of a general economic strategy. Motivation through political consciousness and moral incentives were to be the economic dynamic of planning. Prices, profits and market relations were necessarily bound up with 'individualism' and a denial of the collective ethics and goals of the revolution.

Given the redistribution of income, guaranteed employment, the provision of social services, health facilities and education, economic regulation had to be in large measure based upon moral and collective incentives.

> We are using the almost intuitive method of keeping our ears open to the general reactions in the face of the problems that are posed. Fidel Castro is a master at this; his particular mode of integration with the people can only be appreciated by seeing him in action.
>
> (Guevara 1967a: 17)

On Fidel Castro's 'mode of integration with the people', see Bengelsdorf (1994: 78–84). In this formative 'intuitive' period of democracy, people's opinions and priorities could be expressed through mass organizations: in the workplace, the Confederación de Trabajadores de Cuba (CTC), the Central Organization of Cuban Trade Unions, founded in 1939, and the only one of the mass organizations that pre-dates the Revolution; the Comités de Defensa de la Revolución (CDRs), Committees for the Defence of the Revolution, broad-based groupings organized around neighbourhoods; and certain categories of people, such as women in the Federación de Mujeres Cubanas (FMC), the Federation of Cuban Women, and small farmers in the Asociación Nacional de Agricultores Pequeños (ANAP), the National Association of Small Farmers. Other avenues included the People's Courts, and, 'less tangibly, a general atmosphere of discussion and debate around issues of local and more immediate import' (Bengelsdorf 1994: 85).

There were also such social organizations as the Federación de Estudiantil Universitaria (FEU, University Student Federation), the Federación de Estudiantes de la Enseñanza Media (FEEM, Federation of Secondary Schools Students), the Partido Comunista de Cuba (PCC, Communist Party), the Unión de Jóvenes Comunistas (UJC, Union of Young Communists) and the Unión de Pioneros de Cuba (UPC, the Union of Pioneers, a children's organization). The overwhelming majority of the population belonged to at least one organization. This organizational network covered not only different sectors of social life, but also to an extent a generational continuity.

> In the mass and social organizations, our revolution has a powerful and inexhaustible flow of political and revolutionary energy ... They constitute the great school that develops the consciousness of the millions and millions of workers, men and women, old people, young people, and children.
>
> (Castro, quoted in Medin 1990: 156)

The building of a new social and political culture and the change in individuals' consciousness really began with the nationwide 'literacy campaign' of 1961, which was especially focused on the rural areas. Throughout the 1960s and into the 1970s there has been an emphasis on education in general, and adult education in particular, which is considered to be essential to the creation of a new revolutionary culture. To this end, the content of these education programmes has been 'political', in that people have been encouraged to take an active role in social affairs. For instance,

> the literacy campaign was a training ground for organisational and leadership abilities. In a process of learning by doing, the participants in the literacy campaign learned how to mobilise themselves. People who were able to lead and direct were brought to the fore; and others were provided with strong motivation to participate in organised group activity.
>
> (MacEwan 1981: 77)

In the early 1970s, secondary boarding schools were established in rural areas (escuelas en el campo, schools in the countryside), which combined education with work on the school farm, uniting 'fundamental ideas from two great thinkers: Marx and Martí, [who] both conceived of a school tied to work, a centre where youth are educated for life' (Castro, quoted in Leiner 1989: 451). The schools raised much of their own food and some for the wider community, while emphasizing education in crop and livestock production, as well as more general education. The programme continued to expand in the 1980s, and received much favourable international comment (see CEPAL 1978).

More generally, participation was based, fundamentally, on people's everyday experience, and 'the closer one comes to grass-roots decision making – and by implication the closer one comes to the realities of the vast majority of Cubans – the more frequently this democratic-participative counter-trend is found in operation' (Fagen 1972: 43). Although the 1960s were characterized by participation through the mass organizations, this was participation in the implementation of policies determined by the leadership. Participation was not systematic, 'protected by no guarantees and enshrined in no constitution' (Fagen 1972: 43). The lack of a solidly grounded institutional basis, the exodus of large sections of the bureaucratic administration after January 1959, the inexperience of the newly appointed officials, the contradictory orders and faulty communication all contributed to chaos; a chaos which necessarily implied a paternalistic, bureaucratic centralization that had its own contradictions.

> If it was critical to the paternalism of the Cuban leadership – and particularly Fidel – to fight a never ending battle against the windmills of bureaucracy, the fact was that a decision making structure rooted in paternalism had inevitably to spawn such a bureaucracy.
>
> (Bengelsdorf 1994: 89)

The only recourse was to develop an independent, participative, institutional structure, and to reconcile 'grass-roots' opinion with the need for national economic organization, according to 'social goals', rather than 'individual gain' and market rationality.

How were the social objectives, which transcend the experience of individuals, the objectives of enterprises and even whole sectors of the economy, and to which national economic activity is orientated, to be addressed and taken cognizance of in the organization of economic activity?

Counter to the Soviet Union, in the context of the centralized control of state enterprises, extensive planning and almost complete collectivization of the means of production, economic growth and efficiency were to be achieved by 'socialist consciousness', implying the phasing out of money and material incentives. Consequently,

> the budgetary system of financing is based on centralized control of the enterprise's activities. Its plan and its economic functioning are controlled by central organs in a direct way. The enterprise has no funds of its own, nor does it receive bank credits.
>
> (Guevara, Minister of Industry in the early 1960s, quoted in Hodges 1977: 125)

There was a debate about appropriate economic organization for a socialist society. On the one side of the 1962 to 1965 'Great Debate' was Charles Bettleheim (see Bettleheim 1975a), relying upon 'material' incentives to implement objectives, and on the other was Che Guevara, who saw an evolving socialist consciousness based upon 'moral' incentives as the planning dynamic. Bettleheim had studied the Soviet and Chinese experience and conceived of a system based upon decentralized economic decision-making down to the enterprise on a quasi-profitability basis – sales revenue greater than planned costs. Guevara favoured the 'centralized budgetary' system, where enterprises were centrally planned, controlled and financed, with collective and moral incentives over time replacing personal material incentives entirely. The economy would progressively be 'demonetized', and enterprises would not be geared to earning a profit. Planning would be based on political criteria, and socialist consciousness would be a reflection of voluntary work and participation through the mass organizations. For an analysis of the 'Great Debate', see Silverman (1971).

Guevara's argument prevailed, and he effectively became the architect of the 1960s Cuban model of central planning (see Brunner 1977: 30). The difference in human motivation between people living in capitalist and socialist societies was emphasized. In a socialist society, the social good was to take precedence over individual advantage, the latter being the basis of competitive markets and capitalist society (an argument expounded in Guevara 1967a; reproduced in Gerassi 1968; Silverman 1971; see also Castro 1969). But the 'social good' and production for 'social need' were to be defined by a paternalistic state. There was no mechanism through which people could participate and channel their ideas and opinions into the decision-making process. Cubans did in general accept the demands for voluntary labour, but were perhaps motivated more by the benefits the revolution had brought them, its historical legitimacy and the popularity of the leadership, than by any notion of creating a socialist transformation.

While Che Guevara, as Minister of Industry, had always conceived of moral and collective incentives going hand in hand with central planning to coordinate the economic activity of the island, with material incentives linked to the fulfilment of planned targets, 'over-fulfilment' relied on collective moral incentives. But the limitations of planning in the 1960s had led to the need for *ad hoc* 'mini-plans' to address some immediate problems of production: plans which were not coordinated, exacerbating the problem of overall economic regulation.

> Encouraged to work long and hard while suffering low levels of personal consumption, even the most committed 'new person' could become disillusioned when effort and sacrifice did not result in promised economic results.
>
> (Fitzgerald 1994: 57)

Guevara left Cuba in 1965, going first to the then Congo, where he aided Patrice Lumumba's anti-imperialist movement. In November 1966 he was in Bolivia, leading a guerrilla movement, until being wounded on 8 October 1967 and subsequently executed on the following day by a US CIA-organized Bolivian army operation. In his absence, economic regulation became more and more voluntaristic and chaotic. In the attempt to reduce 'bureaucracy', the administrative apparatus was reduced to a minimum, with fewer personnel, fewer rules, less information sent to or from enterprises and administrators often required to engage in productive manual labour, and at times circulated within the bureaucracy. Enterprises operated semi-autonomously, without either effective central control or decentralized markets. In late 1965, the Ministry of Finance was abolished and the power of the National Bank was limited, as was that of JUCEPLAN. The 'anti-bureaucratic' phase destroyed the accounting system that Guevara had left behind. This phase saw people appointed to positions of management and authority based on political rather than educational or skill credentials, often former guerrilla army officers.

The emphasis was on moral incentives, the building of socialist consciousness by decree: for example, private enterprise was banned by fiat, and not as a result of education or a developing socialist 'consciousness'. The emphasis was upon creating a unified economic organization where the individual was part of a social whole – but how to create social consciousness out of individual experience was never theorized. The result was socialist evangelism, exhorting people to act in the 'social' interest.

The zenith of this period was to have been the 1970 ten million ton *zafra*, or sugar harvest. From 1967 onwards, the planned 1970 record harvest was the economic priority, with the preparation of large cultivation areas, fertilizer and irrigation facilities, preparations which prejudiced the harvests of 1968 and 1969. And the decline in production during these years exacerbated the failure of the 1970 *zafra* to reach the ten-million ton target. Between January and April 1970 it became clear that the harvest would be considerably less than the target, and on 19 May Fidel Castro announced that the target could not be met (on this period see Brunner 1977: 101–9). There was a general mobilization in the island to fulfil the plan, with the social and mass organizations (the ANAP, CDRs, FMC, CTC, etc.) being activated.

> If we fail to achieve the 10 million [tons] ... we shall suffer a moral defeat ... This time it is a whole nation who is to make a superhuman effort to reach a goal which shall be raised as the banner for what we stand for, the banner of socialism, and for which we have fought with a determination with which all revolutionaries need to fight to achieve their goals.
>
> (Castro 19 May 1970, quoted in Brunner 1977: 108)

The revolution's principles and the credibility of the leadership, the pride of the nation and expectations of the future were at stake. Fidel Castro was quick to take responsibility for the failure: 'we alone are the ones who have lost the battle, the administrative apparatus and the leaders of the revolution are the ones who lost the battle' (Castro 1972: 296). He offered to resign.

1970 to 1986: CENTRALIZED PLANNING

Despite everything, the 1970 *zafra* did increase Cuba's import capability over that of previous years. But the economic performance had greater significance than the below-planned sugar harvest. The year 1970 marked a critical threshold in the revolution.

With the rising cost of imports, it became clear that the principles of the revolution could not be achieved through economic development, and therefore industrialization, with the mechanisms of economic regulation in force in the late 1960s. The period of radical experimentation and voluntarism gave way to more structured decision-making, and an emphasis on economic management: 'subjectivism and consciousness were replaced with objective channels' (Azicri 1988: 134). The problem of reconciling the nationalist ethics of Cuban socialism and the exigencies of international economic specialization were brought into sharp relief. And in Guevara's absence, the other side of the 'Great Debate' now assumed dominance.

With regard to the international dimension, the United States had been replaced by the Soviet Union as the major purchaser of the sugar crop, and the major supplier of manufactured imports. Economic planning required that this relation be as stable as possible, and to this end Cuba joined the CAME in 1972. In the socialist world's division of labour Cuba was essentially a sugar producer (and to a lesser extent nickel), and the prices of Cuba's exports were indexed to the prices of imports from CAME partners, most notably Soviet oil/petroleum.

To effect the coordination of the Cuban economy with those of the other CAME members, in 1973 the SDPE (Sistema de Dirección y Planificación de la Economía, the Economic Management and Planning System), modelled on the 1965 Soviet economic reforms, was introduced (for a Cuban account, see Primer Congreso del Partido Comunista de Cuba 1979). The SDPE was intended to be an elaborate system of collaboration between the central planning authorities, regional, industrial and sectoral economic interests, enterprise managers and workers, with limited market coordination and state-enterprise autonomy, planned prices and investment priorities (see Harnecker 1979).

Key economic parameters were centrally defined (output, workforce, productive inputs, etc.), and within these economic parameters, enterprise economic performance was measured by receipts minus costs (at fixed prices) – a quasi-profitability index. This was intended to act as a corrective to the tendency in planned economies for enterprises to limit production to the planned targets and to hoard unused resources. Any surpluses were to finance incentive funds, divided into 'sociocultural' funds, to finance housing, day-care centres, etc., and 'enterprise personal' funds, to provide personal and collective bonuses. For details, see Fitzgerald (1994: 73–80).

Under the SDPE, the first five-year plan began in 1975, and the first 20-year plan, updated every five years, in 1980; these applied to 5 per cent of enterprises in 1979 and 95 per cent of enterprises in 1980 (see Hernández and Nikolenkov 1985). The long gestation period for the implementation of the SDPE planning system reflected the shortage of trained, professional, economic and managerial personnel to formulate, apply and adjust plans, and to manage day-to-day operations.

However, although Cuba was a member of the CAME, international trade on the world market for 'hard' currency was still a priority, peaking in 1974 at 41 per cent of the island's trade (see Eckstein 1980), linked to the record sugar price, which rose from 2 cents per pound in 1968 to 68 cents per pound in November 1974 (see Mesa-Lago 1981a: 188–9). Cuba diverted some sugar supplies from the CAME markets to the world market to take advantage of the high price, increasing the capacity for hard currency imports. On the basis of this relative prosperity, and low international interest rates, Cuba contracted hard currency foreign debt to obtain further, non-CAME investment goods. 'The Western debt rose from $660 million in 1974 to $1,338 million in 1975, and to $2,100 million two years later' (Eckstein 1994: 52).

The hard currency debt rose faster than export revenues when the sugar price dropped, and Cuba, from having one of the best debt/export revenue ratios in Latin America, moved to having one of the worst. Membership of the CAME helped to shield Cuba from the full impact of the downturn in world market conditions, but Cuba was forced to rely once again on the CAME, reinforcing the dependence on sugar as an export crop.

> relations with the Soviet Union were not without their problems ... Aside from Cuba's inability to repay its accumulated Western debt, and aside from the poor quality and high prices charged for items other than oil, the Soviet Union and other Soviet-bloc countries were willing to purchase only a limited range of Cuban products.
>
> (Eckstein 1994: 52)

The pre-revolutionary mono-product export dependence was reinforced. Again there was a contradiction between international economic relations and the ideals of the revolution.

What were the implications for domestic economic regulation?

The operation of the SDPE emphasized material incentives, personal income and financial gain. Enterprises were to be concerned only with their own performance, measured in value terms, and not the general social interest.

> What was profitable to an enterprise ... was not necessarily equally profitable and beneficial to the government ... and projects (such as construction) were left unfinished because the value of the final stages of building were lower than the initial stages. Earth-moving and placement of foundations were worth the most. Indeed at the time of launching of the RP [Rectification Campaign], the number of unfinished projects had allegedly got out of hand.
>
> (Eckstein 1994: 75)

Despite a relatively high growth rate in gross domestic product, estimated by Brundenius to have averaged 7.8 per cent between 1972 and 1981 (Brundenius 1984: 40), there were examples of poor coordination between planning units, the misallocation of resources, administrative and financial difficulties:

> projects weren't being finished and [enterprises] ... wanted to meet the plan in terms of value but not quality ... this system was incapable not only of running the economy efficiently, but of overcoming under-development.
>
> (Castro, quoted in G. Reed 1992: 56, 102)

After the economic chaos of the 1960s, policy had been oriented towards management and technical efficiency in the 1970s. Expertise was stressed over political 'correctness', with more emphasis on material incentives to achieve production targets, though consumer durables as material incentives (refrigerators, televisions, sewing machines, etc.) were still allocated to those judged to be in the greatest need allied to their work record. 'Need' was assessed by workers' meetings and/or trade union committees. Trade unions assumed a more active role in general, such as overseeing the labour councils in workplaces (see Fuller 1987: 140), having been somewhat marginalized in the 1960s (see Pérez-Stable 1985).

> Over 26,000 new union locals [union branches] were established ... worker assemblies were held regularly again ... [and] provided an opportunity to air grievances against management. And workers were formally incorporated into the enterprise decision-making process, through representation on management boards.
>
> (Eckstein 1994: 42)

The Thirteenth Congress of CTC, held in 1973, reflecting that the achievement of targets would be more closely linked to material incentives, officially promulgated the principle of 'to each according to work' (see Fitzgerald 1994: 74). For the majority of Cuban workers, under material incentives wage levels increased, and the availability of consumer goods to purchase also grew, so much so that excess liquidity in the economy (purchasing power greater than things to purchase) was virtually eliminated.

As Brundenius (above) estimates the economic growth rate, the effect was positive. With growth, more goods were available off the ration system. By 1980, consumer spending on rationed items was down to 30 per cent of total expenditure, from close to 100 per cent ten years earlier (see Research Team on the Cuban Economy 1984).

Authoritarian, hierarchical, central control – 'democratic centralism' – was part and parcel of the Soviet planning system and the SDPE. However, the active participation of trade unions in the SDPE system was ultimately limited by the technical parameters set by the division of labour within the CAME. This apparently arbitrary limitation on participation produced a cynicism militating against an evolving socialist consciousness. The more important the decision, the higher up the bureaucracy it was taken. Even Fidel Castro got involved with the minutiae of economic organization.

> Castro often spoke about his personal interventions to detect and solve problems at all levels of the economy; he frequently explained that his staff of 'twenty *companeros*' ... constantly travel, visiting factories, hospitals, schools, *co-ordinating, helping everybody*, and they are not inspectors but people who go around assessing the situation and *co-ordinating one organ with another*.
>
> (Fitzgerald 1994: 127–8, emphasis in original)

Such *ad hoc*, if benign, intervention was not restricted to Castro and his staff. The various ministries were concerned to oversee and organize the particular areas of economic activity that were within their purview, limiting the economic autonomy of enterprises on which the SDPE was supposed to be based. Enterprises, supposed to return a 'profit', would be granted price increases, giving the illusion of financial viability. And the SDPE was in danger of becoming 'a complete farce, as regards enterprise efficiency' (Castro 1986b: 7).

The democratic centralism of the SDPE reinforced the bureaucratic hierarchy of an essentially authoritarian regime, albeit a 'benign' authoritarian regime, precluding the participative intuitions and individual initiatives central to socialist consciousness. On the application and effect of democratic centralism in Cuba, see (Carnota 1974; D'Angelo Hernández 1977; Fitzgerald 1994: 70–3).

> [E]very firm and its plan were part of a central plan. This vertical and authoritarian relation was reproduced within the enterprise, where the director and a small group of managers, without any capacity to innovate, assumed total power with regard to the implementation of planning decisions.
>
> (Dilla 1996a: 25, my translation)

Under the SDPE, enterprises, trade unions, workers' assemblies, etc. were assigned delineated spheres of responsibility within a hierarchy of authority. Initially, economic priorities were to be collectively discussed, so that the economic realities which only people close to the point of production could have full knowledge of, could come to the attention of the decision-makers higher up the hierarchy. It was at this second stage that decisions were made by higher level leaders and planners. Decisions made at too 'low' a level, it was thought, would ignore internal and external factors beyond the experience of the direct producers, leading to less 'optimal' planning. The rationale for planning decisions was to be explained to the workforce, and 'participation' to be encouraged through persuasion:

> the principles of democratic centralism stipulated that, although the masses should not make decisions, they should participate in the pre-decision stage of discussion and in the post-decision stage of implementation.
>
> (Fitzgerald 1989: 286)

The impressive 'economic' turnaround noted by Brundenius in the 1970s continued into the 1980s, when the Cuban per capita national product increased by about a third, compared to a 10 per cent decline in Latin America and a 6 per cent decline in the Caribbean (see Figueros and Vidal 1994: 109). But there were contradictions in the politics of economic co-ordination. Administrative planning procedures, prices, employment and labour allocation, credit policies and other economic variables were not coordinated. There was a particular problem with material incentives being based upon output. 'As far as salaries go, there is chaos all over the country' (Castro 1986a: 9).

The bureaucratic centralism of the SDPE was reflected in the bureaucratic habits and elitist pretensions of planners, with ministries keeping close control of their respective areas of concern, competing with other ministries for resources, which went as far as ministries ordering enterprises not to declare their excess and unused resources as 'superfluous'. Ultimately, the consequence was an arbitrary incentive structure. With employment guaranteed, managers competed to get the best workers, offering higher salaries for lower production targets, or 'norms'. Within the SDPE there was an incentive for managers to 'hoard' labour, making target fulfilment easier, since 'soft' budget and price constraints allowed enterprises to expand their total wage bill. Although enterprises under the SDPE were supposed to be financially responsible for themselves, and, within the confines of fixed prices, to realize a 'profit', if enterprises had losses at the end of the year the National Bank routinely covered them. And disproportionate salaries created disharmony, cynicism and the lack of a sense of collective rights and responsibilities among workers.

> The fact is that there are many instances of lack of work discipline, unjustified absences from work, deliberate go-slows so as not to surpass the norms, which are already low and poorly applied in practice, so that they won't be changed because they are being more than met ... people ... working no more than four or six hours ... The weaknesses and negligence are the responsibility of managers and of all of us who have not set up the most adequate work and salary mechanism and have not known how to organize things and create a certain sense of political and work responsibility on the part of the workers.
>
> (Raul Castro 1979; see R. Castro 1983: 295)

On the problems of the operation of the SDPE, see Fitzgerald (1994: Chapter 6).

1974: PODER POPULAR

The reconciliation of the planning exigencies and bureaucratic tendencies of coordination within the CAME/SDPE with the ethics of the revolution was attempted through Poder Popular (Popular Power). Hitherto, 'direct democracy' had been through the mass organizations, and had been largely structureless. With Poder Popular, democracy was institutionalized, with a more defined role for the party and a rationalization of planning procedures. The Organs of Popular Power (OPP) were initiated on an experimental basis in Matanzas province in 1974, approved by the First Party Congress of 1975, codified into the new constitution of 1976 and extended across Cuba in 1976 and 1977.

The OPP were intended to create the sense of political and work responsibility. The institution of Poder Popular in 1974 to 1976 was an important turning point in the institutionalization of the revolution. Until this time, the mass organizations to which most Cubans belonged (the CDRs, the CTC, the FMC, the ANAP, etc.) were the only avenue for political participation. With Poder Popular there would be elections and formal channels of political representation. The OPP were an attempt to meld the structures of the Soviet based SDPE to the ethics of the revolution: 'to enlarge democracy ... as much as possible' (Che Guevara 1961, quoted in Zeitlin 1970: 78).

Poder Popular decentralized the management of productive and service enterprises and institutions to the areas or constituencies which they serve.

Administrative responsibilities were divided between municipal OPP, provincial OPP and national OPP. Municipalities were further divided into *circumscripciónes*, what we might call electoral wards, in which candidates could be elected to represent the local area on the municipal OPP. In the first national elections in 1976, over 30,000 candidates contested 10,725 delegate positions at municipal level (LeoGrande 1989: 195). Even though voting was not required by law, voter turnout was in the region of 95 per cent. Since 1976, elections to the municipal assemblies have taken place every two and a half years, and delegates were chosen from the municipal OPP for the provincial and national assemblies every five years. The Communist Party (Partido Comunista de Cuba, PCC) is formally prohibited from nominating candidates in these elections, although the majority are members of the party. As members of a 'democratic centralist' party, delegates to the OPP who are members of the PCC are obliged to support party policy.

According to the 1976 Constitution, the first attempt to institutionalize socialist democracy (see Evenson 1994: Chapter 2), the National Assembly approves all laws, legislation, plans and budgets, and is 'the only organ in the Republic invested with constituent and legislative authority' (Center for Cuban Studies 1976: Chapter 7, Article 68). Where appropriate, issues are submitted 'to the people for consultation' (Center for Cuban Studies 1976: Chapter 7, Article 73). In such cases, political issues are widely discussed within the mass organizations, which are explicitly recognized and accorded a role in carrying out state policy. Popular consultation had already been the norm before the approval of the 1976 Constitution. For instance, there was a national referendum, on 15 February 1976, on the Constitution itself, which had been drafted by a party commission in 1974 and circulated in draft form to the mass organizations for discussion and suggested modifications. Such consultation was formalized in the 1976 Constitution, and in the summer of 1990 there were some 89,000 workplace meetings as a preliminary to the Fourth Party Congress of 1991 (see Bengelsdorf 1995: 29). Along with discussions in neighbourhoods, schools and universities, this led to over one million comments, which were processed and circulated to delegates to the Congress (see Blanco and Benjamin 1994: 30). The resultant legislative changes were relatively minor, but the consultation process itself was important in informing people as to the implications of the socialist order embodied in the 1991 changes to the 1976 constitution.

The municipal OPP has the authority to make policy decisions on matters falling within its jurisdiction. It oversees local facilities, such as schools, health facilities, retail outlets, entertainment and factories, although norms and procedures such as school curricula, the scope of health service provision, sanitation standards or wage rates are laid down, according to national policy, by the national OPP (National Assembly of Popular Power). The national OPP also controls national economic activity: the sugar industry, heavy industry, banks, etc. The municipal OPP is able to appoint the management of the facilities under its jurisdiction, and Poder

Popular as an edifice of administration and regulation was, at least formally, constituted from the neighbourhood upwards. Neighbourhoods
vote for delegates to the municipal OPP (there must be at least two
candidates per seat, and the only campaigning allowed is the publication of
biographies of each candidate). Municipal delegates subsequently elected
the delegates to both the provincial and national OPP assemblies. This was
changed in 1992, after the Fourth Party Congress in 1991 criticized OPP for
being overly bureaucratic, formalized and concentrated, and direct elections were established for the provincial and national assemblies, being
implemented in the elections of February 1993.

All OPP delegates are required, twice a year, to report to their electors in
formal 'rendering of accounts' meetings, reporting on their activities and
the pressing issues before their OPP. And delegates can be, and are, recalled
and replaced if their performance is thought to be unsatisfactory. In 1989,
only 45 per cent of delegates were re-elected, and 114 delegates were
recalled (see Lutyens 1992).

There is not space here fully to describe and evaluate the workings of this
attempt at participative democracy, but see Fitzgerald (1994: 80–4), Harnecker (1979), Castro (1991a: 111–25), and Evenson (1994: Chapter 2).

> Overall, the OPPs supply the population with a vehicle for attempting to solve
> problems, especially at the local level, and with a channel for voicing complaints,
> possibly up to national level.
>
> (Fitzgerald 1994: 82–3)

Poder Popular is not conceived of as a 'system' of democracy, but as a
democratic 'process'. With experience in the institutions through which the
population politically participate, these institutions can evolve to reflect
people's potentials and aspirations more fully. The parameters of participation are ultimately constrained by the exigencies of international economic
specialization: trade.

> I sincerely believe, comrades, that by staying on the road we have embarked
> upon with People's Power and staying true to these principles, we are moving
> toward improving our political system, which will be as good as anyone's and be
> the most democratic of any existing in other countries of the world.
>
> (Castro 1991b: 197)

In the 20 years of the operation of OPP institutions, many disagreements
and opinions, both for and against, have surfaced. Perhaps the most
ubiquitous is the apparent inability of local municipal delegates to solve
constituents' problems. Delegates are volunteers who often do not have the
time, or the knowledge, to find their way through the bureaucratic labyrinth
of the state. Delegates lose credibility, and constituents do not feel represented by law-makers, especially at the national level. In a survey of
people's attitudes to Poder Popular (see Carrobello 1990), only 51 per cent
thought delegates had the power to solve their problems, but only 10 per
cent wanted to scrap OPP, 70 per cent thinking it could be improved.

A fundamental problem has been the attempt to avoid the emergence of a 'class' of politicians. Cuba's electoral law stipulates that elected officials cannot be full-time politicians, a legacy from pre-revolutionary times, when 'corruption was the main course of political diet' (G. Reed 1992: 114). But the effect has been that delegates are marginalized from the decision-making process, putting power in the hands of unelected bureaucrats. 'We vote mechanically ... we have ... the tendency to pass legislation simply as a vote of confidence in the commission [that drafted it]' (National Deputy Irma Barrera, quoted in G. Reed 1992: 114–15).

Under the 1976 Constitution it was the municipal delegates, themselves elected within the neighbourhood, who appointed provincial OPP delegates, who in turn chose national assembly deputies. Seventy per cent of the delegates were PCC members. To address the feeling that people were not represented at the provincial and national levels, the Fourth Party Congress in 1991 recommended the direct election of provincial and national delegates to the assemblies of Poder Popular. On 20 December 1992, 1190 provincial assembly delegates were directly elected by secret ballot, and 24 February 1993 saw the first direct, and secret, elections of deputies to the national assembly (see Jeffries 1996: 702–3).

However, the mechanism for coordinating national policy, with local representation involves a complex government/administrative bureaucracy, limiting effective participation, and the Fourth Congress resolved to limit bureaucratic 'formalism', improve 'people's control over government activities ... and enable the Municipal and Provincial Assemblies to fulfil their true role as representatives of the highest state authority at those levels' (Fourth Party Congress 1991c: 121). To this end there were a number of reforms to the institutions of Poder Popular (see G. Reed 1992: 92, 122–5).

The institution of Poder Popular in 1976 was a political reaction to the bureaucratic formalism of the SDPE and the CAME. It was an attempt to maintain the process of democracy at the centre of Cuban socialist development, and to reconcile revolutionary ethics with international economic specialization. 'Our task is to enlarge democracy ... to assure channels of the popular will' (Guevara 1961, quoted in Zeitlin 1970: 78). In 1986, the Rectification Campaign was a reaction to the restricted parameters of popular power within the SDPE system of planning, where enterprise performance was only measured in quantitative, economic terms.

1986: THE RECTIFICATION CAMPAIGN
1990: THE SPECIAL PERIOD

The limitations of the SDPE as a mechanism of national economic organization and the constraints of the CAME as a system of international economic coordination came to a head in the mid-1980s, with the 'Campaign of Rectification of Errors and Negative Tendencies': the Rectification

Campaign of 1986. This process was subsequently compromised by the collapse of the Soviet bloc, the CAME and Cuban trade in 1989 to 1991, giving rise to the 'Special Period in Time of Peace': the Special Period.

The effect of the collapse of the Soviet bloc and CAME and the privations of the Special Period, have already been detailed in Chapter 1 and will not be repeated here. However, the Rectification Campaign and the Special Period were times of radical policy change, which will be addressed below. It is worth prefacing this discussion by highlighting the underlying ethical principles which structured these policy responses.

> [If] Cubans are to be more committed to pulling the economy through [the Rectification Campaign and the Special Period], then they have to have an even greater stake in it, and greater participation in the political decisions that will make or break Cuba's future.
>
> (Fourth Party Congress 1991a: 130)

In the time of the Rectification Campaign and particularly in the Special Period, resources have been limited and in short supply. To try to ensure continued socialist development, and address accumulated social needs and economic development, resources have had to be centralized and used rationally and optimally in the social interest, being directed to urgent national needs. Yet people were to have 'an even greater stake' in the economy. The leadership has had to act quickly and decisively to meet challenges and threats to the revolution, and in this regard has been extremely successful, but this has inevitably placed limitations on representation and accountability. Such limitations were only made palatable by the level of equality in Cuba. But the chaotic incentive system and the somewhat arbitrary distribution of national income of the 1970s and 1980s began to erode the 'national consensus', and demobilize popular support.

> People increasingly look to themselves and their family and friendship networks rather than to the state as the guarantors of their survival. As the project of the revolution, which had everything to do with equality, both economic and social, erodes, so too does the level of popular mobilization in support of that project.
>
> (Bengelsdorf 1995: 28)

Inequality and disillusionment have spawned unrest. At the economic level, there is theft, corruption, speculation, lack of work discipline, poor use of the workday and absenteeism, and a rapid rise in 'black market' activity, from an estimated two billion pesos in 1990 to up to ten billion pesos three years later (see Eckstein 1995: 32). There is emigration: some islanders, travelling under US visas, never return. There have been cases of people in positions of importance taking advantage of the opportunity of official foreign travel to defect. But the highest profile emigration has been the islanders who made the perilous crossing to Florida in unseaworthy craft in 1994. However, interviews indicate that people were escaping the economic hardships resulting from the US economic blockade and the collapse of the CAME leading to the Special Period, rather than 'socialism' (see Eckstein 1995: 31). By September 1994, some 35,000 Cubans had attempted the crossing.

Under a 1984 agreement with Cuba, the USA could grant up to 20,000 entry visas a year. In 1993, only 2700 were awarded and, under the 1966 Cuban Adjustment Act, any Cuban arriving in the US was effectively given political asylum and allowed to stay. To stay 'legally' in the USA, Cubans had to get there 'illegally'. The problem was not the lack of Cuban exit visas – anyone over the age of 20 can apply – the constraint was on the other side. However, after 19 August 1994, all those picked up at sea were taken to the US base at Guantánamo in Cuba; later, some were sent on to camps in Panama. Those making it to the USA were placed in detention centres awaiting 'processing': Cuban illegal immigrants were treated the same as any other nationality. Some Cuban emigrés were subsequently granted entry visas, but the US began returning would-be immigrants in May 1995, the Cuban government having agreed to take no reprisals (for more details, see Jeffries 1996: 700–2).

Additionally, there have been some protest groups, organized around artistic freedom, religious freedom, democracy, etc. Fifty such groups were officially acknowledged to exist in 1992, numbering about 1000 people (see Eckstein 1995: 31). Covert protest is more difficult to identify, but in May 1994, 124 asylum seekers occupied the Belgium embassy, followed by 21 in the German embassy and nine in the Chilean embassy in June. The most serious disturbance involved about 1000 people in the port area of Havana, following a spate of ferry highjackings. About 35 people were injured in the worst outbreak of civil disorder since 1959 (see Jeffries 1996: 701).

The root of the dissatisfaction and disillusionment has been the problem of reconciling participation and economic regulation with 'democratic centralism', the ideological justification of central planning and of the SDPE and CAME. Within the OPP institutions, intended to be the 'highest state authority', democratic centralism had led to nominally independent institutions being party dominated. Although the party did not directly administer the state, or the organs of OPP, party members in OPP were subject to party discipline, and under democratic centralism were obliged to persuade OPP delegates to follow the party line. If this failed at lower levels, then matters would be passed up to the next level of OPP, where, typically, more delegates would be party members. To address this tendency, 'the constitutional reform [of the Fourth Party Congress in 1991] enacted in the 1992 Electoral Law recognises the concept of participation and *abandons the principle of democratic centralism*' (Edelstein 1995: 8, emphasis added).

That the effect of government and the ethics of the revolution were not in tune had been apparent in the late 1970s. There had been tension and impatience with Cuba within the CAME, and frustration within the Cuban government, as the Cuban authorities were more and more reluctant to accept the economic role of sugar (and nickel) producer to the Eastern bloc.

This was a theme expressed by Castro and Guevara back in the 1960s: that economic development rested upon the Cuban economy increasingly being a producer of high technology, manufactured, 'secondary' products. Within the CAME, Cuba was a subordinate raw material, 'primary' producer (sugar and nickel), and economic development was inevitably reliant upon Soviet and CAME aid and economic support.

The growth rate of national income (net material product, or the gross value of output minus productive consumption in the sphere of production) averaged 3.0 per cent from 1976 to 1980, and 8.6 per cent from 1981 to 1985, although beginning to tail off in 1984–5 (see Zimbalist and Brundenius 1989: 81). But in the early 1980s, there were several years of drought and extensive devastation by hurricanes, the world market price of sugar was low, the dollar (in which world sugar prices were denomiated) was depreciating, the world price of oil was low, limiting earnings from the resale of Soviet oil imports, and domestic production costs were rising. The effect was that, in 1986, Cuba was unable to meet debt obligations, estimated at $6–7 billion (see Fitzgerald 1994: 171), to capitalist bankers, and had to call a unilateral moratorium on hard currency debt repayments. The debt/export ratio increased from 117 per cent in 1975, to 272 per cent in 1980, 484 per cent in 1985 and 649 per cent in 1989 (see Eckstein 1994: 222).

With Cuba unable to negotiate new hard currency bank loans, imports from the capitalist world had to be cut drastically, and there was pressure to expand exports, reduce consumption, raise levels of investment and improve economic efficiency.

With the rise to power of Mikhail Gorbachev in Russia in 1985, and under *perestroika* the subsequent increased emphasis on market forces and world market prices, and the unwillingness of the Soviet Union and the CAME to maintain existing trade and aid relations with Cuba, the writing was on the wall. No longer could Cuba assume the solidarity of Russia, the Soviet Union or the CAME (for details of economic problems at this time, see Castro 1986c).

The atmosphere of economic and political isolation had already begun to be apparent in 1983. Maurice Bishop, leader of the Grenadian revolution, whose New Jewel Movement in 1979 was only six years old and with 45 full-time members, seized power from the repressive Sir Eric Gairy while he was out of the country, on 13 March 1979 (see O'Shaughnessy 1984: Chapter 4). Like the 26th July Movement 20 years earlier, the New Jewel Movement asserted Grenada's independence in the face of US posturing.

It is well established internationally that all independent countries have a full, free and unhampered right to conduct their own internal affairs. We do not, therefore, recognise the right of the United States of America to instruct us on who we may develop relations with and who we may not.

(Maurice Bishop speaking on national radio 13 April 1979,
quoted in Bishop 1984: 11)

The radical programme of the New Jewel Movement called for the 'widest possible participation by the people in the Country's decision-making process and the day-to-day administration of the State' (A passage from the June 1983 Draft Constitution, cited in Hart 1984: xvi).

Bishop and the leadership never described their revolution as 'socialist', but the emphasis on free mass education and health provision, full employment, national economic sovereignty, popular political participation and economic assistance from Cuba and the Soviet Union gave clear parallels to Cuba after 1959. The USA was not going to allow another independent thorn in its Caribbean side. However, as a result of infighting within the New Jewel Movement, Bishop was placed under house arrest on 13 October 1983 by a splinter group led by Bernard Coard. The wave of popular support for Maurice Bishop led the Coard faction to panic and order Bishop's execution on 19 October.

> To what extent the American Central Intelligence Agency participated in the events leading up to the killing of Bishop is not yet clear ... The involvement of the CIA in the removal of political leaders disliked by the US Government is too well established for the probability that its agents had a hand in the events leading to Bishop's death to be discounted.
>
> (Hart 1984: xxxvi)

For four and a half years, in secret, the US State Department had been looking at alternative strategies for putting an end to the left-wing government of Grenada. And on 27 October, on the pretext of Bishop's execution, US marines were on the streets of St Georges (the Grenadian capital), after an invasion which included token contingents, to create the illusion of regional unanimity, from Antigua and Barbuda, St Lucia, Dominica and St Vincent, Barbados, Jamaica and St Kitts-Nevis – 300 police and troops in all, out of a 15,000 strong US task force (see O'Shaughnessy 1984: 3).

In the light of the invasion of Grenada, Cuba reassessed its defence capability. Cuba's vulnerability to US military might had been clearly shown during the Cuban missile crisis of 1962, when Soviet-built offensive nuclear ballistic missiles were sited in Cuba. These were first identified by US spy planes on 16 October and the crisis lasted until 28 October, when Russian President Khrushchev caved in to US threats and, without consulting Cuba, agreed to withdraw the missiles (see Kennedy 1969). Clearly, in the event of a US invasion or blockade, Cuba could not expect support from the Eastern bloc.

As a defensive strategy, the role of the professional army was reconsidered. There was a return to the emphasis of the 1960s, to the 'popular defence of the revolution'. Some three million people were trained to take part in militias, and weapons were distributed to factories, farms, universities and neighbourhoods.

> This was a very serious step not only militarily speaking, but also politically and philosophically. Because when you arm the population, you have to make sure

that you have the consensus of the population. It is the acid test for any government ... when you're giving weapons to students and factory workers, when you're creating arsenals in remote places in the mountains, when you're giving access to and control of those weapons to the entire population, you have to be absolutely sure that most of the population is backing up your policies ... this 1984 reassessment of our defence system ... re-activated our original concept of the importance of people's participation in defending the revolution.

(Blanco and Benjamin 1994: 26)

The military vulnerability of the island and the revolution, which were to be underlined by economic difficulties some two years later, prompted a reconsideration of the course of the revolution: the Rectification Campaign. The 1986 economic crisis was the catalyst for rethinking the politics of the revolution.

The egalitarian ethics of the revolution had again been constrained by the basis of Cuba's international economic relations. We have already seen that in the 1960s, the immediate post-revolutionary agenda was to fulfil the promises of the revolution: essentially, national sovereignty and self-determination, and the restoration of dignity to Cubans, *cubanidad*. However, the foreign exchange constraint increasingly impinged on national policy. The world market option being blocked by US economic intransigence, Cuba turned to the Soviet bloc and the CAME. Being part of a planned, system of international technical specialization necessarily implied a planned economy according to technical rather than political parameters: the SDPE. Even though the rigidity of the SDPE was, at least nominally, qualified by the participatory principles of Poder Popular, the ideological underpinnings of the SDPE, democratic centralism, precluded the evolution of power 'from below'. Guevara's agenda of enlarging 'democracy within the revolution as much as possible' was stymied. Hence the 1986 Rectification Campaign.

The most serious error of economic policy put in practice between 1975 and 1985 [the SDPE] was undoubtedly its reliance upon economic mechanisms to resolve all the problems faced by a new society, ignoring the role assigned to *political* factors in the construction of socialism.

(Castro 1987a: 13, emphasis added)

People's conscious political participation in society was reasserted over economic management.

The rectification process constituted the revolution's strategic counter-offensive ... which provoked an extraordinary turnabout in our society, facilitating the revival of the roots, principles and genuinely humane, ideological and *ethical* values that gave breath and life to our own kind of socialism.

(Fourth Party Congress 1991d: 106, emphasis added)

On the specific changes to economic organization, see Fourth Party Congress (1991d: 106–8). The changes were more than changes in economic policy. The political emphases of the early days of the revolution in the 1960s returned:

> little by little we began to recover the idea that the revolution was not only a matter of a more just distribution of wealth, but also a spiritual project to release people's *creativity* and give them a degree of *participation* in society.
>
> (Blanco and Benjamin 1994: 28, emphasis added)

The SDPE system was ended in 1986 for *political* reasons. Economic regulation and control was to be a conscious political process of choosing priorities, and not considered to be the 'inevitable' economic result of technical specialization (see Chapter 6) or the necessary effect of the anarchy of market forces (see Chapter 5).

The political agenda of the Rectification Campaign was to increase productivity, eliminate wastefulness and poor quality products, *and* improve participation and reduce bureaucratic planning procedures. The emphasis was not to be on large-scale investment projects: priority was to be given to housing, hospitals, day-care centres and the like. National economic interests were to prevail over the interests of the enterprise, rural economic conditions were to be improved to stem the tide of rural–urban migration and the incentive system was to be rethought. The majority of material incentives were not removed, but the excesses were ameliorated. A new balance was struck between 'moral' and 'material' incentives.

> We must appeal to people's consciousness, and the other mechanisms, the economic factors ... we must use these economic mechanisms in material production, but with this concept, as an auxiliary means or instrument of political and revolutionary work; because believing that these methods will give us the miracle of efficiency and economic and social development is one of the most ridiculous illusions there ever could be.
>
> (Castro 1987b: 224)

Fundamental to this balance was the emphasis on economic equality. There was a clampdown on certain market relations, particularly targeting 'profiteering'. For instance, the market in housing had led to speculation, and the private use of state resources and raw materials for building. The farmers' markets that had been allowed since 1980 were closed. While these markets had offered wider choice to those who could afford it, they had increased inequality. The private market in services, such as plumbing, electrical and mechanical services, and street vending were reigned in, and self-employment was in general discouraged. There was a renewed emphasis on voluntary labour.

In the drive against corruption, the problem was identified as a lack of popular control of key institutions: 'people are not born corrupt, they get corrupted ... We realized that our system failed to prevent ... corruption because it did not provide for sufficient *popular control*' (Blanco and Benjamin 1994: 29, emphasis added). The Rectification Campaign was conceived of as a long-term, evolutionary process of social change, not an economic policy. Hence, paradoxically, while there was a centralization of the control of the macroeconomy, with national economic needs taking priority, there was also a decentralization of day-to-day economic activity at the micro level. 'The process of change is not a generalised shift toward some abstract notion of "centralization" but a complex process of centralization and decentralization' (Petras and Morley 1992: 98).

To reassert national self-determination, economic dependency had to be reduced. A food plan, the *Plan Alimentario*, was intended to make Cuba more self-sufficient in food. Under the SDPE and within the CAME, agriculture was characterized by extensive mono-crop production for export (sugar), heavily dependent upon imported agro-chemicals, hybrid seeds and machinery. In the early 1980s, scientists at the Ministry of Agriculture developed a critique of agricultural practice in Cuba (see Levins 1991; Rosset and Benjamin 1994a, b). The environmental implications of large-scale, import-intensive, plantation agriculture were examined, and research was orientated towards alternative forms of organization. Although official research policy endorsed a new, small-scale, organic agenda for agriculture in 1986, by the end of the decade little impression had been made on actual agricultural production. It was not until the Special Period after 1990 that the new 'organic' agenda had any real impact (see Pastor 1992).

> While neither the expensive scientific investments in advanced technology [biotechnology] nor the research into agricultural alternatives ... had paid great dividends by 1989, they provided Cuba with crucial resources that are now [1993/4] being mobilised to face the agricultural challenge in the 1990s ... a 'knowledge intensive' strategy based on local technology in order to reshape Cuban agriculture and make it more independent.
>
> (Rosset and Benjamin 1994a: 28)

An economic development strategy was designed to replace the sugar industry as the 'leading edge' in earning export revenues, with extensive investment in biotechnology and other high technology fields starting in 1982 (see Blanco and Benjamin 1994: 28). Again, these priorities have really come to the fore in the period after 1990, in the Special Period.

> We're developing the biotechnological industry, the pharmaceutical industry and the medical equipment industry ... Obviously we can't compete with the Japanese in manufacturing TV sets or cars, and we can't compete with the United States in turning out products of the machine industry or in building planes, but, in the fields I'm talking about, we can compete successfully with ... developed countries.
>
> (Castro, quoted in Borge 1993: 115, 122)

As a source of foreign exchange, increased emphasis was placed on the tourist industry. Foreign investment was sought for joint venture agreements, and such agreements were reached in a number of industries.

Cuban society and the Cuban economy were in the throes of rectification when the Soviet Union began to disintegrate , heralding the Special Period.

However, this collapse was not a complete surprise. In his annual 26 July speech in 1989 in Camagüey, some two years before the demise of the Soviet Union, Castro warned:

> There are difficulties, and tensions and conflicts among the nationalities in the Soviet Union are growing ... If tomorrow or any other day, we should wake to the news ... that the Soviet Union has disintegrated ... Cuba and the Cuban revolution will keep on struggling.
>
> (Castro, quoted in Borge 1993: 108)

The ideological parameters of the 1990 Special Period directly arose out of the 1986 Rectification Campaign. And the Special Period cannot be understood outside of the long-term context of an evolution of the revolution towards greater, popular participation. However, austerity and shortages affected social provision, most of which came under the auspices of Poder Popular. With the catastrophic decline in resources to the municipality, municipal OPP delegates could not even respond to the most basic of problems. Citizens found it was irrelevant to raise problems about transport, maintenance, household supplies and all the other goods and services that were supposed to be under the jurisdiction of Poder Popular, and that going to meetings was a waste of time. People turned to the black market for supplies, fuelled by theft from state enterprises, illegal private sales of agricultural produce and goods brought into Cuba by tourists or obtained from tourists shops by Cubans with access to hard currency.

The party engaged in a host of new initiatives and reforms, trying to revive the idealism of the early years of the revolution:

> the policies guiding rectification, as well as actions undertaken more recently during the special period, exhibit an ideological continuity with Guevara's conception of *lucha* and *conciencia* articulated in the 1960s.
>
> (Dalton 1993: 56)

These conceptions were eclipsed by the period of centralized planning, the SDPE, between 1970 and 1986.

A national commission to study the problems of the SDPE led to a number of experiments in alternative economic organization. The 'minibrigades' of the early 1970s were resurrected, to construct day-care centres, housing, hospitals, etc. 'We re-established the system of minibrigades, which had ... disappeared in that ignominious period of copying the methods used in other places for the construction of socialism [the SDPE system]' (Castro, quoted in Borge 1993: 112). Participation was built into their functioning. For instance, half of the housing was allocated to minibrigade members, the other half being allocated through local, municipal OPP (see Mathéy 1989).

Professional and industrial workers released from their regular jobs on full pay, and people not otherwise employed, such as students, housewives and retirees, made up the minibrigades. The brigades were subsequently widened to include 'social brigades', employing unemployed and delinquent youth in neighbourhood renovation projects (see Hamberg 1986).

The seven and a half million members of the CDRs (the total population is around 11 million) were exhorted to organize contingents to work in the countryside in food production. Various forms of small-scale agricultural production were attempted to increase self-sufficiency, and many of these units were supported by municipal councils, which in conjunction with the Ministry of Agriculture provided training, literature and other support services for the new producers. In a series of inner-city programmes, residents have been supplied with building materials through the municipal Poder Popular to repair homes, streets and the local area.

To extend voluntary labour, in 1987 there was a call by the party for 'forty hours of voluntary work on community projects', and more than 400,000 people contributed 20 million hours of voluntary labour in that year (see Eckstein 1994: 63).

The reorganization of work at the Che Guevara Industrial Complex, known as the 'Revolutionary Armed Forces Initiative', became a model to emulate. Experiments in 1987 with new management techniques and work-styles, incorporating management by consensus and participation in decision-making, showed positive results and were extended to other military enterprises in 1989, and to some civilian enterprises in 1990 (see Frank 1993: 51–5).

There were also 'worker brigades', or 'contingents' (*Contingentes*), the most famous of which is the Blas Roca Contingente (see Rodríguez 1990a). Contingents operated in the construction sector, or where the work was hard and dirty, sectors which had suffered from relatively high absenteeism (see EIU 1988), and saw a project through from inception to completion – for instance, building a whole town – unlike under the SDPE, when it was often unprofitable for enterprises to complete projects. First begun in 1987, as of mid-1990 seventy contingents were functioning (see Carranza Valdés 1992), and in 1993 some sixty contingents with more than 35,000 members were in operation (see Dalton 1993: 58).

> [Previously] projects went on forever and were never completed and of poor quality. It was incredible: a town would be built without streets or a water system, without a nursery and other schools . . . The housing sector contracted an enterprise that wanted to build houses . . . it had to do the same to get the water and sewage systems built. Another sector, with another enterprise, was in charge of building child care centres. It was playing at capitalism . . . believing that those mechanisms would work in socialism.
>
> (Castro, quoted in Borge 1993: 109)

Workers were chosen on their work record, and collectively developed a plan of work and the distribution of the wage fund. Full-time workers, often working a 12 to 15 hour day, were paid 25 to 50 per cent above the average, and had good living conditions in camps attached to the project. More participative, and working with up to 50 per cent of the normal manpower, productivity increased from 130 to 200 per cent, but the contingents were intended to be more than a productive mechanism or a form of enterprise.

They were designed to apply sociological and psychological principles to labour productivity. Experimental studies of influences on moral development had highlighted the importance of goal-orientated small groups, operating under peer pressure, with a sense of dignity deriving from the social value of work tasks (see Dalton 1993: Chapters 4 and 6).

> The Blas Roca [contingent] demonstrated the importance of discipline and how discipline based on dignity, morality and men's pride, the collective spirit of men ... It completely distanced itself from the paternalistic, wordy, and we could even say, over-regulated norms of labor discipline in our country ... It was the collective workers that interpreted and applied discipline with a morality, an authority that even made the ones being disciplined admit to the fairness of their decisions.
> (Castro's speech on the Anniversary of the Blas Roca Contingent, broadcast 4 October 1990, quoted in Dalton 1993: 58)

In 1996, participative strategies for the urban renewal of Habana Vieja (Old Havana), which in places is very run down, were initiated. In the first such scheme the Ministry of Basic Industries 'adopted' an area of Habana Vieja and channelled funds through the municipal OPP, to be distributed to residents to organize themselves to renovate their own environment. This was a pilot scheme, and it is intended that other ministries will adopt different areas of Habana Vieja in similar schemes.

As part of the Rectification Campaign, in 1988 the SDPE system of planning was replaced with a system of 'continuous planning'. The number of commodities subject to planning was reduced, as was the number of directive indicators to the enterprise. The system of 'material balances' was decentralized (see Zimbalist 1993: 127–8). Flexibility, local autonomy and worker participation, allowing greater initiative at the enterprise level in drawing up plans, have been advanced, initially by the enterprise drawing up its own plan. Targets are based on the experience of previous years and expectations for the future. In 1988, 'continuous planning' applied to 32 enterprises; in 1990, 900 more were included, accounting for about 50 per cent of productive outputs and 38 per cent of productive labour (see Frank 1993: 57–61).

More generally, the Rectification Campaign restructured work norms (or *normas*) upon which basic wages were based, which had become so slack they could often be achieved in four or five hours, leading to considerable 'overtime' bonus payments (or *primas*). The complex system of incentives pre-1986 could pay 'the worker twice or thrice for the same work' (see Zimbalist 1993: 125). The subsequent reform of the wages structure, while rationalizing the incentive structure with an increased emphasis on voluntary labour, also raised the wages of the lowest paid in agriculture, as part of a general drive to reduce bureaucracy, administration and management in 1988.

The Rectification Campaign, and by implication the Special Period, has been a 'revolution within the revolution ... [reasserting] Che's ideas, revolutionary thought, style, spirit and example' (Castro, quoted in Liss 1994: 94). Since 1986 there has been more open criticism within the revolution and a revision of short-term priorities, and a new, younger leadership is established at all levels in the state, political organization and social and political institutions. And Fidel Castro has stated his desire to retire in 1999.

The commitment to social and political priorities over the economic interests of the enterprise is not considered to be 'idealistic', but a realistic mechanism of resource allocation given the ethical objectives of the revolution. *Every* mode of resource allocation has an implied ethical agenda. In Cuba, the moral foundations of economic policy are explicit and dominant, not, as with the ethics of economic policy driven by market or technical imperatives, implicit and expedient (see Chapter 4).

In the 1990s, Cuba has had to face: the collapse of the Soviet bloc and the CAME; a tightened US economic blockade; a world economic environment which is now unipolar, dominated by the USA; the economic and social crisis facing less developed countries caught in the 'debt trap'; the ideological hegemony of 'neo-liberalism'; and the need to integrate the Cuban economy with the world market.

> For us, the essential thing isn't just to survive but also to develop ... apart from the privations to which we may be subjected for an indeterminate length of time ... as a matter of *principle* ... resources must be shared amongst us all ... [if workers are unemployed] we will guarantee a large part of their wage. Nobody will be left without support ... [Cuba has been] deprived of more resources than any Latin American country, but we haven't closed any schools, hospitals, polyclinics or medical services at all, and we haven't thrown anybody out of work with no pay.
>
> (Castro, quoted in Borge 1993: 115–16, emphasis added)

ECONOMIC POLICY IN THE SPECIAL PERIOD

Carlos Lage, Vice President and Executive Secretary of the Council of Ministers, is in charge of economic policy in the Special Period. 'There have to be advances in two senses: preserve the socialist achievements and open and modernize the economy, and all this without losing the continuity of the social process that has made our achievement possible' (González 1994: 15).

Before 1991, the JUCEPLAN estimated that imports accounted for some 57 per cent of total human consumption of protein, and 50 per cent of calories consumed (JUCEPLAN 1992: 9). In 1989, 80 per cent of cereals, 99 per cent of beans, 21 per cent of meat, 38 per cent of milk and dairy products and 94 per cent of cooking oil and lard were imported (see Rosset and Benjamin 1994a: 19). Consequently, 'The food question has the number one [economic] priority' (Castro 1991c: 34). The Plan Alimentario (Food Plan), launched in 1989, is intended to reduce this dependency on imported food, working towards self-sufficiency. For instance, it is intended that the city of Havana and the surrounding area, which includes some 30 per cent of the Cuban population, will become as self-sufficient in food as possible. *Agro-ponicas* (urban gardens), which can be individual family gardens on private land, private groups on public land or 'institutional' gardens linked to schools, work places or mass organizations are encouraged (see Rosset and Benjamin 1994b: 92–4).

> The international situation and attempts by our enemies to disrupt economic relations with the Soviet Union make it difficult to forecast the immediate future ... The Food Plan has priority, but will have to be realized with less resources ... Low yields in some lines are partly the consequence of objective shortages, but also due to organizational problems ... There is little time to implement this plan, and any delay will have economic costs and political consequences.
>
> (Adolfo Diaz, Vice President of the National Assembly of Poder Popular 1991)

Plans up to 1995 set increases in output between 121 and 14 per cent. Subsequently, these proved to be too ambitious and were revised, and a number of programmes to construct irrigation systems had to be abandoned because of shortages (see Mesa-Lago 1993b: 242–4).

The intention of the Food Plan is also to reorient food production away from imported agro-chemicals, seeds, machinery and fuel. With regard to the latter, there has been a reversion to ox-power for ploughing, etc., reflecting the lack of fuel oil imports during the Special Period (see Deere 1992). 'The Cuban experiment is the largest attempt at conversion from conventional agriculture to organic or semi-organic farming in human history' (Rosset and Benjamin 1994: 82).

The key to organic agriculture is the management of the soil to ensure 'minimum tillage, rational use of [bio-]fertilizers, the use of soil amendments, crop rotations and crop covers' (Rosset and Benjamin 1994a: 51). To this end the soils of Cuba have been mapped, and many large state farms have been broken into smaller management units, becoming cooperatives. *Unidades Básicas de Producción Cooperativa* (UBPCs, basic units of cooperative production) were established in mid-1993 (the UBPCs are addressed in more detail in Chapter 8).

> With the establishment of these co-operatives, the State sector's share [in 1994] of total agricultural land fell from 75% to 34%, while its share of cultivated land fell from 80% to 25%.
>
> (Ritter 1995: 15)

Production teams work the same piece of land from planting through to harvest, allowing an intimate knowledge of the microclimate of different parcels of land, and the needs of different soils. This has the political advantage of facilitating more direct participation by workers in the production process. In addition to the UBPCs, private agriculture is still relatively important, accounting for some 14 per cent of cultivated land, and providing almost 50 per cent of vegetable output. Incentives to farmers have been increased to encourage production, and in general, agricultural wages have risen, so that agriculture is no longer the poorest paid sector.

Fuel shortages, apart from leading to a conversion from tractor power to ox-power in agriculture, has drastically reduced bus schedules. For transportation, one million bicycles have been imported from China, and sold to students for 60 pesos and workers for 120 pesos (see Eckstein 1994: 112). Five new factories have been set up to produce a further half million cycles over five years (1994 to 1999).

The shortage of newsprint and paper led to reduced publication of newspaper and books, and more generally there has been a return to rationing to ensure equality of sacrifice; people are encouraged to use candles at night and charcoal fires for cooking, and to make their own soap. Free agricultural markets were reopened in October 1994 to try to increase the supply of food to supplement rations.

In order to try to reduce the state fiscal deficit, price subsidies to production enterprises were reduced, with firms having to pay the 'real' price at which inputs are purchased from abroad, although some retail prices were still subsidized. By 1993, about 25 per cent of all enterprises were self-financing.

However, although there have generally been cutbacks, priority programmes in biotechnology and the pharmaceutical and medical equipment industries have been maintained and even expanded, as has the tourist industry. The biotechnology industry was initially developed for Cuba's needs, without foreign involvement, but increasingly, because of the difficulty of overseas marketing, foreign capital has entered into partnerships. Biotechnology exports grew from zero in 1988 to $800 million in 1990, including epidermal growth factor for treating burns, drugs, like PPG for washing cholesterol out of the blood, and meningitis and hepatitis B vaccines.

While these three industries are the core of Cuba's development strategy against economic, and therefore political, dependence, foreign capital has been encouraged to step in, on generous terms, where Cuban economic priorities mean a need is unfulfilled. Pérez-López sees this as giving 'rise to a curious phenomenon: the proliferation of economic enclaves subject to capitalist rules – "islands of capitalism" – within ... an ocean of socialism' (Pérez-López 1994a: 190). The greater the need for the capital, technology, expertise, raw materials or markets in Cuba, the more 'liberal' the Cuban authorities are willing to be with the terms of the investment. In order to counteract the pressure from the USA to discourage foreign investment, foreign capital is being given significant incentives to invest in Cuba. Fidel Castro, in his opening address to the Ninth Havana International Fair (1991) said to the assembled crowd of potential foreign investors: 'I do not believe that any country in the world offers the tax facilities we offer ... [investors] will repatriate their capital [profits] more easily than in any other part of the world ... repatriation ... is automatic' (Castro, quoted in Pérez-López 1994a: 195).

Formally, the legal framework for foreign investment has been established by Foreign Investment Law No. 77, passed by the National Assembly of People's Power on 5 September 1995. Profits are tax free (except for 'joint ventures' and 'international economic association partnership agreements', IEAPAs); profits can be repatriated in convertible currency; investment is guaranteed against nationalization; foreign investment is permitted in all sectors except health care, education and arms-related institutions; investment may be 'direct' or 'equity', 'joint ventures' or 'fully owned'; investors can directly export products and import inputs (customs duties being paid by joint ventures and IEAPAs); free trade zones are being set up.

By the end of March 1997, four 'duty-free zones' had been established: at Mariel, Cienfuegos and two on the outskirts of Havana (City of Havana and Wajay duty-free zones). Licensees and operators in the zones enjoy

> total exemption from taxes for the first 12 years and a 50-percent tax discount the following five years, as well as the possibility of selling up to 25 percent of the goods produced in the domestic market . . . [whereas] other nations recognize tax exemptions for up to 10 years and require that 100 percent of production be marketed abroad.
>
> (E. Rodríguez 1997: 8)

In autumn 1996, Decree Law 165, which defined the legal and financial regime in the zones, reserved the right of the Ministry of Labour to set minimum wages and working conditions, to preclude the zones from becoming 'pools of cheap labour' working under 'sweatshop' conditions, a ubiquitous feature of export processing or duty-free zones elsewhere in the world. Hence the generous tax advantages to maximize investors' returns without resorting to the 'super-exploitation' of labour. Cuba has the added advantage of an educated labour force and political stability. 'I'm convinced that our decree-law is competitive, given that we studied the legislation in other countries with that in mind, particularly what they have to offer in terms of tax exemptions and labor costs' (Octavio Castilla, director of the National Office for Duty-Free Zones, quoted in J. Rodríguez 1997: 8).

Carlos Lage announced in March 1997, at a 'round table' conference on the Cuban economy organized by the *Economist* magazine, that as of the beginning of 1997 there were more than 260 economic associations with foreign capital approved and in operation (45 in tourism, 30 in oil prospecting, 5 in nickel mining, 33 in other mining sectors, 85 in industry and 12 in transport and communications). Forty-two of these associations had been instigated after the passing of the Helms–Burton Act in Washington in March 1996, which had been intended to frustrate the activity of international capital in Cuba (see Lee 1997: 14).

However, it has been made clear by Lage that although foreign investment is being sought, the primacy of socialism is not in question.

> Our opening is not an opening toward capitalism, but rather a socialist opening toward a capitalist world. It is based on certain principles that guarantee the

preservation of socialist order over our economy and our ability to meet our economic and social objectives.

(Carlos Lage, quoted in Pérez-López 1994b: 191)

Since 1987, before the announcement of the Special Period, CUBANA-CÁN has been aggressively promoting foreign investment in tourism. Joint ventures have been established with Spanish, Canadian, Chilean, Finnish, Irish, Jamaican, German, Austrian, French, Mexican and Swiss partners. It seems that the bulk of foreign investment has been within the tourist industry.

Another area for import substitution to reduce trade dependency is oil (and petroleum). In 1991, net imports of petroleum accounted for 93 per cent of supplies and 67 per cent of total primary energy supply (see EIU 1991: 23). The subsequent reduction in imports caused widespread disruption: cuts in public transport, cutbacks in manufacturing output, general power cuts, etc. In December 1990, Cuba granted off-shore oil exploration rights to a French consortium, with the French partners supplying the capital, technology and expertise, in return for a share of any output. Since 1990, reportedly, similar deals have been arranged with Swedish, Canadian, Brazilian and Mexican economic interests. Italian, Spanish and Latin American firms have been involved in retooling the steel industry, and Canadian interests are developing the nickel industry (see EIU 1991: 37).

Within the parameters of highlighting future growth sectors, the foreign exchange balance of payments has to be managed competently. The value of imports cannot exceed the value of exports by any significant amount now that Cuba has lost development assistance and credit provision from the Soviet Union. No longer can trading deficits be rolled over into debt, and credit from commercial banks and official sources is virtually impossible to obtain since the 1986 unilateral moratorium by Cuba of debt amortization and servicing. To become eligible for foreign loans and credits, hard currency (essentially US dollar) payments of debt obligations must be honoured by Cuba. In an attempt to regain access to international finance, particularly from Japan, the United Kingdom and Mexico, Cuba has offered to renegotiate outstanding debt through purchases of Cuban goods. Debt for equity swaps with Mexican and Argentinian companies have been made in tourist, industrial and citrus fruit undertakings. It is not clear how successful these initiatives have been, but with pressure from the US blockade, Cuba finds it almost impossible to raise hard currency loans and credits, and relatively expensive 'suppliers' credits' for imports have been the only source of foreign finance. Cuba is not a member of the international institutions that could provide credit and assistance.

Foreign exchange structures have been decentralized, and new corporations established to encourage foreign trade (for instance, in 1989 there were some 300 enterprises involved in foreign trade, in 1991 over 500). Imports are controlled to reflect development policy priorities, and industrial policy is orientated to relieve import dependency through import substitution.

Because of shortages, the 'black market', which operates in dollars, became a necessary aspect of daily life in Cuba. 'We all resort to the underground [black] market because the authorised quotas in the state stores are sufficient for perhaps 12 of the 30 days of the month' (Calderon 1995: 19). Consequently, trading in dollars was legalized for domestic transactions, in order to decriminalize people's daily existence. There has always been some 'informal', black market, economic activity, but the severe shortages of the early 1990s in state-owned shops expanded such activity. In September 1993, after a summer of blackouts and simmering discontent, possession of dollars was decriminalized, and while pent-up tension was temporarily relieved, other social and economic forces were released.

While the most common source of dollars comes from remittances from relatives abroad, workers in the tourist industry also have privileged access, producing such anomalies as a waiter at a tourist resort earning (including tips) more than a professor or a surgeon. In a society that has always emphasized educational opportunity, such arbitrary inequality creates tension. Those who are skilled and educated now earn less because their income is in Cuban pesos rather than US dollars. The majority of Cubans without regular access to dollars can only look on at the minority who can enjoy the fruits of the dollar economy. Not only is the economy distorted, but the 'every man for himself' morality of the dollar economy is in contradiction to the socialist ethic of 'to each according to need'. 'I think that the people who express frustration are, above all, the people who grew accustomed to the paternalism of the state ... They expected the state to resolve everything, and now feel betrayed' (Arturo Arango, editor of *La Gaceta*, quoted in McFadyen 1995: 22). It is the hustlers, workers in the tourist industry, prostitutes and managers of joint ventures with foreign capital who enjoy the material higher standards of living, rather than those committed to the revolution.

> The present conjuncture has stimulated the creative juices of the island's intelligentsia, prompting them to rethink the meaning of socialism ... For the average Cuban, however, the last five years have been merely difficult and confusing.
>
> (McFadyen 1995: 22)

With the decriminalization of holding dollars, the reduction of goods on sale due to the Special Period and the large fiscal deficit, the unofficial peso/dollar exchange rate rose from 7 in 1989, to 30 in 1991, 50 in 1992, 100 in 1993 and 120 in 1994 (see Pérez Villanueva and Marquetti Nodarse 1995: 37). However, there have been active attempts to make the peso more valuable and economically useful. On 1 October 1994, 121 'free' agricultural markets were opened throughout Cuba (there have been others since this time), in which the transactions are in pesos. And the peso is now more valuable. With economic recovery, as the Cuban economy produces more and more for the domestic economy, the value of the peso is expected to rise and the importance of the dollar to fall. The unofficial peso/dollar exchange rate improved to 50 in 1994, and by February 1996 it had reached just 23.

In part, the relatively high black market prices reflect the 'monetary overhang': the money in circulation exceeding the commodities to purchase. In market-based societies, such 'excess liquidity' would be absorbed by price inflation, but where prices are regulated, excess balances accumulate as savings. Such 'forced' savings, which effectively cannot be spent, tend to undermine material incentives intended to increase production. There has been a concerted effort to reduce the overhang by reducing the state fiscal deficit. Enterprise subsidies have been cut, and an extended taxation system has been designed and is currently (1998) being implemented. Trading in pesos in the free agricultural markets has also had an effect on 'excess liquidity'. In the fiscal year 1994–5, the state deficit was reduced, 'with a virtual balance between spending and income' (Pérez Villanueva and Marquetti Nodarse 1995: 37).

ECONOMIC RESULTS OF THE SPECIAL PERIOD

On 23 July 1996, Carlos Lage gave a press conference 'to provide information on the situation of the Cuban economy at the end of the first half of 1996' (Lage 1996: 5). Lage reported that the trend to economic recovery, greater efficiency and improved economic organization was demonstrated by a growth of gross domestic product of some 9.5 per cent. This growth was from a very low level: between 1990 and 1993 gross domestic product fell by 34.8 per cent, with a 0.7 per cent increase in 1994 and 2.5 per cent growth in 1995. However, it was not expected that economic growth would be as buoyant in the latter half of 1996; because of climate variations the sugar harvest takes place in the first half of the year. In January 1997, José Luis Rodríguez, Minister of the Economy and Planning, reported to the National Assembly of Poder Popular that the 1996 annual growth rate had been 7.8 per cent, (see J. Rodríguez 1997: 4).

Andrew Zimbalist notes that, although the encouraging growth statistics include previously unrecorded 'informal' economic activity, and the statistical methodology for compiling the figures is unclear,

> growth in the informal market during 1994 was robust and most of it probably was not recorded, so, on balance, the level of economic activity was likely to be similar to the government estimate. Moreover, official estimates of 2.5 percent growth in 1995 and projections for 5 percent growth in 1996 seem reasonable.
> (Zimbalist 1996: 3)

Because of the economic blockade, Cuba has access only to short-term, high-cost, high-interest loans, costing about 30 per cent above the free market rate and absorbing a disproportionate part of the gains from economic recovery. However, Cuba's population growth of 0.8 per cent, less than half the Latin American average, and reflecting the social development strategy of the revolution, means that the growth in per capita gross domestic product is more reflective of the aggregate growth rate.

In the first half of 1996, the prices of products sold on the ration card remained stable. Sales in hard currency stores increased by 33 per cent while free market prices, reflecting supply and demand, tended to fall. For instance, compared to the first half of 1995, sales in farmers' markets increased by 27 per cent while prices fell by 35 per cent. Domestic growth has not been accompanied by inflation, as is common in market economies.

During this period, capital formation, or investment, grew by 13 per cent, and the production of goods and services for export by 34 per cent. In this latter category, sugar was particularly important, showing an increase in production in 1995–6 for the first time in the Special Period and reaching almost 4.5 million tons, despite unfavourable weather conditions. However, this level is still considerably below the potential for this sector.

Tourism has increased at an annual rate of 17 per cent since 1991, well above the 6.8 per cent for the Caribbean in general and 3.9 per cent for Central America. The effect of tourism on the national economy has always been mitigated by the cost of imported inputs to the tourist industry. But in the first half of 1996, with a growth of 46 per cent, 'tourism's effect on the reactivation of the domestic economy, measured by the financing contributed to national production and services by the tourism industry, grew by 18% in relation to last year' (Lage 1996: 6). The gross income from tourism in 1996 exceeded $1.3 billion (see Anoceto 1997: 6).

Excluding sugar, industrial production increased by 10.9 per cent, and of particular importance was the revival of the nickel industry, a 23 per cent increase in cement and a 19 per cent rise in steel production. Perhaps most significant, given the Plan Alimentario and the drive towards food self-sufficiency, was the 25 per cent increase in root and garden vegetables. There was also an increase in tobacco production of 30 per cent, indicating an increase in cigar exports in 1997 after the long treatment and drying process. There was a 10 per cent increase in citrus production, and the exports of juice and citric concentrates increased.

However, international market prices have not been in Cuba's favour. The price of imports, principally foodstuffs and oil, increased by about 13 per cent, while the prices of exports fell by 7 per cent. Measures to address the 'monetary overhang' and excess liquidity include: raising the prices of non-essential items; introducing taxes in the state sector and to self-employed persons in the private sector; reducing gratuities; reducing subsidies to enterprises. This reduced total liquidity by some 24 per cent or 250 million pesos, further reducing the informal peso/dollar exchange rate to 22 in mid-1996 (and 19.2 by the end of the year; see J. Rodríguez 1997: 4). Since 1994, the peso became effectively six times stronger as a currency. Overall budget expenses remained within planned limits as state institutions exhibited greater financial discipline, and the budget deficit as a percentage of GDP fell from 33.5 (5.05 billion pesos) in 1993 to 3.5 (775 million pesos) in 1995 (see Castro 1995). In 1996 it fell further to 2.4 per cent of GDP, and is expected to fall by another 19 per cent in 1997 to 'approximately two per cent of GDP' (J. Rodríguez 1997: 5).

Overall, the effect on Cubans' lifestyles has been limited.

> It can be said that the economic results of the first half of the year [1996] are not reflected primarily in consumption ... [being] directly mainly towards the solution of the economy's fundamental problems, the most important being the lack of hard currency; however to a modest degree, they also reflected somewhat in the population's standard of living.
>
> (Lage 1996: 6)

There are still many consumer goods shortages in food stuffs and medicines, and material limitations, especially in transport services. The American Association for World Health concluded in March 1997, after a year long study, that the US economic blockade 'has dramatically harmed the health and nutrition of a large number of ordinary Cuban citizens' (AAWH 1997: 67). Surgical services face shortages; a shortage of parts and treatment chemicals has led to a deterioration in water quality; there have been delays in obtaining drugs for the treatment of AIDS; Cuba is effectively barred from obtaining nearly 50 per cent of new world class drugs; and so on. In the attempt to ameliorate these problems during the period 1989 to 1996, while the national budget remained static, public health spending increased by 30.4 per cent at the expense of other sectors of the economy (AAWH 1997: 14). 'Consequently, in the 1990s Cuba's health statistics more closely approximated those of the nations of Europe and North America than of developing countries ... The infant mortality rate in Cuba is [still] roughly half that in Washington DC' (AAWH 1997: 12).

The number of power cuts has been reduced. Income has for many stayed the same, the overall growth of 7 per cent being particularly directed to the *campesino* and cooperative sector, while the average income has grown in the state sector by 2.7 per cent.

The primary economic constraint remained the lack of convertible currency: the deficit in the external financial balance. And world economic trade conditions have not favoured Cuba. In 1996, 'the negative effects of the Helms–Burton Act coincided with a deterioration in the terms of trade by 21.3%' (J. Rodríguez 1997: 5). Almost a third of the money spent on imports goes towards purchasing oil, and the growth of fuel consumption was about 10 per cent over this period, slightly over the growth rate. The principal use is in the generation of electricity, though the steel, cement, nickel and sugar industries are also large consumers. There have to be further efforts to economize on fuel consumption.

For 1996 overall:

> the Cuban economy crossed the threshold of its recovery. Not only was it able to

grow and even surpass many of the goals set ... but we are now in a position to regulate our growth in a planned way ... without sacrificing our social achievements.

(J. Rodríguez 1997: 5)

On 31 March 1995 the *Miami Herald* could print a story based on a Pentagon study of Cuba that concluded that Cuba had weathered the worst of the crisis consequent on the collapse of the Soviet bloc and CAME (see M. Castro 1997: 91).

For further details of economic performance in 1996, see J. Rodríguez (1997).

The recovery of the Cuban economy is to be contrasted with the situation in the former Soviet Union, Central Europe and the Balkans, where the 'transition' has been characterized by 'rampant poverty, family breakdown and sexual abuse, alongside rising juvenile crime, murder and suicide rates, and the reappearance of tuberculosis and diptheria' (*Guardian* 22 April 1997: 8; reporting on a UNICEF report published the previous day).

INTERPRETING THE CUBAN ECONOMY

This chapter has offered a particular interpretation of the Cuban development process. It has shown the attempt to reconcile the collective ideals and ethics of the revolution with the necessity of trading with partners who do not share the objectives born of a uniquely Cuban socialism.

Different stories could be told. The same experience could have been interpreted to highlight other aspects of human development: for instance the extent to which government economic intervention frustrates individuals from maximizing 'personal' utility; or the problems of Cuban development reflecting inappropriate management of 'technical' resources for production. These criteria can be, and have been, used to evaluate Cuban development strategy.

Social and economic development implies social and economic change, and hence people's changed behaviour. Each analytical perspective argues from distinct assumptions about human motivation, which necessarily highlight the significant aspects of experience to be taken into account and analysed. The relevant 'facts' are defined, as is 'development', suggesting strategies for 'progress'. The important reality is an *abstract* reality: *why* people relate to each other in different ways. This abstract reality has to be 'theorized' to be understood, but it is no less 'real' for that. We actually *do* relate to each other, and there are 'intellectual parameters' to this dimension of the 'real' world, and hence to development theory and policy.

This implied intellectual agenda has to be made explicit if we are to understand, and therefore be able to compare and contrast, the alternative development strategies open to Cuba. It is to the identification of the intellectual parameters that underlie analyses of the Cuban development process to which we now turn in Chapter 4.

CHAPTER 4

THE INTELLECTUAL PARAMETERS
OF CUBAN DEVELOPMENT

UNEXAMINED AND UNEXPRESSED ASSUMPTIONS

Although there is general agreement on the seriousness of Cuba's economic predicament, there is no unanimity as to the causes, consequences or solutions.

Such disagreement is not peculiar to Cuban studies in particular, or what some specialists refer to as 'Cubanology'. It is a common trait within economics and development studies in general, and indeed across the whole spectrum of social analysis. It is argued that such variance is characteristic of *all* scientific inquiry.

> Scientists, like other intellectuals, come to their work with a world view, a set of preconceptions that provides the framework for their analyses of the world. These preconceptions enter at both an explicit and an implicit level, but even when invoked explicitly, unexamined and unexpressed assumptions underlie them.
>
> (Levins and Lewontin 1985: 267)

This book is concerned to understand the development options open to Cuba, and is not the place to engage in debates on the philosophy of scientific inquiry in general, or of economic analysis and development theory in particular (but see Diesing 1982; Rose 1984; Cole 1993, 1995: Chapters 1, 6 and 7). However, identifying the 'unexamined and unexpressed assumptions' that underlie analyses of the world, and hence of Cuba, is elementary to understanding, evaluating and comparing the development options open to Cuba. *All* development strategies, concerned to allocate and utilize resources to achieve particular ends, act to the advantage of particular social and economic interests. Bias is inevitable and unavoidable. Searching for the chimera of the correct, neutral analysis is a pointless exercise, since distinct analytical perspectives operate with different parameters of 'scientific' inquiry: different philosophies of science associated to distinct ideologies of knowledge.

The late Professor Dudley Seers, a respected 'mainstream' development economist, maintained that the neutral, objective analysis of development is an impossibility.

> Let me first dispose of the question whether any economic [or development] theory is, or can be 'correct'. Students often ask me which theory is right? This is

an inappropriate question because there is no objective way of assessing whether any theoretical school is right ... the main ones are self-contained systems, perfectly logical on their own premises ... Empirical tests are not very relevant ... because the objectives ... are derived from the theories ... The crucial questions are: *Whose interests does a theory serve?* How does it serve them?

(Seers 1983: 33, emphasis added)

Essentially the same experience is interpreted differently: there can be no recourse to empirical data as the final arbiter. The same 'facts' have different significance for theorists working within different theoretical perspectives: different 'intellectual parameters' of scientific inquiry. The essential reality is an *abstract* reality of relationships, which can only be understood theoretically: there are no unambiguous 'facts' to see. But relationships are none the less real for that. We are concerned to explain relations *between* people. It is not a question of what people do, but of how they affect each other, and what people perceive these effects to be. Hence, having identified the shared, material conditions which are the parameters within which people make choices and adopt options, we are concerned to understand *why* people, faced with the same constraints, behave and react in different ways. Such implicit understandings of human motivation and behaviour are at the basis of theoretical interpretations of, and policy prescriptions for, development objectives.

We cannot begin to define economic and development objectives for society, how to bring about the 'good' society and what is 'just', until we have, at least implicitly, a notion of what people are in the first place. What motivates people's behaviour; what is fundamental to 'human nature'? The implied conceptions of human nature are the 'unexamined and unexpressed' assumptions that underlie scientific inquiry. And these assumptions specify the moral, ideological and political implications, and hence the bias, of theoretical analyses.

That there are fundamental disagreements within economic and development theory is a commonplace. 'If you laid all economists [and development theorists] end-to-end you wouldn't reach a conclusion' (George Bernard Shaw). Economists have different 'visions' of economic behaviour and development theories, and understand the process of social change differently (see Heilbroner and Milberg 1995). The terms in which economic 'reality' (see Bell and Kristol 1981) and hence the development process (see Preston 1996), are defined are different, which makes reasoned debate between competing economic and development perspectives at best difficult, leading to what Paul Deising calls 'distorted communication' between theorists working within different perspectives (see Diesing 1982: 5). More generally, on the bias in scientific inquiry in economic analysis see Cole (1995: Chapters 1, 2, 6 and 7).

Theorists using the same words, such as 'value' and 'development', mean different concepts. This chapter attempts to understand the conceptual basis of economists' and development theorists' disagreements, and the implications of the different interpretations of economic activity for development policy.

Human existence is social existence. And social life is characterized by a technical division of labour, with people specializing in particular economic functions. This specialization reflects the particular social and environmental parameters of human life in each location. In economic terms, people do not consume what they produce, and for social existence there has to be some form of exchange of products between producers and consumers. Economics is the study of this relation of exchange between consumers and producers. And development studies is concerned to understand how this relation might be better regulated, managed or organized to achieve higher and/or more secure and more desirable standards of living.

In the economic relationship of exchange between consumers and producers, what determines the rate of exchange? Is it the preferences of consumers? Is it the technical exigencies of the production process? Or is the relation between consumers and producers one of interdependence, the behaviour of each defined in terms of the other? Since consumers and producers are party to *every* economic transaction, economic data can *always* be interpreted within three perspectives, the distinct analyses reflecting the assumed 'dynamic' of economic activity. Of course, there are more than three 'schools' of economic thought (see Cole 1993, 1995: 35–6).

In Chapter 1, I cited a number of different assessments of the Cuban 'predicament':

> The 1990–93 macroeconomic crisis in Cuba has arisen essentially as a result of the elimination of the subsidization of the Cuban economy [by the Soviet Union].
>
> (Ritter 1994: 69)

> The proximate cause of the present predicament is not hard to identify. Cuba has a small and heavily trade-dependent economy. In the presence of the US embargo, Cuba came to depend on the former Soviet trade (CMEA) bloc for over four-fifths of its imports. Without access to the US market, with access to other markets restricted and with imports from the former CMEA countries reduced by roughly two-thirds, Cuba's economy and its people are struggling to survive.
>
> (Zimbalist 1992a: 407)

> Decisive as the revolution has been ... it has not produced an effective system of participation ... With respect to the deficiencies of the existing regime, the debates and preoccupations with it reflect a need not to replace the regime but to improve it by deepening its ideals and its socialist project.
>
> (Heredia 1993: 75–6)

It is the intellectual project of this chapter to make explicit the 'unexamined and unexpressed assumptions' that underlie these interpretations of the Cuban predicament: to highlight the 'intellectual parameters' of the Cuban 'reality'. The ideological and political implications of these analyses will be highlighted, making purposeful theory 'choice' possible.

THE CONSUMER AS ECONOMIC DYNAMIC

In the relation of exchange between producers and consumers, it can be assumed that the price paid for a commodity, and hence the income of producers, essentially reflects the tastes and preferences of consumers. 'Economists proceed on the fundamental *article of faith* that the economy is a structure that exists for the benefit of the individuals in it as human beings and, therefore, for *consumers*' (Lancaster 1974: 216, emphasis added).

Individuals are 'assumed', it is an article of faith, a belief, to be innately endowed with a unique set of tastes and talents; and humans are naturally motivated to fulfil their own ends – to enjoy themselves, to maximize 'utility'. It is 'natural' to be selfish. But this understanding of human nature is not a 'fact', it is an interpretation, based upon a casual, empiricist (reflecting the positivist philosophy of science which underlies this perspective) observation of human behaviour, allegedly identifying characteristics and traits that are universal to all humanity: 'the nature of economic analysis ... consists of deductions from a series of postulates ... which are almost universal facts of experience *whenever* human activity has an economic aspect' (Robbins 1984: 99–100, emphasis added).

These 'universal facts of experience' are:

1. Every individual is different, being innately endowed with a unique set of tastes and talents, defining his or her subjective preferences, which are peculiar to him or her. Individuals in their essentials are *not* social products but are *in*dependent beings.
2. Every individual attempts to enjoy himself or herself, according to his or her own preferences. This is what economists refer to as 'maximizing utility'.
3. Individuals like to choose between alternative sources of 'utility'. 'Diminishing marginal utility' is part of the human condition. Our enthusiasm begins to wane the more we have of any one source of utility: the pleasure from each extra unit declines – marginal utility diminishes. Hence we prefer a 'basket' of alternatives to choose between – 'moderation in all things'.

Now, everyone I know fits this description, it really seems to be a 'universal fact of experience'. But the subjective preference theory of value goes one step further, arguing that these 'universal' human characteristics *determine* value, and hence prices. They are not merely descriptive of the human condition, but they *determine* human behaviour. The 'universal facts of experience' are the *dynamic* of economic activity: '*value depends entirely upon utility*' (Jevons 1970: 77, emphasis in original).

The assertion that these 'universal facts of experience' determine value and price does not logically follow from the 'description' of 'universal' human characteristics. It is an axiom of economic analysis, a *belief* in human motivation, an *article of faith*. Economic policies which derive from this interpretation of economic activity are orientated towards creating an economy, and a society, in the image of this belief; a society in which independent individuals are 'free' to act according to their assumed nature, and maximize utility according to their 'subjective preferences'; free to choose.

Social and economic policy should be driven by individuals' quest for personal pleasure. If this is how individuals 'naturally' behave, then the creation of a social environment in which people can be 'natural' is a moral imperative. The theory of free markets becomes an 'ethical' principle. And the 'science' of economics, which allocates resources to maximize individuals' or utility, fulfilling the purpose of human life, is morally justified. 'Economics is the science which studies human behaviour as a relationship between ends and scarce means which have alternative uses' (Robbins 1984: 16). Development is a process by which resources are better allocated to achieve higher states of independent individuals', utility maximization. It is assumed (believed) that price, and therefore value, is determined by the hedonistic expediency of consumption: the *subjective preference* theory of value (see Cole *et al.*, 1991: Chapters 3 and 4; Cole 1995: Chapter 3).

Economic policy is intended to control individuals' selfish intuitions through 'incentives': to harness individuals' unique talents in production to satisfy consumers' preferences; to maximize utility. Hence there must be 'free' markets. If individuals are to consume according to their own subjective preferences, then they must be able to choose freely between alternatives. Individuals as talented producers have to receive an income which compensates them for the discomfort, the 'disutility', of work, which is also subjective. In free markets the disutility of production is compensated by the utility of consumption, and consumers reward producers with an income commensurate with the pleasure they have provided as a reward for the disutility suffered in production. 'The theory ... is entirely based on the calculus of pleasure and pain; the object of economics is to ... [purchase] pleasure ... at the lowest cost of pain' (Jevons 1970: 91).

DEVELOPMENT AS FULFILLING INDIVIDUALS' POTENTIALS

Economic development requires modernization of the mind. It requires revision of the attitudes, modes of conduct and institutions adverse to material progress ... economic achievement and progress largely depend upon human aptitudes and attitudes.

(Bauer 1976: 84, 41)

Economic development will be consequent on producers responding to consumer demand, as indicated by market forces. Individuals must acquire the attitudes and intuitions to offset 'costs' and 'benefits', to maximize profit. Individual 'responsibility' must prevail over social 'accountability'.

Independent individuals are the development dynamic as well as the economic dynamic. As a perspective on development this goes right back to Adam Smith in the eighteenth century. But more recently, the 'modernization' school of development theory is concerned to create societies which maximize the freedom of individuals (see So 1990: Part 1). Contemporary modernization theory has its roots in Walt Rostow's *The Stages of Economic Growth: An Anti-communist Manifesto* (Rostow 1960). Development is presented as a natural, evolutionary process from 'traditional', backward society, to 'modern', advanced society, examples of the latter being the United States or Western Europe. The key stage in this evolution is the 'take-off', where scientific research is applied to production, dramatically increasing productive efficiency. What is essential for take-off? 'It is evident that the take-off requires the existence and the successful activity of some group in society which is prepared to accept innovations. (Rostow 1960: 50). Entrepreneurs motivated to maximize profit and, responding to the markets forces of consumer demand (utility) and producer supply (disutility), are the development dynamic, and are to be encouraged.

There is not space here to go into all the ramifications of development as modernization, to allow for the purposeful activity of entrepreneurs to raise living standards. But the contemporary manifestation of this development ideology is the International Monetary Fund and World Bank inspired 'structural adjustment' programmes for indebted developing economies: 'A structural adjustment program can be defined as a set of policy measures that attempts to permanently change relative prices of tradable to notradable goods in the economy, in order to reallocate . . . productive factors' (Edwards and Van Wijnbergen 1989: 1482). It is market exchange guided by appropriate relative prices which allocates resources to achieve economic growth – a precondition for take-off and development.

> [E]conomic growth . . . remains the unquestioned imperative of development strategy and that the benefits derived from economic growth can best provide the means for addressing ancillary concerns [poverty relief, environmental protection, etc.].
>
> (D. Reed 1992: 4)

John Pilger gives a graphic account of the process of 'reallocation of productive factors' in the Philippines:

> [T]he Philippines has been 'structurally adjusted' . . . almost all the forests will be lost by the end of the century [being exported as timber to earn export revenues] . . . 500,000 will lose their jobs this year . . . an increase in child labour is anticipated . . . 399,000 children would be denied milk and vitamins, and 103,000 tuberculosis suffers medical treatment . . . tens of thousands of children will die 'silently' and 'unnecessarily'.
>
> (Pilger 1992: 161–2)

For detail on the suffering caused and the inequality created in Latin America by these policies, see Green (1995).

There is currently a great deal of intellectual effort being put into trying to understand why the theoretical promise of the maximization of utility is being experienced as an increase in misery, low pay and unemployment, and not as something that might be described as 'development'.

> Evaluating the effects of ... structural adjustment programmes ... depends on the method selected [the 'intellectual parameters' of 'reality'] ... are the disappointing results to be attributed to the poor execution of the programme or to the programme itself? ... it is not clear how much time has to go by before the adjustments affect macroeconomic development ... [and] the indicators ... used to evaluate the effects ... are disputable.
>
> (Lensink 1996: 97)

However, for those sinking into absolute poverty, suffering and dying, the indicators of the effect are not quite so opaque and disputable.

Academics, consultants and theorists within the modernization perspective are not oblivious to this suffering, and are concerned to discover why these programmes have not delivered something that could be unambiguously defined as 'progress'. The problem is being addressed by a school of thought known as the 'New Institutional Economics' (see North 1990; Stiglitz 1992; Harriss *et al.*, 1995). It is argued that individuals' behaviour reflects their understanding as to how the world functions, an understanding based on people's experience of the world. However, experience of, and hence intuitive understandings of, the world differ. The different intellectual parameters of 'reality' create uncertainty, and 'institutions are formed to reduce uncertainty ... [but] institutions [become] ... a critical constraint ... [since] individuals ... with bargaining power as a result of the institutional framework have a crucial stake in perpetuating the system' (North 1995: 18–20).

So, Rostow's evolution towards modernity is thwarted by institutional constraints intent on 'perpetuating the system' and maintaining an iniquitous society. Development strategy should now be geared towards overcoming the cultural and institutional limitations on individuals' 'freedom' to choose, constraints which are particular to each social context. To this end, the World Bank emphasizes 'good governance', defined as governments establishing 'the rules that make markets work efficiently and ... correct for market failure' (World Bank 1992: 1). According to the US State Department, this requires: building a national identity; fostering democratic values; constructing democratic institutions; ensuring 'honest' government administration; competition for political power between political parties; and civilian control of the military (see Agency for International Development 1990: 3).

With regard to the Soviet bloc economies in 'transition' from central planning, a category to which Cuba is thought to belong, the goal of transition 'is the same as that of economic reforms elsewhere: to build a thriving market economy capable of delivering long-term growth in living standards' (World Bank 1996b: 1). For William Robinson (1996), the emphasis on political, multi-party democracy is a reaction to the instability and unrest created by spiralling global economic inequality. Neo-liberal economic regulation, based on the theoretical conclusions of the subjective preference theory of value, understands that utility will be maximized if economic activity is organized according to the free market economic imperative, which is a precondition for democracy. But

> the world's productive resources are owned by an ever smaller circle of human beings ... by the year 2000 some 400 transnational corporations will own about two-thirds of the fixed assets of the planet ... Such tremendous concentrations of economic power lead to tremendous concentrations of political power at a global level. Any discussion of 'democracy' under such conditions becomes meaningless.
>
> (Robinson 1996: 385)

Such economic power is justified within the subjective preference theory of value by 'market forces', reflecting human nature, the resultant distribution of which is a consequence of genetic superiority (natural selection), which is not amenable to political control. It is an ideological justification of economic inequality. With the emphasis on the 'democratic' organization of political life, which does not threaten or question the unequal social and economic status quo, conflicts over economic inequality are side-tracked into political avenues which cannot address the problems of economic inequality; problems which derive from the control of economic resources, not something which people 'vote' about. This is a strategy which has its contradictions.

For instance, in Latin America there has been a dramatic shift from military dictatorships to elected civilian governments, a development that has heightened expectations of the poor majority that political representation will alleviate their poverty. But as their economic position fails to improve, there will be a return to military dictatorships as the poor seek economic justice by non-electoral means (see Castañeda 1993: 245; Lambie 1997: 12).

However, the World Bank is more optimistic about the benefits of economic 'freedom', and increasingly defines development priorities in terms of particular institutional initiatives needed to address poverty, asserting that 'No country has had a sustained impact on reducing poverty without continuing positive economic growth' (World Bank 1996a: 10). The problem is in ensuring that growth is 'broad-based', which particularly means addressing the needs of the 'microentrepreneurs' who 'are of tantamount importance to ensuring broad-based growth' (World Bank 1996a: 11). It is essential to the functioning of a market process of development that small producers have access to 'essential factors of production', especially credit, and it is stated that since most of the poor live in rural areas (although by the year 2000 most people in the world will live in urban environments), access to land and land reform is critical.

So, it is not the natural propensity of individuals to compete to maximize their own advantage that is the problem, but the institutional, and hence cultural, context within which self-interest is exploited. The emphasis is to change institutions so as to reduce the constraints on individual choice: a return to Rostow's 'modernization' project.

Hence, with regard to the quote above from Archibald Ritter, the fact that the Cuban economy has not functioned for nearly 40 years on the basis of 'free' exchange inevitably has meant that individuals have been institutionally denied the opportunity to fulfil their potentials and maximize utility. This has only been accepted by Cubans because of Soviet subsidies, which have artificially inflated their living standards, compensating for the 'authoritarian' limitation of 'freedom'. Dependency on state (ultimately Soviet) largesse has militated against the development of an entrepreneurial culture in Cuba. Individuals' economic complacency will only be overcome if people have to respond to individual, economic incentives, 'modernizing the mind'.

> In the long run there appears to be no reasonable alternative to a substantially marketized, mixed-ownership, and externally orientated system. In the absence of intensified movement in these directions, Cuba could look forward to a productivity decline, growth slow-down, excessively slow diversification and expansion of exports, and sluggish response to new economic opportunities.
>
> (Ritter 1990: 144)

Susan Eckstein (Eckstein 1994) develops this line of argument, asserting that Fidel Castro's political authority and power has been maintained in the face of the controls on individuals' economic liberty by his 'charisma'. Political power itself is a reflection of the 'individual' characteristics of Fidel.

> By the 1990s, it appeared that his [Fidel Castro's] role had become intensely conservative. He now seems to be intent on preserving the political and economic status quo ... Ultimately, Cuba *has no alternative* but to embark on a process of economic reform in the direction of marketization and economic liberalization.
>
> (Ritter 1994: 83, 91, emphasis added)

Where the relevant interpretation of economic and development experience is defined in terms of the activity of independent individuals, whose behaviour and nature are biologically determined, then the purpose of life is to maximize personal satisfaction: personal consumption and 'utility'. It is thought that Cubans' tolerance of the lack of a 'free' society, in which they might better fulfil their individual potentials, has been 'bought' by Soviet largesse. Cuba's predicament is therefore the ending of the Soviet subsidization of Cubans' living standards.

THE IDEOLOGICAL IMPLICATIONS OF THE 'CONSUMER' AS ECONOMIC DYNAMIC

Starting from the conception of human nature that individuals are bio-logically endowed with tastes and talents, and motivated to maximize utility, it can be logically argued that individuals *only* have to know the price of commodities to be as happy as possible. If the relationship between consumers and producers is conducted through competitive, free markets, which are ideally 'perfectly competitive', then utility will be maximized, under a condition known as 'general equilibrium' (see Cole 1995: Chapter 3).

Of course, 'perfect competition', in which consumers determine what is produced, and are able to consume according to their individual prefer-ences, is impossible (see Cole 1995: 63). But the theory is not meant to *describe* any actual economy. *If* individuals are as assumed, *then* perfect competition is the image of utopia, the standard of 'development'. This is an image which acts as a template for policy formulation, attempting to make the 'real' world more like the 'ideal'. 'The Utopian theoretical construct of perfect competition ... becomes relevant as a reference point by which to judge the health of an economy, as well as the remedies suggested for its amelioration' (Lal 1983: 15).

As an economic methodology, the subjective preference theory of value, in consequence of the intellectual parameters set by the 'preconceptions that provides the framework' for the analysis, considers *only* 'individual' con-sumer choices in the ceaseless quest to maximize utility. Value is *qualitatively* defined as reflecting each individual's subjective preferences for utility. Hence economists cannot say anything 'quantitative' about distribution within free markets, and are interested only in consumer choice between competing sources of utility. The aggregate *amount* of utility enjoyed is not the problem. All that can be said about inequality is that in 'free' markets poverty reflects individuals' endowment of talents for sat-isfying consumers' subjective preferences for utility. The relevant data for economic policy formulation mean that economists are concerned only with the *marginal* effects of individual choice. Indeed, the subjective preference theory of value is often described as the 'marginalist' school of econom-ics.

Essentially, each economic transaction can logically be considered inde-pendently of other economic activity. It is just another aspect of utility being maximized subject to individuals' choices. As far as the subjective prefer-ence theory economist is concerned, economic exchange is a series of independent events, each a reflection of individuals' tastes and talents.

As a scientific methodology it is reductionist, believing that the parts (individuals) explain the whole (the economy) (see Rose 1984). The imma-nent theory of knowledge is 'positivist': for knowledge to be scientific and valid it must predict future 'events' (see Popper 1959; Magee 1975). It is not necessary to explain those events – only to correlate them to other, essentially independent, phenomena. As Karl Popper, the 'doyen' of the positivist theory of knowledge, writes: 'without a carefully protected free market, the whole economic system must cease to serve its only rational purpose, that is, *to satisfy the demands of the consumer*' (Popper 1962: 348, emphasis in original).

The subjective preference theory of value as an analytic, economic methodology is: methodologically *reductionist*; legitimated as 'valid knowledge' by a *positivist* philosophy of science; morally *individualist*, justifying 'self-interest'. And it is ideologically and politically *conservative*: as long as there are 'free' markets the rich deserve to be rich, and the poor have only themselves to blame (see Cole 1995: Chapters 1, 2 and 6):

> our society is as equal as it can be, given the natural inequalities between people. According to this view, the political and social revolutions of the eighteenth and nineteenth centuries destroyed artificial hierarchies and allowed the natural differences in ability to manifest themselves.
>
> (Lewontin 1982: 89)

By addressing *only* individual responsibility and utility maximization, this perspective cannot even frame meaningful questions about social accountability. The social 'status quo' is not under investigation, only how well people 'choose' to fulfil their personal objectives *within* society. The criticism that this theory is unrealistic, that 'free' markets do not exist, does not dent the conservative theoretical edifice. The fact that perfect competition is not a reality does not diminish the 'free' market emphasis within economic policy.

For instance, where inequality is a result of imperfect markets, and *all* markets are imperfect by definition,

> a tax/subsidy system based on *income* differences which aimed at legislating for a desired income distribution would ... affect the choices individuals make at the margin between work and leisure ... [which] would impair the productive efficiency of the economy.
>
> (Lal 1983: 14, emphasis in original)

In compensating those who lose through 'imperfect' economic transactions by redistributing income to achieve a 'fairer' distribution of income, there is no reason to believe that the increase in economic 'welfare' should compensate for the loss in economic efficiency. All that governments can do is to correct competitive imperfections for the future rather than retrospectively address economic injustices which only serve to compound economic 'distortions' (from perfect competition).

But the idea that economic policy should be intended to make economies more 'perfect' is coherent *only if* it is assumed (believed) that individuals are biologically endowed with unique tastes and talents and are motivated to maximize personal utility. Such assumptions justify and legitimate social inequality, since as long as free markets obtain, poverty and disadvantage are the product of personal inadequacy. The victims are to blame. The rich have nothing to be ashamed of. 'Simple though this view is, its appeal derives from its political message which is that those who have money got it by dint of merit and effort and those who do not have only themselves to blame for it' (Desai 1982: 293).

THE PRODUCER AS ECONOMIC DYNAMIC

Alternatively, relations of exchange between producers and consumers can be interpreted as reflecting the technical exigencies of production, rather than consumers' preoccupation for 'satisfaction'. Production is fundamental to survival, and fundamental to production is specialization: the 'technical division of labour'. Markets are not now considered to be *mechanisms* through which individuals 'compete' to maximize utility, but *systems* by which individuals with particular specialist talents can 'cooperate' to produce: to this end economic activity has to be coordinated. 'Most people think of themselves first of all not as consumers but as producers' (Galbraith and Salinger 1981: 164). Value and price now reflect the costs of production: the amount of resources used to produce a commodity, and hence 'technology'; and the price of those resources, reflecting the incomes of producers, and hence 'distribution'. This is the cost-of-production theory of value (see Cole *et al.*, 1991: Chapters 6 and 7; Cole 1995: Chapter 4).

Individuals are not now 'free to choose' as independent consumers, but have to fit into a cooperative system as dependent producers. While income in part reflects individuals' abilities, it is also contingent upon their place in the technical division of labour, which is beyond their volition and control. It is not a question of 'choice'. Individuals' fortunes do not merely depend upon their innate tastes and talents; rather, individuals are now assumed (believed) to be 'socialized' to fit into the social system in general, reacting to the technical needs of the economy, and in particular responding to the material incentives of the price system. People 'adapt' to the needs of society. Human nature is not fixed by biological determinism, but is, within limits, 'malleable'.

> Man is innately programmed in such a way that he needs a culture to complete him ... Man is like one of those versatile cake mixes that can be variously prepared to end up as different kinds of cake ... just as a cake has to be baked, so a baby has to be exposed to a specific, already existing, culture.
>
> (Midgely 1978: 286)

The economy now has to be managed in the 'general' interest to create a cooperative environment. For an environment to engender cooperation implies full employment and standards of 'fairness' and equality. 'The outstanding faults of the economic society in which we live are its failure to provide for full employment and its arbitrary and inequitable distribution of wealth and income' (Keynes 1936: 372).

There are two policy objectives for the cost-of-production theory of value: the efficient utilization of economic resources and the 'fair' distribution of income. Economic policy now has to be 'realistic', reflecting the actual technical conditions within which producers cooperate, and the institutional context which determines income distribution. Policy is not a consequence of comparing the 'actual' economy to a model of the ideal ('general equilibrium' or 'perfect competition'). Indeed, as technology evolves to achieve higher levels of efficiency, implying that individuals become ever more technically dependent upon each other as the division of labour expands, techniques of economic management must also change. Economic activity has to be coordinated within ever less flexible technical parameters, making free exchange by independent individuals in their own 'subjectively' defined interest ever less a rational option where cooperation reflects a wider, technical rationality. Free markets become less and less relevant as policy options for social and economic coordination and development.

The state is now concerned with the evolving, general 'aggregate' interest of the *macro*economy, and not the 'marginal' interests of individuals in the *micro*economy. 'Macroeconomics is the study of how whole economic *systems* function. What is ultimately at issue are such things as the determination of *national* income, output, inflation and unemployment' (Godley and Cripps 1983: 13, emphasis added). The dynamic of economies is 'technically' defined, to be managed in the 'general' interest. If economic activity is measured in 'value' (price) terms, then management of the economy is conducted through a 'mixed economy' model of economic activity, with the economic aggregates of employment, investment and trade being controlled through the manipulation of state expenditure/income (effective demand), the interest rate and the exchange rate. Value is a *quantitative* concept to be managed and accounted for, it is not subjectively defined and *qualitative*.

An alternative to quantifying output in value terms is to define economic activity in physical (technical) terms, and then economic management and regulation is through central planning, reflecting the dependence of different specialized sectors within a technical division of labour. In either case, an elite of economists or planners manages and controls the economy in the general interest.

DEVELOPMENT AS STRUCTURAL CHANGE

As with the subjective preference theory of value, the cost-of-production theory of value has an analogous conception of development.

> The primary objective of long-run development ... [is] sustainable economic growth *combined with* social justice. Development involves structural

transformation of the economy and society ... as developing countries acquire *technological* capability ... special efforts are needed to ensure ... a wide spread of economic opportunities and an appropriate *distribution* of social goods.

(Stewart 1994: 98, emphasis added)

Development has to be managed to achieve structural change: 'structuralism' (*not* structural adjustment). The social structure is to be 'engineered' by experts, by planners and economists, managed to be compatible with an advancing technical division of labour. Development, contingent on technical change, can be approached through such policies as 'import substitution industrialization', producing technically advanced goods which were hitherto imported (see Prebisch 1962).

> Policy recommendations centre on finding ways in which governments can intervene to help private producers change ... [the economic] structure ... via the promotion of import substitution in individual underdeveloped countries and the establishment of common markets among underdeveloped countries.
>
> (Hunt 1989: 122)

Policy initiatives are institutionally based to effect social and economic management of production, and not orientated towards augmenting individuals' freedom of choice in consumption.

However, the 'radical' structuralists, or 'dependency' theorists, who now consider themselves to be part of 'world systems theory' (see Chew and Denemark 1996), are not optimistic that structural transformation and institutional change will be possible, at least in the short term. In the contemporary world, economic activity is effectively institutionally controlled to ensure the profitability of transnational corporations:

> competitive capital accumulation remains ... the ultimate determining process of ... [w]orld history ... [and is characterized by] shifts in trade routes, centers of accumulation ... these places and peoples temporarily enjoyed privileged cultural, social, economic ... and political positions.
>
> (Frank 1996: 44–5)

However, the radical structuralists have a problem in defining policy alternatives. If development reflects the ebb and flow of world economic exploitation and the institution of the 'world market', what can individual people, or even nation states, actually do to improve their fortunes and develop?

More generally, within the structuralist perspective on economic development, there is confusion over why, after so many resources have been invested in the economic development of the 'Third World', the plight of the world's poor is demonstrably getting worse. We saw that within the subjective preference theory of value and the 'modernization' approach to development, working within the New Institutional Economics, theorists are also attempting to explain this apparent anomaly. However, structuralist theorists believe themselves to be in a 'theoretical impasse', and are working towards a 'new' paradigm for development (see Long and Long 1992; Schurrman 1993; Booth 1994).

Theory and policy have to adapt to the changing technical and institutional conditions of economic cooperation. Effective management of social and economic systems requires accurate and relevant models of systems: models which reflect the best scientific 'paradigm' to explain 'development'. Existing development models and paradigms are anachronistic, referring to a post-war reality that has moved on in the course of incessant technical change. And revised 'intellectual parameters' imply a new theoretical context, a new paradigm for understanding development, which would highlight new policy emphases.

In the quote on Cuba from Andrew Zimbalist (1992a: 407) cited above, the Cuban economic predicament is essentially one of coordinating, through trade, with the wider world technical division of labour, which has changed with the collapse of the Soviet bloc and CAME. It is a 'management' problem. Indeed, within the context of the cost-of-production theory of value, the system of control through physical, central planning was already anachronistic, exhibiting increasing signs of inefficiency, and poor coordination and cooperation between producers: 'certain features of the centralized model were of special value. It was essential [in the early years] to ensure an extraordinarily high degree of concentration of means . . . on a small number of key goals' (Brus 1972: 83). The 'key goals' of the Cuban economy had been coordinated by planners within the CAME, a system increasingly under strain. Similar tensions, the consequence of central planning, ultimately led to the collapse of the Soviet Union, the Eastern bloc and the CAME in 1989 to 1991.

For Zimbalist, the Rectification Campaign of 1986, begun before the collapse of the CAME, is part of the inevitable cycle of reform in centrally planned economies. This reflects the need for economic policy and the techniques of economic management to adapt to the technical exigencies of economic activity.

> [The] initiation of the rectification campaign is . . . [a] moratorium/retrenchment in the reform cycle of a centrally planned economy (cpe). Periods of liberalisation [under the SDPE] in cpe's *inevitably* generate economic, political and social tensions as well as outcomes that are antithetical to the stated goals of socialist society.
>
> (Zimbalist 1993: 124, emphasis added)

If the state is to maintain central control, these tensions are addressed by reasserting central authority: the Rectification Campaign. Through the Campaign, the Cuban authorities nipped in the bud the tensions that led to the disintegration of the Soviet Union. That the Rectification Campaign was *inevitable* indicates an economic determinism that precludes economic organization according to conscious political choices, which ideologically justifies economic regulation and social organization by a technocratic elite.

THE IDEOLOGICAL IMPLICATIONS OF THE 'PRODUCER' AS ECONOMIC DYNAMIC

Believing human nature to be an adaptation to the needs of the social and economic system implies that the economic system has to be expertly 'managed' to achieve the full utilization of economic resources, and a 'fair' distribution of income to ensure social harmony (see Cole 1995: Chapter 4).

There is still a role for markets and competition where economic activity is measured in value terms, to ensure the efficiency of individual production processes. But the competitive exigencies of the enterprise geared towards the maximization of profits cannot be permitted to override the more general interest: such objectives as full employment and 'fair' distribution take precedence. A mixed, part-state and part-private, economy is called for, the precise mix changing with the evolving technical and institutional parameters of the production process. 'Economics is a science of thinking in terms of models joined to the art of choosing models which are relevant to the contemporary world' (Keynes, quoted in Moggridge 1976: 26).

As an economic methodology, the cost-of-production theory of value addresses the technical and distributional aspects of production. Economists are concerned with the *aggregate* effects of the changes in economic activity, not the 'marginal' expression of individual choices. As a scientific methodology it is *holist*, rather than reductionist, believing that the whole (the economy) structures the behaviour of the parts (individuals); that individuals have to adapt to the needs of society or the economy, rather than vice versa. Human nature is not simply biologically determined, but is analogous to a 'versatile cake mix' (which gives a whole new meaning to describing deranged individuals as being 'as nutty as a fruit cake'), adapting to the cultural needs of the 'system'. The immanent theory of knowledge is *paradigmatic* rather than positivist. Even if forthcoming 'events' are not predicted accurately, that paradigm, or model, which best resolves problems of the system is considered to be the current standard of a 'scientific' analysis. And as the system evolves and encounters hitherto unexperienced problems, there is a theoretical impasse, calling for a 'scientific revolution'. A new paradigm is developed which defines the problem to be solved, and more adequately explains experience and manages the system. 'The existence of the paradigm sets the problem to be solved' (Kuhn 1970: 27). The dominant paradigm defines the 'intellectual parameters' of reality.

The cost-of-production theory of value as an analytic, economic methodology is: methodologically *holist*; legitimated by a *paradigmatic* philosophy of science; morally committed to a mixed, welfare-based economy, in the *general interest*. And it is ideologically and politically *social democratic*. The (changing) general interest is identified through 'pluralist' political institutions, through which distinct economic 'interest' groups, technically defined (miners, farmers, bankers, students, doctors, etc.), arrive at a social compromise over the distribution of the national economic product.

It is an elitist ideology, legitimating the role of experts in managing social and economic life. In the coordination of economic activity, the only 'political' aspect is in the distribution of the technical product, affecting the costs of production, which are addressed through pluralist political institutions. Otherwise, economic (and development) problems are 'technical', being 'rationally' solved by trained 'experts' (economists and development theorists).

> In practice governments begin with consultation. They seek agreement from the principal groups in the economy ... However, having done everything possible to reach consensus, the government must also retain the power to enforce the result.
>
> (Galbraith and Salinger 1981: 121)

However, where the institutional framework of political control is centralized and authoritarian, then the quantitative measure of economic activity is not in terms of 'value', but is 'physically' defined: the *number* of things produced, the *weight* of resources used, etc. And social change and development is purely a technical, 'natural', exigency. 'The social movement ... [is] a process of *natural history*, governed by laws not only *independent* of human will, consciousness and intentions, but, rather, on the contrary *determining* the will, consciousness and intentions of men' (Lenin 1963: 166, emphasis added).

Human nature is not a 'versatile cake mix'; it is defined by subsistence (a 'bread' mix). There is not now the institutional flexibility to reconcile different interests. Society is determined by the technical parameters of production. The social and political 'superstructure' is determined by the economic (technical) base, and the management of society in the common interest is a function of a 'vanguard' party, which essentially manages the institutional and technical conditions of productive processes. And the vanguard party, by means of technical planning, and therefore the central, planned control of production, creates the technical preconditions upon which will emerge a 'communist' social and political superstructure. 'Class political consciousness can be brought to the workers *only from without*, that is, only from outside the economic struggle ... it is our bounded duty to guide *these* "activities of the various opposition strata", if we desire to be the *"vanguard"'* (Lenin 1969: 78 and 84, emphasis in original).

This approach is similarly 'elitist'. The vanguard party is to manage development on behalf of the masses. But what is the interest of the vanguard party? It is not, and cannot be, a unified, homogeneous political unit. There is a myriad of conflicting technical interests to be represented, which has led Alec Nove to characterize this form of government as 'centralized pluralism' (Nove 1977: Chapter 3). Ministries and enterprises effectively become discrete 'interest groups', and it is the role of planners to achieve compromise between them in the general interest.

> [In] late 1984 . . . the draft plan for 1985 came under heavy criticism from . . . Fidel Castro . . . [and] a final high-level meeting in late November, attended by members of the Party's Politburo and Secretariat, vice-presidents of the government's Executive Committee, economic and other ministers; provincial party secretaries and Poder Popular presidents; the heads of mass organizations such as the trades unions . . . [approved the plan]. If one is seeking an 'economic decision making elite' in Cuba, then this group is probably it.
>
> (White 1986: 9)

In Cuba under the SDPE, the planning process was organized into four stages (see JUCEPLAN 1981):

1 Based on information from ministries, a macro, directive, technical plan was produced based on 'material balances'.
2 The feasibility of the plan was commented on by enterprises, and where relevant by appropriate mass organizations and the organs of *Poder Popular*.
3 Suggested modifications to the plan went to JUCEPLAN via the relevant ministry.
4 JUCEPLAN produced a definitive version of the plan, which became law through the National Assembly of Popular Power and was binding on all subordinate units.

The practice was not so smooth.

> All those years, ever since we made our first efforts in planning and development, a sectional spirit prevailed in all the state agencies, in every ministry and, in the end, in practice the plan was not necessarily rational or optimal. Rather it reflected the sum total of each sector defending its interests before the planning agencies and vying for available resources . . . each sector claimed that its needs were the most essential . . . and . . . important . . . a war [was] being waged by each agency, a struggle, a battle for what limited resources we had.
>
> (Castro 1985: 35)

Hence the Rectification Campaign, a process which for some commentators is 'a renewed commitment to perfect planning mechanisms' (Deere and Meurs 1992: 836).

For the cost-of-production theory of value/structuralist perspective, during the Special Period, when central control has been necessarily weakened, 'informal pluralism' provides the basis for political consensus and social order.

> Where should one look to find informal politics? The answer is broad: everywhere. The issue is not were to look but what to look for, because informality coexists and operates even within formal bureaucratic institutions and processes . . . discourse (public versus private transcripts); humor; the black market (or the

second economy); dissimulation and formalism; informal neighbourhood net-
works; fashion (clothes, hairstyle); art (music, films, painting literature);
sabotage; religion; labor (low productivity, absenteeism); the daily life of women;
and 'criminality'.

(Fernández 1994: 74)

THE CITIZEN AS ECONOMIC DYNAMIC

Instead of assuming (believing) either the independent consumer or
dependent producers to be the economic dynamic, as economic actors,
producers and consumers can be understood to be *interdependent*. It is the
citizen, who is both consumer *and* producer, who is the 'economic dynamic'.
Both consumer and producer are the condition and effect of the other.

> Production mediates consumption; it creates the latter's material; without it,
> consumption would lack an object. But consumption also mediates production,
> in that it alone creates for the products the subject for whom they are products . . .
> Without production, no consumption; but also, without consumption, no pro-
> duction.

(Marx 1973a: 91)

The specialization of producers into certain lines of production satisfying
consumers' particular preferences, necessitating exchange between consumers and producers, means that relations of social reproduction are
'commodity relations' – the exchange of products. 'What I proceed from is
the simplest social form in which the product of labour in contemporary
society manifests itself, and this is the "commodity" ' (Marx, quoted in
Dragsted 1976: 44).

The commodity is essentially a social relation, the value of which is both
qualitative and quantitative. In relations of 'commodity exchange' between
producers and consumers, to the independent, individual consumer the
commodity is a source of utility, a 'use value', qualitatively defined; to the
dependent, technical producer the commodity is a source of income, an
'exchange value', quantitatively defined. Value itself is a social relation, a
dialectic of the (qualitative) subjective preference and (quantitative) cost-of-
production theories of value. Each is the condition and effect of the other,
reflecting different aspects of the *same* reality. And citizens are *interdependent*.

As 'relations', the *commodity* and *value* are 'concepts', which can only be
conceived of abstractly, in theory. Actual social behaviour, what people *do*,
has to be interpreted to make explicit the social relationships which give
meaning to that social activity: *why* people do what they do and what is the
effect of their activity. '[All] science would be superfluous if the outward
appearance and essence of things coincided' (Marx 1972a: 817). As a social
relation, the commodity has value, which is both a qualitative use value and
a quantitative exchange value. And it is because commodities are values

that the productive activity of a mass of individual labourers can be coordinated to respond to the needs, wants and preferences of independent consumers through market exchange. 'The central characteristic of the capitalist mode of production . . . is that the private labour of individuals is not directly social, but must be rendered social by the exchange of products as commodities' (Weeks 1981: 29).

Value as a social relation between people is like weight: quantitatively it can only be determined by comparison. What a commodity is worth (how heavy it is) reflects what it will exchange for (is compared to a standard of weight, e.g. 1 kilogram). Value can be expressed only as *exchange value*: what the commodity will exchange for. But for qualitatively different commodities (as use values) to be compared and exchanged (as exchange values), there must be a common quality in terms of which they are commensurable. And this common quality is that *all* commodities are produced by *labour*. Use values may not also be exchange values, and thus not commodities: for instance, 'air' is not normally produced by labour and therefore is not a commodity, but is still very useful. 'The equalization [and therefore comparison and exchange] of . . . different kinds of labour can be the result only of . . . reducing them to their common denominator, viz, expenditure of human labour-power or human labour in the *abstract*' (Marx 1974: 78, emphasis added).

'Private' *concrete* labour, the actual work done by labourers, through exchange, becomes 'social' *abstract* labour. The concrete labour of the individual is socially (abstractly) valued, denoting its worth as indicated by the price realized by the commodity in exchange. Value, which is a social relation, exists *only* in exchange, as an exchange value; and exchange value is manifested as, but not the same as, price. 'Price taken by itself is nothing but the monetary expression of value' (Marx 1975: 39). On this perspective on value and price, see Cole (1995: 118–30).

The 'amount' of abstract labour, representing the value of a commodity, will affect (but not determine) the price of the commodity, and is *socially* defined. Value reflects the 'socially necessary abstract labour time' embodied in a commodity. Social necessity reflects the social demand (in market economies, individual need backed by purchasing power, or effective demand) and social supply (the ability of society to utilize technically resources to produce wanted commodities). Social demand: 'For a commodity to be sold at its market value . . . the total quantity of social labour used in producing the total mass of the commodity must correspond to the quantity of the social want for it, i.e. the effective social want' (Marx 1972a: 192). Social supply: '*the quantity of labour necessary* for its production in a given state of society, under certain average conditions of production' (Marx 1975: 38, emphasis in the original).

It is, then, an *abstract labour theory of value*, which is a dialectic of the subjective preference and cost-of-production theories of value. All interpret the *same* experience according to different intellectual parameters of 'reality'. Different 'unexpressed and unexamined' assumptions provide the framework for the analyses: assumptions which rationalize social behaviour within a moral, ideological and political context.

> Every product of labour is, in all states of society, is a use-value; but it is only at a definite historical epoch in a society's development that such a product becomes a commodity . . . *when the labour* . . . becomes expressed . . . *as its value.*
>
> (Marx 1974: 67, emphasis added)

Essentially, the market is not merely an incentive mechanism so that producers can satisfy consumers' subjective preferences; nor do markets merely systematically coordinate the economic activity of producers divided by a technical division of labour. Rather, the market is a process through which independent individuals' 'concrete' labour is transformed into social, 'abstract' labour. The concrete labour time actually worked by individuals is abstractly valued by society, in turn influencing the allocation of economic resources by producers trying to maximize their income. 'Concrete labour refers to the unique productive process undertaken by an individual, while abstract labour describes the social value of that labour as it is expressed through the exchange of commodities in the market' (McNally 1993: 177). Money is the 'general equivalent', representing human labour in the abstract, and 'mediates every transaction and quantifies the social value of each and every act of concrete labour' (McNally 1993: 178).

It is necessary to exchange the commodity for money, for producers to receive an income, allowing concrete labour to be valued as abstract labour, in which process market competition is essential. The rationale for production in an economy based on commodity exchange is to maximize the economic surplus (surplus value), which in the capitalist mode-of-production appears as profit. 'It must never be forgotten that the production of . . . surplus value . . . is the immediate purpose and compelling motive of capitalist production' (Marx 1972b: 243–4).

Through competitive market exchange, resources are allocated into those lines of production, and to those producers, which produce the greatest social surplus over and above the reproduction of society. The production process consumes the labour power of workers (variable capital, v) and produced inputs (raw materials, machinery, etc.), the means of production (constant capital, c). A surplus is produced (surplus value, s) over and above the value consumed in production ($v + c$). Labour power, the ability to work, is a commodity, which is sold on the labour market by labourers, who do not control the means of production, to capitalist employers, who do. The value *of* labour power reflects the value of the commodities that are consumed to reproduce the ability to work: subsistence, housing, clothing, training, recreation, etc. In the production process labour power produces more commodities, and hence values, than it itself is worth – this is surplus value. And the value of labour power (variable capital) is reflected in the payment to labour (income). And labour power is reproduced and renewed by consuming utilities bought with the income: the surplus value produced

goes towards expanding the economy through the reinvestment of profits.

Hence the value of commodities, while being determined by social demand
and social supply, is given by $v + c + s$ – the variable and constant capital
consumed, and the surplus value produced in the labour process – but the
magnitude of this value is revealed *only* in the process of exchange between
consumers and producers, and *does not exist* prior to exchange. 'The necessity
of translating concrete to abstract labour, of exchanging commodity for
money, makes competition an essential feature of the relations between
individual producing units' (McNally 1993: 179).

Value is a 'relationship'. Where the social means of production are owned
by individuals, surplus value appears as profit, but as with value and price,
surplus value and profit are distinct concepts. Apart from profit, surplus
value also appears as interest and rent: all incomes reflecting property
ownership and not the production of use values. Hence values differ from
prices (see Weeks 1981: Chapters 1, 2 and 3; Harvey 1982: Chapters 1 and 2;
McNally 1993: Chapter 4).

> The discrepancy between price and value . . . is an essential feature of any system
> of commodity production . . . This is not a defect, but, on the contrary, it makes
> this form the adequate one for a mode of production whose laws can only assert
> themselves as blindly operating averages between constant irregularities.
>
> (McNally 1993: 163–4)

There is constant competitive pressure on capitalists to maintain the rate
of profit and therefore remain in business by 'efficiency savings'. Costs have
to be reduced. Ultimately, the same output has to be produced by less
labour (variable capital) input: v as a proportion of total investment in
production $(v + c)$ declines. Unemployment rises or wages are reduced,
though there are limits to how far labour can be devalued. 'There can be no
market regulation . . . without a labour market, the wages system, and the
unplanned drive to accumulate for the sake of further accumulation'
(McNally 1993: 183).

At some point the amount of labour employed falls relative to the
investment in constant capital (c), reducing the potential for producing
surplus value: remember, value (and surplus value) is produced by variable
capital (labour power). Surplus value is distributed as profit to the most
efficient enterprises engaged in commodity exchange, and as a consequence
the least efficient firms become less viable economically, suffer declining
profits, becoming bankrupt and going out of business. 'Surplus value
originates in the productive process by virtue of the class relation between
capital and labour, but is distributed among individual capitalists [as profit]
according to the rules of competition' (Harvey 1982: 61). Hence enterprises
have to adopt the latest technology to maintain relative competitivity:
'competition puts a further obligation upon the capitalist to keep pace with
the general process of technological change' (Harvey 1982: 88).

The process of technical change economizes on labour, and production becomes more 'capital' intensive – what Marx conceived of as a rising 'organic composition of capital' (see below). While the individual enterprise may become *more* profitable through investing in labour saving techniques, the economy as a whole will be less able to produce a viable rate of return, a rate of profit: surplus value (s) as a rate of return on total investment in production ($v + c$). And unless labour is exploited more to produce relatively more surplus value, the *rate* of profit to capital in general will decline, even though the rate of profit may rise for the most efficient enterprises, and the overall absolute *amount* of profit may increase.

> [T]he gradual growth of constant capital [c] in relation to variable capital [v] must necessarily lead to a *gradual fall of the general rate of profit* so long as the rate of surplus value, or the intensity of exploitation of labour by capital, remains the same.
>
> (Marx 1972a: 12, emphasis in original)

Labourers are exploited, they are denied control over the product of their labour, even though they are paid their 'value', what they are worth to society.

Relations of commodity exchange apply at the world level, and if there is a secular tendency for an increasing organic composition of capital, and a tendency for the rate of profit to fall, this can only be observed by interpreting world trade and production; as world accumulation impoverishes the 'Third World' to subsidize the profits of transnational corporations and banks.

Labour power is a commodity. It is sold by labourers and bought by employers who own the means of production, which comprise: the 'object' of labour – raw materials – which are transformed by labour power into use values; and the 'means' of labour – tools, techniques and technology – through which the natural environment is transformed into utilities. And labour produces value. The contradiction in the capitalist mode of production is between: the 'qualitative' use value of labour power, i.e. the amount of value produced for the purchaser, the capitalist employer; and the 'quantitative' exchange value of labour power, i.e. the value of labour to the seller, the wage payment to the labourer. There is a contradictory qualitative/quantitative dialectic within labour power as a commodity, which, like all commodities, is a social relation, a relation through which society develops: in the capitalist mode of production the relation of 'capital'. Commodity production generates the production of surplus value on which the viability of the capitalist mode of production depends. But the competitive dynamic of commodity exchange makes the production of surplus value dependent upon ever increasing capital intensity of labour: in Marx's terms, a 'rising organic composition of capital'.

> By the composition of capital we mean ... the proportion of its active and passive components, i.e. of variable and constant capital ... The value-composition of

capital inasmuch as it is determined by, and reflects its technical composition, is called the *organic* composition of capital.

(Marx 1972a: 145–6, emphasis in original)

However, the rising organic composition of capital, implying a declining rate of profit, can be offset by increased exploitation of labour power: the same investment in *v* producing more *s*, producing greater social conflict within the capitalist mode of production. 'The real barrier to capitalist production is *capital itself*' (Marx 1972a: 259, emphasis in original).

There is, then, a tendency for the rate of profit to fall (see Clarke 1994), although with a changed relationship between capital and labour, implying increased exploitation, there can be an upturn in profits. There have been four 'long waves' of capital accumulation, with buoyant profitability in the periods 1793 to 1825, 1848 to 1873, 1894 to 1913 and 1945 to 1966, followed by periods of declining profitability in 1826 to 1847, 1874 to 1893, 1914 to 1939, and 1967 to the present (1998) (see Mandel 1975: Chapter 4). Declining profitability, implying economic crisis, unemployment and depression, essentially redefines the capital–labour relation. Remember, commodity, value and capital are social relations. And the redefining of such relations may include wars of conquest, the extension of the area of operation of capital, class struggles, counter-revolutions, etc.

> Thus our general conclusion is that the 'technical' possibility of a new strong upturn in the long-term rate of capitalist growth will depend on the outcomes of momentous battles between capital and labour in the West, in some of the key semi-industrialized countries of the so-called third world, between national liberation movements and imperialism, and between the noncapitalist countries and imperialism ... the similarity to the 1930s is striking.
>
> (Mandel 1980: 118–19)

DEVELOPMENT AS POWER STRUGGLE

Within this perspective, human beings are understood to be socially creative individuals. People are certainly biologically endowed with particular characteristics, but only become aware of their potentials *through* social experience. Consequently people change as they learn more about themselves through social activity. 'The properties of individual human beings do not exist in isolation but arise as a consequence of social life, yet the nature of that social life is a consequence of our being human' (Rose *et al.*, 1984: 11).

In the biological determinism of the subjective preference theory of value, and the process of socialization in the cost-of-production theory of value, there is very little room for manoeuvre for individuals to control their own lives. However, for the abstract labour theory of value, biological and social determinants are interdependent. The relationship is *dialectical*: one of mutual causation. Selfishness is not 'natural' or 'socially induced', but is one of many possibilities in the dialectical relation between genetic inheritance and social experience. People, as a result of their experience, constantly change. It is possible, theoretically, to understand this process, and collectively and purposely to intervene to alter the course of events, to organize society to fulfil more completely individuals' *changing* social potentials.

As the potentials of individuals change, so does society, which in turn changes people's social environment and experience, and they in turn, in some small way change, etc.; so the process continues. This is the dialectic of development. But people have different interests within society. Fundamentally, for change within a society based upon commodity exchange, the contradiction is between those whose incomes derive from surplus value (profits, interest and rent), a result of the exploitation of labour, and those who labour to produce commodities, and hence value. 'Class' is defined by the control of the means of production: the means and object of labour. There are those who employ labour to produce value, and those who own only their labour power to be sold as wage labour. But importantly, the concept of class is *not* descriptive, describing lifestyles, but is explanatory, identifying shared (abstract) class interests. There are of course some people who do not fit into this bipartite classification of society: monks, priests, kings and queens, self-sufficient subsistence producers, hermits, students, etc. The abstract labour theory does not deny their existence, but states that their lives and experience will not be pivotal in the process of social change and development.

As societies change, reflecting the imperative to maximize profits through commodity exchange, the capitalist 'class', which owns the means of production, is to a degree able to protect itself from the adverse effects of social change, and normally better able to fulfil its creative potentials. Although the nature of commodity exchange forces them to compete among themselves for a share of surplus value, and bankruptcy relegates some to join the ranks of the working class. However, the latter, the working class, who do not own economic resources, other than their ability to work, suffer the full effects of economic crisis: unemployment, job insecurity, inflation, the effects of reduced state expenditure on services such as health and education, etc. Economic crises, a consequence of the competition between capitalists for a share of surplus value as profit, are endemic to the capitalist mode of production (see Cole 1995: 142–50). 'The antagonism between each individual capitalist's interests and those of the capitalist class as a whole . . . comes to the surface' (Marx 1972a: 253).

Economic regulation is necessarily biased towards different economic interests: different economic theoretical perspectives assume that the consumer, producer or citizen is the dynamic of economic activity. Archibald Ritter's call for a 'substantially marketized . . . system', facilitating the extraction of surplus value from labour as profits (see Cole 1995: 127–42), understands the consumer to be the pivotal actor in the economy, with economic policy acting to the class advantage of those who hope to become 'owners' of the means of production in the 'new' Cuba. Andrew Zimbalist, however, sees decisions in the sphere of production as fundamental, and emphasizes the importance of management and expertise, albeit to achieve a 'fair' society. But both perspectives address only one half of the dialectic of social reproduction within the community: one aspect of commodity relations. Abstract labour theorists, however, concerned with the interests of the direct producers, address both the qualitative and quantitative dimensions of the dialectic of development. The struggle for a 'just' society in which people can fulfil their potentials is at the heart of the development process.

> For dialectics the universe is unitary but always in change; the phenomena we see at any instant are parts of processes, processes with histories and futures whose futures are not uniquely determined by their constituent units. Wholes are composed of units whose properties may be described, but the interaction of these units in the construction of the wholes generates complexities that result in products qualitatively different from the component parts . . . in a world in which such developmental interactions are always occurring history becomes of paramount importance.
>
> (Rose *et al.*, 1984: 11)

Change and development is understood to arise, ultimately, from the struggle by the disadvantaged to fulfil their individual, changing, creative potentials. Commodity exchange tends towards economic crisis, and because of the differential power of the exploiting and exploited classes, the brunt of the crisis is felt by labour. Living standards fall, unemployment increases (in November 1996, the International Labour Organization estimated that worldwide unemployment had reached one billion, a third of the workforce) and social welfare provision is cut back (in the developed market economies, a reduction in the welfare state; in underdevelopment societies the incidence of malnutrition and starvation increases). Hand in hand with this goes a rise in crime, alcoholism, violence, drug abuse, etc. The 'economic' crisis becomes a 'social' crisis (see O'Connor 1987).

Social change and development is a dialectical process of creative individuals attempting to fulfil their potentials in the face of social constraints. The dialectic is *within* people. Human nature is understood to be a consequence of individuals' biological potentials being revealed and realized *through* social experience. And it is when people are denied individual fulfilment by social forces beyond their control, resulting in anger and frustration, that they may be motivated to organize and struggle to change society. People can, collectively, manage the course of their lives: the future is not determined and beyond their control. This is the Marxism of Karl Korsch and Antonio Gramsci, not Lenin and Althusser (see Boggs 1976; Goode 1979; Smith 1996).

There is not a determinate logic to change and development: people are unique *creative* beings. (On the indeterminacy of Marxist analyses see Cole and Yaxley 1991; Cole 1995: Chapter 5.) Change is ultimately the result of frustration. These frustrations can be turned inwards, psychologically, and ultimately physically, destroying the individual (see O'Connor 1987: Chapter 1). Or this inner anger can be turned outwards, and individuals combine and organize with similarly frustrated people, people who share their 'class' interest, constructively to progress and change society: they develop. This raises two issues.

First, how is social experience analysed to identify those constraints and resultant frustrations which give common cause, a shared 'class' interest around which there might be organization and mobilization to challenge the social status quo? 'The materialist conception of history starts from the proposition that the production of the means to support human life and, next to production the exchange of things produced, is the basis of all social structure' (Engels 1970: 57). The materialist conception of history understands the basis of production to be the 'mode of production'. 'The mode of production of material life conditions [n.b. *not* "determines"] the social, political and intellectual life-process in general' (Marx 1976: 3).

A person's 'class' position is defined with respect to the degree to which he or she controls the social 'means of production'. So, if people experience the economic crisis as unemployment, or longer hospital waiting-lists, or larger classes in schools for their children, or reduced pensions for retired people, or reduced development assistance, or reduced grants for students, or homelessness and starvation, these people have a shared 'class' interest. Inequality and disadvantage have different manifestations. In capitalist society there is one ultimate cause: the organization of economic activity to exploit labour to realize profit, rent and interest for the bourgeoisie. To reorganize society to utilize resources more fully to meet people's needs, to advance the 'forces of production', will necessitate a change in the social, cultural and political dimensions of existence, the 'relations of production': 'as men develop their productive forces, that is, as they live, they develop certain relations with one another and ... the nature of the relations is bound to change with the change and growth of these productive forces' (Marx 1975: 34). And these 'certain relations' are relations of power within society. It is the task of theoretical analysis to reveal these 'relations' of power. As 'relations' they are abstractions and can *only* be comprehended theoretically.

Identifying the 'battleground' only precedes the struggle. This brings us to the second issue.

> We either choose to be observers of history, thereby lending our weight to the forces now in control or we choose to be participants, actively building a new culture based on human values.
>
> (Lappé and Collins 1977: 327)

The theorist has to become an 'activist', working towards building a movement to redefine power relations in society. But for people to be willing to get involved and organize, they must believe that change is possible. While people conceive of human nature and motivation as beyond control and immutable – either biologically determined (the subjective preference theory of value) or socially adapted (the cost-of-production theory of value) – the present form of social organization appears as inevitable, and fundamental change as impossible. People need to understand the world as capable of change because *people* can change. People have potentials for collective organization as yet unrealized and unexpressed (the abstract labour theory of value).

> [None] of us can live fully ... as long as we are overwhelmed by a false view of the world and a false view of *human nature* to buttress it. Learning how a system can cause hunger then becomes, not a lesson in misery and deprivation, but a vehicle for a great awakening in our lives.
>
> (Lappé and Collins 1977: 329, emphasis added)

Such a realization and awareness of the potentials of class power is a product of cultural change. The 'common sense' understanding of social inequality alters, seeing it as a 'class' issue, rather than one of individuals' indolence, a consequence of technical change, just bad luck or whatever. The intellectual parameters of people's 'real' world changes:

> only by degrees, one stage at a time, has humanity acquired consciousness of its own value and won for itself the right to throw off the patterns of organization imposed on it by minorities ... this consciousness was formed ... as a result of intelligent reflection ... every revolution has been preceded by an intense labour of criticism, by the diffusion and spread of ideas amongst masses of men.
>
> (Gramsci, quoted in Foracs 1988: 58–9)

The Cuban predicament is then a 'moment' in the process of change which is Cuban development. Necessarily in the context of world economic specialization, Cuba can develop *only* by becoming increasingly integrated into a more extensive international division of labour. And we saw in Chapter 3 how the development of Cuban development strategy had been a process of compromise between the ideals of the revolution and the exigencies of world trade. 'One major aim of Marx's analysis of capitalism is to explain how people can make their own history and be made by it at the same time, how we are both free and conditioned, and how the future is both *open* and *necessary*' (Ollman 1993: 89, emphasis added).

The social, economic and political context of life in Cuba has changed, and previous forms of social coordination are anachronistic and not appropriate to reconciling the moral principles of the revolution with the new material, world reality, which is the international division of labour. This is to be addressed by new ways of social integration and participation. 'With respect to the deficiencies of the existing regime, the debates and pre-occupations with it reflect a need not to replace the regime but to improve it by deepening its ideals and its socialist project' (Heredia 1993: 76).

THE IDEOLOGICAL IMPLICATIONS OF THE 'CITIZEN' AS ECONOMIC DYNAMIC

Believing that destiny is not beyond purposeful human control, is a pre-condition for people's participation. 'The poor learn from ... conflicts ... and its members ... grow in consciousness and political power ... In this process, the poor themselves define and control their own struggle ... development becomes radically participatory' (Wisner 1988: 15 and 26). But participation itself is a process. In the experience of participation individuals realize new social potentials: things they could not do by themselves. And this subjective awareness of the possibilities of participation raises new, unpredictable potentials, needs and ambitions, which hitherto have only been immanent. To be aware of and realize this potential, people must understand what they are capable of: it is fundamentally a process of self-awareness:

> people are not machines ... there are subjective processes in the making of decisions ... it is not classes but individuals who make choices ... the conscious-ness of an individual is not determined by his or her class position but is influenced by idiosyncratic factors that appear as random, those random factors operate within a domain and with probabilities that are constrained and directed by social forces.
>
> (Lewontin and Levins 1997: 68)

People become increasingly self-conscious and understand their own *social* experience, in as far as they can differentiate themselves from others, becoming aware of their unique potentials but also the shared parameters of their social experience. To 'know' themselves people have increasingly to 'know' other people. Subjective awareness is central to transformation and development: 'one cannot conceive of objectivity without subjectivity ... To deny the importance of subjectivity [understanding] in the process of transforming the world is naïve and simplistic'(Freire 1972: 27). Knowledge should be a product of experience, reflecting the differential activity of different people:

> theory ... becomes a material force once it seizes the masses, theory is capable of seizing the masses once it demonstrates *ad hominem*, and it demonstrates *ad hominem* once it becomes radical. To be radical is to grasp matters by the root, but for man the root is man himself.
>
> (Marx 1970: 137)

'Science' is now understood as *praxis*, which is *not*, as many 'radical' theorists use the term, the same thing as *practice*. Practice is what people *do*, praxis is how experience changes people's *consciousness* or awareness. Lessons are learnt from social activity; self-consciousness and intuition evolve.

> Problem posing education is prophetic, and as such it is hopeful, corresponding to the historical nature of human beings. It affirms people as beings who

transcend themselves, who move forward and look ahead ... for whom looking at the past must only be a means of understanding more clearly what and who they are, so that they can more wisely build the future.

(Freire, quoted in Hope and Timmel 1995: 20)

Theory and practice go hand in hand. This differs from a 'paradigmatic' theory of knowledge, in that for those theorists paradigms change when there are 'new' unpredictable problems to be addressed. Change comes as a surprise. For 'praxis', because society is composed of creative individuals, social experience and human understanding is permanently in change, which is to be expected. This process of change, understood theoretically, highlights the *potentials* yet to come, and what might be the courses of action to realize these possibilities.

The theoretical agenda of the positivists, describing and correlating events without attempting to explain them, is knowing without understanding. Not highlighting the conflict that underlies social change and development only serves (passively) to preserve an (iniquitous) social status quo. 'Washing one's hands of the conflict between the powerful and the powerless means to side with the powerful, not to be neutral' (Freire 1972: 96).

THE INTELLECTUAL PARAMETERS OF CUBAN DEVELOPMENT

Implicit assumptions and meanings ... guide, and circumscribe the types of questions and testable hypotheses to be raised and the interpretation given to empirical data, even beyond the conscious intent of the researcher ... [It is essential to] make explicit underlying meanings, expose assumptions, and uncover key political and ideological notions.

(Robinson 1996: 359)

By making explicit the 'unexamined and unexpressed' assumptions that underlie various analyses of the Cuban development process, the 'intellectual parameters of Cuban development', I have attempted to highlight the moral, ideological and political implications of alternative understandings: each of which is 'rationalist', 'realist' and 'activist'.

'Rationally', analyses have a logical coherence running from assumptions to conclusions. Each follows a distinct philosophy of knowledge – positivism, paradigms, praxis – which defines the assumptions that underline the theoretical practice. It is not that science is distinct from ideology: there are different ideologies *of* science. It is more a question of 'plausibility', of being able to account adequately for personal experience in particular, and the world in general.

'Realistically', plausible coherent analyses cite particular events and behavioural traits: the intent to maximize utility according to personal choice; the exigency to cooperate technically to produce; the creative dialectic between individuals' unique biological inheritance and social experience. The 'relevant' facts are theoretically abstracted out of the innumerable 'possible' observations of social existence.

Based upon ideologically defined interpretations of human existence, the 'activist' can propose policy prescriptions for problems, which are in keeping with the moral pretensions that derive from a theoretical perspective. The implicit beliefs in human nature, the 'unexamined and unexpressed' assumptions which define the analysis, legitimate the policy conclusions as appropriate to developing a society in which people can fulfil their 'natural' potentials. It is a circular argument. The conclusion justifies the assumptions from which it derives.

Ultimately, theory choice is a matter of belief. The choice is *political*:

> what is the best response to the perennial problem of theory choice? The problem arises because, in many significant instances in science, there are no objective criteria according to which competing theories may be compared, ranked and evaluated; in a phrase, there is no algorithm of choice ... the theory choice problem is a real one in economics.
>
> (Caldwell 1982: 7)

In the next three chapters we look in detail at the analysis of the Cuban 'predicament' in the terms of each theoretical perspective. By making explicit the theoretical preconceptions, we will then be able to compare and contrast the various assessments and conclusions, and understand the political implications of each programme. Theory choice is a question of political awareness.

CHAPTER 5

THE COMPETITIVE MARKET OPTION

NO ALTERNATIVE TO THE MARKET

Archibald Ritter thinks that 'Cuba has no alternative but to embark on a process of economic reform in the direction of marketization and economic liberalization' (Ritter 1994: 83). This is a commonly held interpretation, not just of the Cuban predicament, but of development theory in general and economic theory in particular, especially as applied to economies defined as being 'in transition' from central planning to market regulation. The 'transition economies' are listed by the World Bank (World Bank 1996b) as: the countries of Central and Eastern Europe (Albania, Bulgaria, Croatia, the Czech Republic, Hungary, the Former Yugoslav Republic of Macedonia, Poland, Romania, the Slovak Republic, Slovenia, Bosnia–Herzegovina, the Federal Republic of Yugoslavia); the newly independent states of the former Soviet Union (Armenia, Azerbaijan, Belarus, Estonia, Georgia, Kazakstan, the Kyrgyz Republic, Latvia, Lithuania, Moldova, Russia, Tajikistan, Turkmenistan, Ukraine, Uzbekistan); and Mongolia, China and Vietnam. Cuba has yet to make 'meaningful' reforms to qualify to be on this list.

What are the assumptions that underlie this analysis, and what are the aspects of the development process that are highlighted as significant for policy initiatives? Further, what are the ideological implications of adopting such an approach to social and economic analysis in general, and to the analysis of Cuban development in particular?

We saw in Chapter 4 that some economists 'proceed on the fundamental *article of faith*' that economies exist for the benefit of consumers. This preconception is not a 'fact', it is an interpretation of human motivation, an assumption, a belief in 'human nature'. Such an interpretation of economic activity is based upon a casual, 'empiricist', observation of human behaviour, identifying properties and characteristics which are thought to apply to *all* human beings.

The state of 'perfect competition/general equilibrium', to which there will be a trend if free markets obtain, will allow individuals to behave 'naturally' and fulfil their own potentials. This is a motivation which 'modernizes' society as economic activity responds to consumers' preferences. Hence,

> policy changes [towards free markets] are *essential* if former CPEs [centrally planned economies, and therefore Cuba] are to prepare themselves to reap the

long-term benefits associated with a market economy and their insertion into the world economic system.

(Pérez-López 1992: 367, emphasis added)

State economic intervention, which by definition cannot accurately reflect independent individuals' *subjective* preferences, means that prices cannot reflect individuals' enjoyment of utility. Relative prices cannot therefore act as efficient incentives, encouraging individuals to suffer the 'disutility' of production, and to work hard and efficiently, in order to spend their income and enjoy the positive utility of consumption. Therefore the economy cannot efficiently allocate scarce resources between competing ends. As a consequence, individuals will not fulfil their potentials. Had prices been allowed to reflect individuals' subjective preferences, without interference from the state, then output would have been maximized, as the disutility of production would be 'adequately' rewarded by consumption. There would be an incentive to work hard and fulfil individuals' potentials, leading to economic development.

In this context, Archibald Ritter (1995) discusses the 'bifurcation' of the Cuban economy.

> In the first half of the 1990s ... Cuba's economy became increasingly split between the traditional [state controlled] socialist economy ... and the rapidly expanding internationalized dollar-based economy together with the domestic market-based peso economy ... [which] interacted in a number of ways to generate a severely *dysfunctional structure of incentives* shaping people's economic energies in counterproductive ways.
>
> (Ritter 1995: 114, emphasis added)

Jorge Pérez-López (Pérez-López 1995, 1997), making a similar theoretical point, refers to the 'second economy' as those private activities outside of the centrally planned 'first economy': the 'bifurcation' of economic activity. And these 'two parts of the economy interacted so as to generate a number of *pathological* [i.e. caused by a 'disease'] economic and social phenomena' (Ritter 1997: 151, emphasis added).

The 'pathogen' is the denial of free consumer 'choice'. The prognosis? Without a transition to free markets it will probably be terminal: the destruction of Cuban society, as people through corruption and crime try to compensate for their loss of utility and declining standards of living. Order will only be restored through repression. The cure? Both Archibald Ritter and Jorge Pérez-López argue that these two aspects of economic activity have to be reintegrated according to market priorities, through a whole range of policy initiatives, including price decontrol and enterprise liberalization. The trend should be towards the ideal of 'perfect competition'. 'Reunification of these parts of the economy into a market-oriented system is *vital* if economic recovery, adjustment and transition [to the world economy] are to occur' (Ritter 1995: 114, emphasis added).

The Cuban authorities' wanton disregard for individuals' 'natural' proclivity to be selfish is judged to be at best a short-sighted attempt to prop up a regime that is inevitably doomed.

> Initially [under the Special Period following the collapse of the Soviet bloc] there appears to have been a paralysis in public policy making which lasted from 1990 to mid 1993 ... The government *only seems to have become* fully aware of the increasing dual currency bifurcation of the Cuban economy after the decriminalization of the use of the US dollar in the summer of 1993.
>
> (Ritter 1995: 124, 122, emphasis added)

The problem is one of incentives. For those involved in the dollar economy, such as bartenders in hotels or taxi drivers, earnings can be substantially higher than for people working in the state provision of services, such as education and health. With the decline in per capita income and the increase in shortages during the Special Period, there has been an increase in crime, prostitution, hustling, corruption, etc. All this is seen as tending towards the collapse of Cuban socialism as people 'naturally' react against state restrictions on individual activity.

Because the option of subsidization from the Soviet Union no longer exists, the state has been forced to reduce the fiscal deficit, for instance, from about 5.1 billion pesos in 1993 to about 1.4 billion in 1994 (from about 28 per cent to 8 per cent of GDP) (see *Granma International* 4 January 1995; Ritter 1995: 123). State subsidies to enterprises have been reduced, with a concomitant drive towards enterprise self-financing and price rises. As such there have been increased charges for electricity, telephones, postage and transport. Charges have also been introduced for meals in workers' dining rooms and for school lunches, and entry fees are charged for sporting events, museums, art galleries, etc. A tax system, Law Number 73, promulgated by the National Assembly of Poder Popular on 4 August 1994, has been introduced to tax incomes outside the purview of the state, to try to maintain economic equality and the egalitarian nature of Cuban society (see R. Rodríguez 1995).

However, for Archibald Ritter and Jorge Pérez-López these are all measures which reduce consumers' utility, individuals' tolerance of restrictions on free exchange and the fulfilment of independent individuals' potentials. As a consequence of these and other 'reform' measures, such as the decriminalization of the holding and use of US dollars by Cubans in August 1993, the liberalization of self-employment in September 1993 and the re-establishment of agricultural markets, it is interpreted within the intellectual parameters of the subjective preference theory of value that, finally, state economic (and development) policy is bowing to the inevitable. Individuals' human nature as essentially *independent* beings, 'naturally' intent on maximizing personal utility, is prevailing over bureaucratic expediency, and 'modernizing' Cuban society. 'There are few, if any, instruments of government policy which are non-distortionary, in the sense of not inducing economic agents to behave less efficiently' (Lal 1983: 15).

Policy-makers have had to recognize that individuals are essentially concerned with their own pleasure. The maximization of utility is the
underlying motivation to human behaviour in general and economic activity in particular, and human nature overall.

In agricultural markets, prices are now allowed to reflect the 'forces' of
supply and demand, and all types of producers, including private, state and
cooperative farms, are eligible to use them. The agricultural market reform,
together with the liberalization of transport, the legalization of industrial
and artisanal markets in 1994 and increased self-employment, it is argued,
will lead to an unstoppable trend towards the market. Once market rationality takes a hold, individuals will not willingly give up their new found
'freedoms': minds will have been 'modernized'. When 'the benefits of
marketization are increasingly apparent, adherence to the traditional system in Cuba will be unsustainable' (Ritter 1992: 143). The alternatives will
be further market liberalization or repression.

However, the 'intellectual parameters' of this perspective selectively
interpret Cuban economic experience, theoretically defining the 'real
world'. Only those aspects in accord with the assumptions/beliefs of the
subjective preference theory of value are highlighted and included in the
theoretical analysis.

NEW INSTITUTIONAL ECONOMICS

Reflecting the 'marginalist' emphasis of the subjective preference theory of
value, the essential economic effect of the collapse of the Soviet bloc was a
change in relative prices.

> What makes the structural changes [towards free markets] inevitable is the
> dramatic shift in *fundamental relative prices* recently experienced, in particular for
> oil and sugar, as a result of the demise of the centrally planned systems in Eastern
> Europe and the Soviet Union.
>
> (Betancourt 1991: 7, emphasis added)

Although the trend towards liberalization (and modernization) is 'inevitable', particular responses within Cuban society will reflect the unique
institutional context of change within Cuba: in particular the distributional
effects of economic institutions. The 'theory of the firm', the theory of the
logic of individual entrepreneurs' decision-making to maximize profit, is a
central tenet of the subjective preference theory of value. Apart from the
known conditions of supply and demand, reflected in market prices and
therefore revenues and costs, because perfect competition and general
equilibrium never obtain, there are *always* implicit 'opportunity costs'
(depressing the overall enjoyment of utility) attached to exchanges which
impact on individuals' enjoyment of utility. And market imperfections
reflect the degree to which institutional constraints limit individuals' free
choice, imposing 'opportunity costs' on market exchange. Such costs can be

generally grouped under the general heading of 'transactions costs' (see Stiglitz 1993: 583–4).

The concern is with identifying 'equilibrium contracts' – for instance, in the market for factors of production – focusing upon

> the high opportunity cost of time [the alternative way in which individual producers could spend their time]; the increase in the number of households due to the decreased role of extended family structures; the increase in the number of households with multiple earners. Of these three factors the last two are relevant to the Cuban economy.
>
> (Betancourt 1991: 19)

This is an application of New Institutional Economics (highlighted in Chapter 4) to the Cuban experience of 'modernization', and to the writing of a new Cuban constitution, based upon market principles, in which the issue of returning assets nationalized after 1 January 1959 to their previous owners would be addressed (see Mueller 1991; Thomas 1992).

In keeping with the subjective preference theory of value, it is not noted that price rises, reflecting reduced subsidies to enterprises, have as far as possible been restricted to 'non-essentials', such as cigarettes, cigars and rum. But then, within this perspective 'essential' only has meaning with regard to the satisfaction of consumers' utility as indicated by relative prices, and is not a question of survival.

Neither is the attempt to mitigate any increased inequality, as a consequence of the increased reliance on market forces to allocate scarce resources, through extended rationing considered to be relevant. Distributive and economic inequality is defined in terms of free choice by individuals to consume: if free exchange obtains then poverty is not a problem. That the Cuban government would want to equalize economic hardship is beyond the purview of the intellectual parameters of the subjective preference theory of value.

The Rectification Campaign of 1986 is dismissed as merely an institutional, ideological ploy to try to restore work discipline in the absence of material incentives, stressing work as a 'revolutionary duty' rather than for personal gain. As early as 1982, articles in the newspaper *Granma* were emphasizing the importance of 'socialist consciousness' and 'ideology', reasserting Guevara's legacy of the 1960s and preparing the ground for the critique of the SDPE. The SDPE, with an emphasis on decentralized decision-making and enterprise financial autonomy, threatened economic control by the CPP in general, and Fidel Castro's power in particular. 'If [these] mechanisms [the SDPE planning system] were to solve everything, what was left for the Party to do? . . . These ideas involved a negation of the Party' (Castro 1987, quoted in Mesa-Lago 1989: 101).

Carmel Mesa-Lago argues that the Rectification Campaign was not a success: in 1986–7 gross investment fell by 5 per cent over the previous year; sugar production declined by one million tons in 1986 to 1988 from over eight million tons in 1984–5; more than half the products reported annually by the National Bank of Cuba declined in output in 1987; labour productivity declined between 4 per cent and 9 per cent, and wages by 2 per cent in 1987, etc. The government attributed this disappointing economic performance to adverse weather conditions, a decline in world sugar prices, falling world oil prices (affecting the resale of Soviet oil), the devaluation of the dollar, affecting export revenues, a lack of hard-currency loans, etc. And the Rectification Campaign was 'officially considered to be a positive factor that compensated somewhat for the adverse ones. But this article has presented evidence to support the opposite hypothesis' (Mesa-Lago 1989: 125).

The evidence is interpreted within the intellectual parameters of the subjective preference theory of value, assuming economic activity to be a consequence of independent individuals' motivation to maximize utility. Hence, worker brigades, contingents, agricultural cooperatives and construction minibrigades, all promoted by the Rectification Campaign, have merely been attempts to maintain the regime in power by encouraging 'unpaid' work to offset the underperformance of the centralized, planned economy, which reached such levels of inefficiency in 1985 that the outstanding Cuban hard currency debt reached $3.6 billion (rising to $7.3 billion by 1989) (see Eckstein 1994: 222). This prompted a 'fiscal crisis of the state' (see Eckstein 1990), requiring Rectification. 'The Rectification Process is ... the result of Castro's political struggle to retain power' (Cardoso and Helwege 1992: 27). A free market economy reflects 'human nature'. And there will naturally be a 'modernizing' pressure to evolve towards a free society, characterized by a political system of 'representative democracy' (one-person-one-vote and periodic elections) and capitalistic free markets.

As economic and development policy continues to deny individuals' interests and 'human nature', social unrest is the inevitable outcome. The chickens will come home to roost. The only alternative to political repression is a policy purposefully designed to integrate Cuba into the world economy. Cuba is in an unstoppable transition from central planning.

> Transition economies have made great strides in liberalizing their domestic markets and foreign trade regimes and in freeing up entry into private business. Many are trying to define property rights more clearly and to ... create ... institutions to support efficient markets.
>
> (World Bank 1996b: 142)

Essentially, 'private property' rights have to become the basis of economic activity. There are two stages to this strategy: 'stabilization' and 'liberalization'. However, as a precondition, institutions have to be created which will create labour and capital markets, restructure and privatize state enterprises, liberalize openings to foreign investment, institute a legal system which is orientated to the protection of private property, create a comprehensive taxation system, facilitate a whole range of regulatory institutions to ensure free enterprise, etc.; and, 'once they settle upon a financial structure, they will find change [back to socialist regulation] difficult and costly. Vested interests arise which will quickly attain political and economic influence' (Stiglitz 1992: 184). Capitalist development is a one-way street.

ECONOMIC STABILIZATION

Stabilization is the correction of macroeconomic 'imbalances' between spending and income. State spending, whether it be on social welfare, health care, education, economic development, law and order or defence, should not exceed state income from taxation or borrowing. No longer is Soviet 'largesse' available to subsidize state spending. And in foreign economic transactions, imports have to be paid for out of export revenue or international borrowing. Foreign exchange deficits can no longer be rolled over into long-term debt as in the 1970s and 1980s within the CAME. Economic stabilization is a necessary but not sufficient condition for liberalization and structural adjustment. It is a dual process of fiscal policy and trade policy.

The fiscal debt, state expenditure in excess of state income, should be reduced to lessen public debt. Such debt 'distorts' interest rates, 'crowding out' private investment, by channelling savings into state sponsored projects, rather than schemes which are commercially viable, which would clearly indicate that consumers' preferences are being addressed.

Inflation will also be reduced by reducing the public debt, as the money supply will be more in line with actual purchases, reducing excess liquidity or the 'monetary overhang'. In the past, inflation has been suppressed in Cuba, as prices have been fixed, and excess liquidity could only be accumulated as virtually useless savings, distorting any possible incentive effect of differential incomes. It is believed that the elimination of 'crowding out' by the public debt, and the renewed incentive effect of market prices, would increase entrepreneurial activity and the rate of economic growth, leading to development.

Achieving a fiscal balance will reduce public expenditure, deflating the economy and leading to unemployment. But as business activity responds to the 'enterprise culture', people will be absorbed into work which is profitable, rather than being a drain on public finances. More and more state services will be privatized and 'commoditized', facilitating 'consumer power' in the allocation of economic resources. Any residual government expenditure will come out of taxation, and hence the public authority will, through periodic elections, be held accountable to consumers for spending priorities.

Trade policy is the other component of 'stabilization'. Stabilizing the balance-of-payments so that expenditure on imports reflects income from abroad, and changing the trade regime to remove 'distortions' away from choices that would have been a reflection of world market prices, will, it is predicted, in conjunction with fiscal stabilization, create the incentives to stimulate export growth. Such a belief in the efficacy of economic stabilization on foreign trade and the powerful incentive effect of market forces on exports has been central to IMF/World Bank inspired structural adjustment programmes, which have been applied to most Latin American economies. But by

> 1995, after 13 years of debt crisis, adjustment and undoubted pain, most Latin Americans are still waiting for the long-promised benefits of structural adjustment to 'trickle down' to their neighbourhoods ... the rich have had a vintage decade, [but] most of the region's people are poorer and more insecure ... Neoliberals ... insist that the pay-off lies just around the corner.
>
> (Green 1995: 111)

In the 1980s there was a naïve belief in the 'automatic' incentive effects of market forces on economic activity, which would lead to growth and development. But as we saw in Chapter 4, the failure of the free market growth dynamic, has led to research, spearheaded by the New Institutional Economists, on the institutional constraints which prevent people from benefiting from behaving 'naturally'. And the World Bank is looking to 'microentrepreneurs' to generate 'broad-based' growth, as a precursor to the elusive development. The promise of the free market is now more circumspect.

> There is growing doubt as to whether macro-economic policy can move from adjustment to growth, whether reforming the trade regime can move from removing distortions to stimulating dynamic export growth, and whether private sector reforms will increase output and employment sufficiently to meet the wider social goals of social equity, political participation and environmental balance.
>
> (IADB 1993: 35)

But, of course, within the 'intellectual parameters' of the subjective preference theory of value and the neo-liberal development agenda, there can be no other interpretation of economic activity.

The CAME system of trade within COMECON was based upon 'technical specialization', essentially defined in 'physical', technical terms, rather than in values: so many tons of sugar exchanged for so many tons of oil. Increasingly during the 1980s, the market value of trade came to be more and more important. However, in adapting to the post-CAME world economic environment, market prices are central, and according to the subjective preference theory of value, trade has to be based upon 'comparative advantage'. This means that specialization is determined by world market competitivity: market prices become the arbiter of economic specialization and trade. For production to reflect competitive advantage and to be based upon market incentives, the national currency, the peso, cannot be 'over' or 'under' valued. The international value of national currencies should 'float', the value of the Cuban peso being determined by market forces, reflecting the demand for pesos to buy Cuban goods and the supply of pesos to pay for imports to Cuba.

This means that the international value of the currency cannot be used as a variable in development strategy. For instance, where countries have followed an 'import substitution' industrialization strategy, producing in the domestic economy commodities that were hitherto imported, currencies had often been deliberately 'over valued': the effect is that exports are relatively more expensive, and hence typically demand falls, but imports are relatively cheap. Where the industrialization strategy involves the import of expensive capital equipment, the gains from cheaper (in terms of national currency) imports frequently outweigh the loss of export revenues from reduced international sales.

However, for the subjective preference theory of value, the peso should float and trade reflect Cuba's comparative advantage. The theory of comparative advantage argues that economies should specialize in producing those commodities in which they are relatively more efficient. And 'relative efficiency' is defined by 'opportunity cost': that is, the disutility suffered by producers in providing the commodity. If producing, say, bicycles, takes resources away from the production of sugar cane, such that the same resources earn less foreign exchange, then the policy should be to export sugar cane and import bicycles. Of course, such an analysis assumes full employment, so that there is a real cost to producing bicycles in that other products have not been produced. Moreover, world market prices are taken to be the standard of efficiency. The assumption that (world) market prices are effective as incentives to individuals requires an acceptance of the belief in human nature that underlies the subjective preference theory of value, with all the ideological implications that this entails.

Prices only reflect efficiency in the provision of utility to consumers in conditions of 'perfect competition' and 'general equilibrium'. As we have already seen, this is the conception of utopia within the parameters of the 'subjective preference theory of value'. It is not a description, nor could it be, of *any* actual economy. And the belief that a move towards such a competitive economy will lead to an improvement in welfare, and individuals' enjoyment of utility, is just that, a *belief*.

The logical impossibility of such a utopia is lost in the translation of economic theory into economic policy. It is implied that there is no alternative to world market prices being the arbiter of national productive specialization and development strategy. Consumers' decisions, which are supposed to determine international market forces, should determine productive decisions: 'consumer sovereignty'. Yet the economic success of the developed market economies has not been a reflection of their international comparative advantage. The relevance and significance of market forces has been denied. More than this, the world market has been deliberately 'distorted' away from the choices which are suggested by the resources, both raw materials and labour skills, that would confer a comparative advantage on the developed market economies.

> The United States, in particular, has always been extreme in rejecting market discipline. That is how it developed from the beginning, including textiles, steel, energy, chemicals, computers and electronics, pharmaceuticals and biotechnology, agribusiness, and so on, gaining enormous wealth and power instead of pursuing its comparative advantage in exporting furs, in accordance with the stern principles of economic rationality.
>
> (Chomsky 1996: 101)

The principle of 'comparative advantage' is currently being championed by the Bretton Woods institutions – the International Monetary Fund (IMF), the World Bank and the General Agreement on Tariffs and Trade (GATT) – as the basis of development strategy, and being imposed on the lesser developed economies through the 'structural adjustment' conditions attached to loans (from the IMF) to offset balance of payments disequilibria, aid disbursements (World Bank), or negotiations on 'liberalizing' trade (GATT). Of course, any system of 'free' trade acts to the advantage of those producers who are relatively efficient, denying the lesser developed economies the right to define their development strategy and decide in which sphere productive potentials will be concentrated.

There is an

> institutional framework that corresponds to specific social relations and class interests . . . the 'open' economy is not equally open to everyone. It is an economy open to money and the owners of money . . . borders can be 'held open' to inflows and outflows of money-capital only if everyone submits to certain objective 'rules of the game' . . . *The International Monetary Fund [and the World Bank and GATT] is merely the embodiment of this objective logic.*
>
> (Mandel 1978: 190, emphasis in original)

It is only by denying the principle of comparative advantage that Cuba has been able to lay the foundations for the future to overcome dependency on sugar, and look towards biotechnology, pharmaceuticals and medical equipment as a knowledge-intensive, high value added alternative to labour-intensive, low-income primary production (sugar cane).

ECONOMIC LIBERALIZATION

Economic policy within the intellectual parameters of subjective preference theory of value is intended to make the 'actual' economy more like the 'ideal': perfect competition. In the transition from central planning to market economies, thousands of prices have to be realigned to reflect the calculus of pleasure and pain, utility and disutility, supply and demand, and an 'expeditious and straight-forward approach [in Cuba] is to liberalize foreign trade and allow world prices to guide domestic economic actors' (Pérez-López 1992: 386).

For competition between enterprises to be effective in allocating resources to maximize utility, payments to productive inputs, factors of production and hence wages to labour must reflect the disutility endured in production and the positive utility enjoyed in consumption – the 'marginal productivity theory of distribution'. To this end, factor markets, and hence labour markets, have to be competitive (on the theoretical limitations and contradictions of the theory of distribution according to market forces, see Cole 1995: 195–8). 'The persistence of weak [i.e. not competitive] labour markets has complicated the problem of worker discipline and incentives' Pérez-López 1992: 390). Ideally there should be 'flexible' labour markets: workers should be easily hired and fired by capitalist employers. Labour 'discipline and incentives' is a euphemism for low wages with no trade union protection. With the trend in the rest of Latin America towards economic regulation by market forces, between

> 1980 and 1990 real wages fell in Venezuela and Argentina by 53 per cent and 26 per cent respectively ... By 1994, average real wages in Peru ... were down to just 47 per cent of their 1980 value ... [and] had still not recovered their 1980 value in Argentina, Mexico, or Costa Rica ... [which were seen] as neo-liberal [subjective preference theory] triumphs.
>
> (Green 1995: 95–6)

It is accepted by subjective preference and neo-liberal liberal theorists that policies of structural adjustment, and policies for transitional economies to move from planned to market economies will be unpopular.

> It will take strong and enlightened governments and much public explanation of the need for reform to keep the process going. The need for public explanation will be particularly strong in justifying policies aimed at reducing government expenditures.
>
> (Tanzi 1993: 2)

This 'enlightened' move towards (perfect) markets will bring its reward in the long run: there is no 'gain' without 'pain'.

Such was the promise of the economic, social and political reforms that followed the lowering of the red flag over the Kremlin in Moscow on Christmas Day 1991. What is the effect at the time of writing (May 1997)? There are soaring crime levels and the emergence of a strong mafia; output has plummeted; inequality has widened (seven bankers and tycoons are said to control half of the wealth of Russia); declining health going hand in hand with economic disadvantage has decreased longevity (see Steele 1996). And Russia's fledgling democracy? Corruption is rife; gross electoral fraud is common; broadcasting is controlled by Boris Yeltsin, effectively censoring political opposition. 'Russia today is a political and economic disaster, with one major difference from the Soviet period. At that time the West bore little responsibility for what was going wrong. Since 1991 the Russian show has been Western-inspired' (Steele 1996b: 16).

The hyperinflation resulting from the liberalization of prices in January

1992 – 350 per cent in one day – has led to the non-payment of millions of people's wages and pensions in an effort to reduce the money supply, the subjective preference theory of value believing that inflation is a 'monetary phenomenon'.

Inflation is a disease . . . a disease that if not checked in time can destroy a society . . . substantial inflation is always and everywhere a monetary phenomenon . . . produced by a more rapid increase in the quantity of money than in output . . . a reduction in the rate of monetary growth is the one and only cure for inflation.
(Friedman and Friedman 1980: 299, 398, 316)

Hyperinflation wiped out savings, and investment has dried up. The IMF predicts that economic growth will begin again in 1997 – five years after the overnight liberalization of the economy – but in 1996 output still fell by about 8 per cent. Prime Minister Victor Chernomyrdin predicted that growth will not revive until the next century (see Steele 1996). This should be compared to the Cuban economic recovery detailed at the end of Chapter 4.

Jonathan Steele, in his assessment of liberalization in the former Soviet Union, is not bound by the intellectual parameters of the subjective preference theory of value. Commentators who are have a very different interpretation of the Russian experience: 'progress is remarkable' (Layard and Parker 1996a). The market has taken over from the state, with little chance that this tide will ever be checked. Private enterprise is now entrenched, and the vested interests which Stiglitz predicted are now there to protect any challenge to 'their' property. The liberalization trend is predicted to continue, with

a continuation of 'muddling through' in politics and market deepening in economics . . . Whatever happens there will be strong economic growth, based on private enterprise . . . [and] foreigners will reap good returns . . . [especially] from the current undervaluation of Russian assets.
(Layard and Parker 1996a)

For further argument along these lines, see Layard and Parker (1996b).

CHAPTER 6

THE MANAGED ECONOMY OPTION

PLANNING AND SCARCITY PRICES

In Chapter 4 we saw that the policy imperatives of the cost-of-production theory of value and the structuralist conception of development are: managed production and technical change and a 'fair' distribution of income. Producers' decisions are fundamental to economic activity, rather than the hedonistic expediency of consumers' preferences. Production is defined within a technical division of labour. Producers specialize and are dependent on the wider economic system, which has to be managed in the general interest to ensure technical efficiency and a 'just' distribution of income. Cooperation, rather than competition, is the dynamic of economic activity and development.

Central planning was an attempt to manage economic activity, where such activity is measured in technical, quantitative terms, rather than as value. With economic development, as more and more goods circulate in the economy, it became increasingly difficult for planners to coordinate the activity of millions of producers. For instance, it is asserted by Smith and Zimbalist (1991: 329) that over two million different goods circulate in the Cuban economy. With the inevitable problems of physical coordination, there is necessarily *ad hoc* decentralized planning, economic coordination through values and some market exchange, and producers making informal deals with each other to obtain scarce supplies. These 'adaptations' to the limitations of planning exacerbate the problem of allocation, and plan fulfilment gets ever more improbable.

In the Special Period, economic strategy has to be oriented towards becoming an 'effective participant in the world market ... [requiring the coordination] of both domestic and international components ... to introduce greater efficiency and flexibility into the economic mechanism' (Zimbalist 1992b: 92). Economic coordination through physical planning is not sufficiently flexible to integrate with the world economy, where economic integration between a myriad of producers, suppliers and markets is just too complex; an inevitable consequence of which is increasing economic inefficiency. When one enterprise underfulfils targets, a chain reaction sets in: other producers fail to receive planned inputs, and ultimately there is a shortage of consumer goods. Accustomed to input shortages and the need to queue for goods in short supply, workers reduce their effort and leave work early to locate goods in short supply, etc. Quantitative planning techniques have no internal mechanism for adapting to an imbalance between supply and demand. No signals are generated to guide producers, and to diverge from the plan.

> In the presence of these and other obstacles, the conventional project of central planning grows more and more inefficient and untenable as an economy grows in size and complexity. The imperative for decentralization becomes increasingly apparent.
>
> (Smith and Zimbalist 1991: 331)

As we saw above, Wlodzimierez Brus argues that when the economy is relatively inefficient and undeveloped, the central allocation of resources to achieve a few strategic objectives has a rationale. But central planning becomes increasingly irrelevant as economies become more and more technically sophisticated with economic development. And as the centrally planned economies have developed and become more complex, there have been a number of attempts, especially since the death of Joseph Stalin in 1953, to reconcile central planning with market forces (see Nove 1983, 1988; Bergson 1987, 1989; Ellman 1989; Lane 1996).

It was not until the late 1970s that Cuba had a stable, institutional basis to planning. The SDPE, based on the 1965 reforms to the planning mechanism in the Soviet Union, began in 1977. The Soviet reforms had attempted to address the rigidity imposed on producers by central planning (quantitative techniques of 'material balances'), and were based on the work of Yevsi Liberman, who in 1962 had written an article in *Pravda* proposing that enterprise profits should be instituted as a 'success' indicator of economic performance, to act as a guide to enterprise economic decision-making (see Dyker 1976: Chapter 4).

The SDPE was orientated towards putting enterprises on a self-financing basis, with the aim, within the parameters of planned prices, of realizing a profit on sales, implying a degree of decentralization to achieve higher technical efficiency. But prices were still determined by planners according to political objectives, and did not reflect 'scarcity'. 'Enterprise autonomy and cost accounting . . . make little sense without scarcity prices' (Zimbalist 1993: 130; emphasis added). That is, a 'rational' price structure has to provide adequate incentives to mobilize productive resources as inputs into the production process to satisfy consumers' demands. Higher prices, and incomes, should be paid for those inputs in short supply to encourage their application in production. And the SDPE system, while attempting to put enterprises on a self-financing basis, encouraging economic decentralization and increasing autonomy from the centre, and thereby promoting efficiency, did little to enhance the scope of actual decision-making. Prices were still centrally set every five years, making it impossible to identify, through a profitability index, well-managed enterprises. Shortages were commonplace, and managers behaving rationally hoarded inputs, exacerbating problems of economic coordination.

Profitability was not a consequence of efficiency, but a question of the serendipity of planning targets and administratively determined prices; and planners, on equity grounds, had to take action to control excessive profits, weakening any incentive effect. Since profitability was not an indication of high-quality production in accordance with consumers' demands, new administrative regulations were devised to allocate productive resources. Investment projects were still centrally planned, although enterprise funds to implement the plan came out of bank accounts, which began to replace financing by the state budget, increasing from 1 per cent of total investment financing in 1981 to 30 per cent in 1985 (see Banco Nacional de Cuba 1986: 6).

In the end, profits as a system of incentives became hopelessly complicated, and the centre still planned investment projects. The SDPE did not imply a decentralization of capital allocation to meet shortages. There were a number of reforms 'Cubanizing' the SDPE system. 'Resource fairs' in 1979 and 1980, where enterprises could freely trade surplus stocks between one another, were designed to mobilize hoarded stocks. Self-employment was liberalized, and farmers' markets were introduced in 1978. However, overall, the SDPE did not have a 'rational' basis reflecting supply and demand, prices did not reflect 'scarcity' and the contradictions became ever more obvious: shortages, irrational incentive structures, lack of coordination between ministries, labour absenteeism, enterprise over-staffing, corruption among officials, etc.

These contradictions came to a head in 1986 in the Rectification Campaign. This campaign, for structuralist theorists, was confused: on the one hand, because the centralized control of the economy had been weakened by the limited decentralized decision-making under the auspices of the SDPE, the political leadership apparently felt the need to reassert its authority, which, for Zimbalist, is an inevitable consequence of the 'reform cycle of a centrally planned economy' (Zimbalist 1993: 124). Another example of this was the abolition of free peasant markets on 15 May 1986.

At the same time as the recentralization of *economic* decision-making, there was a process of increased *administrative decentralization*. Production brigades, which had first appeared in agriculture in 1981 and industry in 1983, and by 1986 numbered some 2500, were given greater emphasis. These were sub-units within enterprises, operating as self-accounting (and to become self-financing) and self-organizing entities, intended to enhance worker participation and productivity (on the internal structure of brigades, see Ghai 1986).

Enterprises were also increasingly organized into *Uniones de Empresas*, to achieve joint economies of scale in the provision of common products and services (for example, research and development costs), and these *Uniones* were organized independently of central planning. In existence since 1977, in 1988 the Comisión Nacional del Sistema de Dirección de la Economía (National Commision for Economic Direction) called for the extension of *Uniones de Empresas* to more sectors of the economy. Between 1988 and 1989 the number of economic units directed by the ministries of transport, food, basic industry, metallurgy and light industry fell by 43.2 per cent (see Zimbalist 1992b: 102).

As part of this 'administrative' reorganization, in 1986 the planning system was decentralized, with the number of planning directives to enterprises being reduced (see JUCEPLAN 1988). In 1988, experiments started with 'continuous planning', with a greater role for the enterprise to set targets: a reform extended to a third of all enterprises by the mid-1990s (see CNS 1989; Zimbalist 1992b: 102–3). However, the reformed system of economic management and administration still did not address 'scarcity' prices, and 'In sum, although rectification has signified an effort to re-balance the importance of moral vs. material incentives, the basic incentive structure of the SDPE has been retained' (Zimbalist 1993: 125).

This analysis of the significance of the Rectification Campaign as a 'management' problem is to be contrasted with the understanding within the intellectual parameters of the subjective preference theory of value. Following the analysis of the crisis of the Special Period being essentially one of decreased Soviet subsidies, the Rectification Campaign is seen to be similarly prompted by the 'state attempting to address its fiscal needs' (Eckstein 1990: 83). The contradictions resulting from the lack of free markets led to the Rectification Campaign, which was 'economically ir-rational' (Eckstein 1990: 73).

From the 'structuralist' vantage point, the 1990 Special Period in Time of Peace added a new dimension to an increasingly chaotic productive envi-ronment: the imperative to reconcile and locate the productive structure of the Cuban economy within the world market, following the breakdown of trading relations within the CAME.

Problems with the Cuban economy are not, fundamentally, questions of limited, individual consumer choices, but reflect 'structural' obstacles to 'efficient' production within a technically defined world division of labour. Value is defined 'quantitatively' (rather than the 'qualitative' notion within the subjective preference theory of value), and economic management is based upon quantitative accounting within a 'rational' pricing mechanism. This price mechanism reflects technical specialization and the institutional context of distribution – the costs of production – with distribution organ-ized to provide appropriate incentives, offering 'fair' rewards to producers and mobilizing 'scarce' resources.

The economic structure is technically and institutionally defined, and is disrupted when these parameters change suddenly.

These basic structural features – nearly mono-culture exports and reliance on imported intermediates to feed an industrial structure driven by domestic demand – meant that the Cuban economy was open to negative external shocks.

(Pastor and Zimbalist 1995: 706)

A shock was delivered by the collapse of the Soviet Union and the socialist trading system (CAME). The Cuban authorities reacted by cutting demand (the Special Period), with cuts in industrial energy consumption and petroleum consumption and the extension of the rationing system, etc. On the supply side, there was a drive to reduce food imports, efforts to increase biotechnology and pharmaceutical exports, expansion of tourism, incentives to foreign investment, etc.

While there is an attempt to manage production (supply) and consumption (demand), there are more deep seated institutional problems with regard to distribution:

> political contradictions have been mounting. Distribution has worsened despite a stringent rationing system . . . economic agents have realized that their best bet at income earning and wealth preservation involves engagement in dollar-earning activities.
>
> (Pastor and Zimbalist 1995: 708–9)

As a consequence, socialism, which is essentially a question of 'equitable distribution', can no longer be maintained and managed. 'The contribution of worsening distribution, a shrunken economy, and political anomalies has therefore been a recipe for the erosion of the goal of socialism and the moral authority of the Party and the Revolution' (Pastor and Zimbalist 1995: 709). 'Systemic' change, reflecting a change in the structural parameters of economic activity (the collapse of CAME), is inevitable. And a renewed emphasis on economic liberalization has begun: the transformation of state farms into smaller cooperatives; the extension of self-employment; depenalizing the use of the dollar, which has legalized black market activity; the re-emergence of farmers' markets; attempts to reduce the state deficit; and so on.

For the structuralist interpretation of economic interaction and development, there is a dual policy agenda: production and distribution. While there have been attempts to engineer an upturn in production, with managed changes in the conditions of demand and supply, distributional issues are *institutional* problems. Institutionally, people have been guaranteed certain standards of welfare, leading to a large public deficit. This needs to be cut, since the deficit generates incomes for which there are insufficient commodities for wage earners to purchase: monetary overhang. As a consequence, because prices are the only viable method of coordinating exchange relations between producers and consumers as specialization and the technical division of labour extend with economic development, it is necessary to 'absorb' the accumulated monetary balances, which reflect years of purchasing power exceeding the supply of commodities. Because prices have been controlled, these balances have not been absorbed by price inflation but have been 'saved'. With free market 'scarcity' prices, this pent-up demand, which is the monetary overhang, will be an inflationary 'time bomb'.

Hence the budget deficit has to be reduced, and the monetary overhang eliminated, before any liberalization of prices reflecting 'scarcity', a precondition for an increase in productivity, can be contemplated. Thereafter the price mechanism will 'provide the automatic inflation/*redistributive* mechanisms that restore [the] internal balance in market economies' (Pastor and Zimbalist 1995: 711, emphasis added). The liberalization of markets will require the privatization of state assets, and it is maintained that such a policy is compatible with equality and the maintenance of state welfare benefits.

The post-1986 economic reform programme (the Rectification Campaign) is understood to be a cynical attempt by the leadership to hold on to power in the light of economic chaos and the 'inevitability' of market reform, and not a serious attempt to address the developmental needs of Cuba: 'this toying with capitalist style incentives would be tossed away if another "oil-daddy" could be found to replace the Soviet Union' (Pastor and Zimbalist 1995: 710). Apparently, 'the *systemic* problems have not been recognised at the leadership level' (Pastor and Zimbalist 1995: 710, emphasis added). The Cuban authorities have not recognized the importance of 'ownership patterns and hence the material incentives [scarcity prices] for increasing domestic output' (Pastor and Zimbalist 1995).

MARKET SOCIALISM CUBAN STYLE

A variant of this structuralist thesis is the 'market socialism' of Carranza Valdés *et al.* (1995). Their book, *Cuba: Restructuración de la Economía*, has provoked considerable debate within Cuba.

It is acknowledged that with the collapse of the CAME, the Cuban economy is at a 'crossroads', and has to adjust to a new basis of international specialization. It is argued that Cuba must be transformed from one 'model' of socialism to another. And the new model will be 'a decentralised market economy with a high level of state participation. State and private enterprises alike would operate according to a market dynamic that would demand a high level of efficiency and profit' (Carranza 1995: 31). But market regulation need not be at the expense of the socialist achievements of the revolution:

> the theory is intended ... to increase the rate of economic growth and economic efficiency, and to reintegrate the Cuban economy into the world economy, without diminishing or threatening the achievements of the Revolution or compromising Cuba's independence.
>
> (Carranza Valdés *et al.*, 1995: 16, my translation)

It is argued that there is limited potential in expanding revenues from the expansion of the primary export industries: sugar, nickel, tobacco and citrus fruits. Rather, emphasis has to be given to import substitution, in particular in the use of petroleum, an increase in food production, an expansion of the tourist industry and an increase in foreign productive investment.

However, more fundamentally, economic regeneration will depend upon internal changes to the functioning of the Cuban economy. An economic 'dynamic' has to be established based on incentives to work (scarcity prices), incentives which will work towards economic efficiency in production. Current economic strategy, intended to equalize economic hardship through rationing, and to maintain people in employment, only leads to state deficit financing and a 'monetary overhang' – more money in circulation than there are goods to buy – militating against any incentive to work, and encouraging 'informal' economic activity, speculation and black market activity.

The effective existence of a 'dual economy', Archibald Ritter's bifurcation of the Cuban economy, the stagnant peso economy alongside a dynamic dollar economy, is not conducive to achieving economic efficiency. Inevitably individuals' economic activity is drawn to the pecuniary benefits of operating in the dollar economy rather than working for the social good in the peso economy, acting against the provision of the crowning achievements of the revolution: individuals' right to free health care, free education, a substantial degree of economic equality, etc.

The market dollar economy, has to be integrated with the planned peso economy. Cuba has to adapt to the market, but a market managed under very strict conditions, and very differently from the conclusions of Ritter and Pérez-López discussed in Chapter 5. Unregulated markets are not the answer: consumer demand is not the dynamic of the economy. Instead, 'an alternative, socialist, economic model has to be designed' (Carranza Valdés et al., 1995: 61, my translation). In this model there are different forms of productive property: state, cooperative, mixed social/private and individually private (the category private property includes that under foreign ownership). Large-scale enterprises (monopolies) would be state property, and centrally controlled and planned, fulfilling social objectives, though with much more autonomy to earn profits which would be distributed as incentives to the workforce.

Medium-sized enterprises (oligopolies) could be state, private or mixed property. They would not be subject to central planning but subordinate to the relevant Poder Popular assembly – national, provincial or municipal – although also responsive, in some unexplained way, to market signals.

Small enterprises, similarly, could potentially be any form of property, and while formally administered by Poder Popular, they too would be fundamentally orientated to market signals, although 'it is the function of government ... to create the conditions for markets to function efficiently' (Carranza Valdés et al., 1995: 94–5, my translation).

The dynamic of markets is not individual consumer choice, but the state coordination of production. 'Efficiency' is not a reflection of consumers' utility maximization, but is defined technically in production. The price level has to be regulated to achieve the full utilization of economic resources in production, and a fair distribution of income. Yet the market, in an unspecified way, is to operate according to the profit incentive.

The emphasis on market rationality, and the profit motive, necessitates that the Cuban economy is 'stabilized', and 'liberalized'. This would be a more or less gradual, phased, coordinated and managed process of reform, each phase being the precondition for subsequent phases. Phase 1 has two stages: financial stabilization and the beginnings of economic restructuring. Financial stabilization requires that deficit spending is cut. Demand would be contracted to reflect supply more closely, through policies of austerity, reduced subsidies to enterprises and taxation. To minimize the threat of inflation consequent upon the liberalization of market forces, the monetary overhang, which is pent-up effective demand, must be eliminated. Because the austerity of the first stage of phase 1 and the restriction of demand would necessarily have social and political repercussions as standards of living decline, engendering unrest and discontent, it should be achieved in as short a time as possible: a month. So that there can be no unintended, 'windfall' benefits from the hoarding of money as savings, the currency would have to be changed. And so as to maintain the socialist ideal of 'equality', the 'old' money would be changed into 'new' money progressively: the larger the bank balance of individuals, the lower the rate of exchange (less new money would be exchanged for old).

Economic restructuring would begin by ending subsidies to enterprises, although the state would still set investment objectives. How the state direction of investment would reflect scarcities revealed by market forces is not specified. Instead individuals would be guaranteed a minimum wage or social security: people, not enterprises, would be subsidized. Enterprises would be decentralized and survive by market criteria, which would generate unemployment as the market identifies scarcity. The unemployed would be entitled to social security payments, and as the economy picks up would be reabsorbed into the productive economy. To minimize economic 'distortions', as far as possible national prices would be linked to free trade prices. Yet a prices and incomes policy 'would reform prices in the state sector to eliminate distortions' (Carranza Valdés et al., 1995: 138, my translation). How?

The understanding of what constitutes a 'distortion' is at best confused, at worst contradictory. It appears to mean when economic activity does not conform to an intended, planned, 'fair' set of economic outcomes. Yet, increasingly, market incentives and therefore prices are to allocate resources, implying competition, which will inevitably create inequality and 'unfairness'. The supposed compromise between planned prices and market forces is the worst of both worlds. People's expectations cannot be met and government commitments will be unfulfilled, leading to disillusionment and the collapse of the social cohesion that is fundamental to any 'socialist' project.

However, the preconditions for phase 2 are now in place. A market is now established for intermediate products/means of production, requiring enterprises to interact by market exchange, and state enterprises have to abide by the 'forces' of supply and demand. How this is to be achieved, with such enterprises pursuing social planned objectives, is nowhere explained. Any excess over and above the plan could be sold to act as incentives to the workforce, and where enterprises are not financially profitable they would be allowed to go 'bankrupt' and cease trading; although there would be 'strategic' subsidies to socially important loss-making enterprises. Again, how these would be funded within an economy based on profitability is not explained. The logic is as confused as that over price 'distortions'.

Following phase 2, phase 3 would 'be the normal functioning of the economy. The government would reserve ultimate power to regulate the economy in the social interest, with an economically decentralized state sector coexisting with various forms of property' (Carranza Valdés *et al.*, 1995: 161, my translation). The state's strategic role in managing the market economy to fulfil social(ist) objectives would be, in an undefined and unspecified institutional context, reconciled to people's participation through Poder Popular.

This rhetorical genuflection to the principle of Poder Popular is little more that an attempt to give the market principles, which lie at the heart of the analysis, the illusion of being compatible with the ideals of the revolution. And it is this contradiction which underlies the confused analysis of 'price distortions', and the reconciliation of 'bankruptcy' with 'strategic sub-sidies'.

Fundamentally, socialism, the 'revolution', is defined as a 'social-welfare state' – 'the preservation of a social-welfare state ... is so fundamental that the day it disappears, it won't make sense to talk of revolution anymore' (Carranza 1995: 31). This vision of a social-welfare state includes: state control of the 'fundamental' means of production; the state 'strategically' plans economic development; the state represents the interests of the country *vis-à-vis* foreign capital; and the state guarantees social spending to 'impede the emergence of acute poverty' (Carranza 1995: 31).

Socialism is an issue of 'fair' distribution. 'This does not mean that income differences will be eliminated. There would simply not be extreme poverty and extreme wealth' (Carranza 1995: 31). All enterprises, state and private, would compete, and profitability would define 'efficiency'. Ultimately, unemployed resources and 'scarcity' prices will establish the 'internal balance' of the economy, so central to the Pastor and Zimbalist strategy (see Pastor and Zimbalist 1995: 711). But extremes of wealth and poverty will be avoided by state spending, which will be financed by a progressive taxation system.

THE PROMISE OF MARKET SOCIALISM

As an economic strategy, Carranza Valdés *et al.* spell out the implications of the Pastor and Zimbalist 'structuralist' thesis, making the policy initiatives explicit of what is essentially a variant of the economic agendas of the developed, social-democratic, market economies of the 1960s and 1970s (e.g. Australia, Germany, Japan, Canada, Sweden, the United Kingdom; see Therborn 1986, who compares the economic policy of 16 countries from which these six examples are a selection).

The 'liberal collectivist' ideology that underlay these strategies (see Cutler *et al.*, 1986) made a social commitment to certain politically defined minimal objectives of social welfare and employment. In *every* case the role of the state in guaranteeing these minimum standards of living has been compromised in the attempt to maintain the profitability of enterprises, whether they be state owned or private. An understanding of the 'tendency of the rate of profit to fall' was addressed in Chapter 4. This analysis is outside the intellectual parameters of the theory of market socialism, being a consequence of 'value' understood as a dialectical relation between use value, qualitatively defined (the subjective preference theory of value), and exchange value, quantitatively defined (the cost-of-production theory of value). Market socialism is a school of thought in the latter perspective.

As a consequence of the accumulation crisis in capitalism, state expenditure has been 'rolled back', and the neo-liberal agenda of free competition, individual utility maximization and inequality has moved to centre stage.

For the cost-of-production theory of value, value is conceived of as a merely quantitative concept, reflecting the technical utilization of productive resources in an institutional context, and prices are the indices of technical efficiency and 'fairness'. Profits are understood as a 'technical' surplus, the product of improved efficiency, a consequence of technical evolution. And where the concerns of 'fairness' require it, relatively 'inefficient', loss-making enterprises can be subsidized by taxing the more efficient, profitable enterprises. It is a quantitative accounting problem to be solved by management expertise.

Such an economic strategy would repeat the experience of the developed market economies since at least the early 1970s. The 'consensus politics' of post-war social democracy, based on Keynesian macroeconomic management and the expansion of the welfare state, and geared towards full employment and a 'fair' distribution of the national product, was seemingly successful in the 25 years up to 1970. But this 'success' was bought with economic growth. Political consensus was built upon a 'fair' distribution of a *growing* economic product, a consequence of buoyant profitability in the period 1945 to 1966 (see Mandel 1975: Chapter 4). The 1950s and 1960s saw average economic growth rates, in the developed market economies, of around 5 per cent; while price inflation stayed below 4 per cent until the late 1960s and unemployment was below 3 per cent. State sponsored full employment was the equivalent of the Carranza Valdés *et al.* 'strategic subsidies'. This went hand in hand with an unprecedented expansion in expenditure on social welfare: 'an extended period of prosperity for which it is impossible to find a precedent' (Shonfield 1965: 61).

It was this climate of sustained economic growth, and a growing economic surplus, that made the resolution of distributional conflicts and consensus politics possible. By the early 1970s, the halcyon days of economic prosperity were over. In the OECD (Organization for Economic Cooperation and Development) economies – Austria, Belgium, Canada, Denmark, France, Germany, Greece, Iceland, the Republic of Ireland, Italy, Japan, Luxembourg, the Netherlands, Norway, Portugal, Spain, Sweden, Switzerland, Turkey, the UK and USA – average economic growth for the decade from 1974 sank to 2 per cent. By 1975 unemployment reached 15 million, doubling within ten years, to maintain a flagging growth rate; inflation accelerated, and most of the OECD experienced growing balance of trade deficits. 'Governments *throughout the developed* West found themselves simultaneously failing to achieve the four major economic policy objectives – growth, low inflation, full employment and balance of trade – on which the post-war order had been based' (Pierson 1995: 36, emphasis added).

The only way to manage the Cuban economy to meet the market socialist objectives of Carranza Valdés *et al.*, combining full employment with economic equality and low inflation in a market economy, is by some mechanism of demand management. However, the viability of such interventionist economic strategies was called into question with the emergence of 'stagflation' – the coincidence of high unemployment with rising inflation – in the early 1970s in the OECD economies. This combination is logically impossible according to cost-of-production principles of economic management. The basis of this economic perspective, and of the cost-of-production theory of value, is that value is a 'technical' product, a quantitative concept, questions of management essentially being issues of the distribution of this technical product. Economic decline and stagflation were initially blamed on 'exogenous' shocks to the economic system, caused, principally, by the fivefold rise in oil prices in 1973, which OPEC (Organization of Petroleum Exporting Countries) was able to impose on the world economy (similar to the 'shock' to the Cuban economy of the collapse of the Soviet bloc).

However, attention has now turned to contradictions *within* the social-democratic post-war political consensus, as the harbinger of economic decline. The economic crisis was increasingly apparent from the late 1960s (before the OPEC price hike). The end of prosperity was not precipitated by an external 'shock' to the economic system, but was '*inherent* in the social, political and economic order of the social democratic consensus and especially in its ameliorating institutions for the management of economically based political conflict' (Pierson 1995: 38, emphasis added). It is to these 'inherent' difficulties that we now turn.

CHAPTER 7

THE SOCIAL PARTICIPATION OPTION

NEED, EQUALITY AND POTENTIAL

According to the Food and Agricultural Organization of the United Nations (FAO), and the United Nations Children's Fund (UNICEF), 800,000 children that could be saved, die every year in Latin America, and none of those children die in Cuba ... Thirty million children are homeless, in Cuba there are none; there are tens of millions of beggars, there are none in Cuba.

(Castro 1991d: 51, my translation)

Abstract labour theorists look at the 39 years since the triumph of the revolution in 1959 in terms of a process through which Cuban society has, or has not, moved towards people achieving greater freedom to fulfil their own creative potentials. Fundamental to this is improving health service provision and education, particularly to the young.

In 1992, Tomás Borge, Minister of the Interior in the Sandinista Government in Nicaragua between 1979 and 1990, engaged in a series of conversations with Fidel Castro (published as Borge 1993), of which he says: 'I was particularly impressed by his ... reflections on humanity, the human condition and human beings as the protagonists in the inconstancy of history' (Borge 1993: 5). The implication is that there is a 'faith', a belief, in people's creativity, and that Cuban development strategy can be interpreted as a process of political evolution to define methods of governance by which to achieve a just social order, in which individuals can fulfil their social potentials. Opportunity becomes less and less the preserve of a privileged minority, whether that advantage comes from wealth or political influence.

Of course this is a very different interpretation of the course of the Cuban revolution in general, and the motivations of Fidel Castro in particular, from those implied by the development perspectives already discussed. 'It must be taken into account that Cuba is a totalitarian state, Stalinist style. Castro has the repressive capacity and the ruthless will to use it that is required to prevent a revolt' (Ernesto Betancourt, quoted in ASCE 1991: 2). Or, as Pastor and Zimbalist imply, government policy has been a cynical attempt to buttress a political elite in Havana, and 'this toying with capitalist style incentives [the Rectification Campaign] would be tossed away if another "oil daddy" could be found to replace the Soviet Union' (Pastor and Zimbalist 1995: 710).

Underlying these alternative assessments are 'beliefs', which colour the perception of behaviour. These are the 'unexamined and unexpressed assumptions' (Levins and Lewontin 1985: 267) that provide the analytical 'framework', that define the 'intellectual parameters of the real world'. Tomás Borge empathizes with Fidel's attitudes and values, whereas Ernesto Betancourt fundamentally differs in his understanding of human motivation, seeing Castro as frustrating individuals' concerns with their legitimate 'self-interest'. And Manuel Pastor and Andrew Zimbalist, recognizing the need for social and economic coordination and management, interpret policy initiatives as attempts by the ruling elite to manage the economy in the face of problems, so as to maintain the political status quo.

The 'objective' is always understood 'subjectively', reflecting cultural norms, standards and morally acceptable beliefs. Knowledge is a social product: '*just as* society itself produces *man as man*, so is society *produced* by him. Activity and mind, both in their content and their *mode of production* are *social*: *social* activity and *social* mind' (Marx 1973b: 137, emphasis in original). For 'abstract labour' theorists, development is a process of class struggle against a ruling elite by the disadvantaged, through which people are able to realize new potentials. 'Praxis', the dialectic of knowledge and experience, creates a consciousness where people become aware of the possibilities of collective, cooperative activity. People evolve as creative beings, becoming increasingly conscious of the ideological limitations on 'freedom': 'communist [socialist] production by society as a whole ... will both require and generate an entirely different kind of human material. Communal operation of production cannot be carried out by people as they are today' (Engels 1977: 19–20).

The significant features of the evolution of Cuban development strategy, since Batista fled the island on 1 January 1959, have been: (a) the extent to which policy has evolved to reflect more nearly people's changing needs; and (b) the commitment to equality.

THE EVOLUTION OF POLICY AND NEED

[The] task of the revolutionary is first of all to arm people's minds, arm their minds! Not even physical weapons can avail them if their minds have been armed first.

(Castro, quoted in Medin 1990: 5)

It is, first, a question of people becoming aware of their own potentials. Second, it is about people being conscious of their interests, and those of their allies, in realizing shared objectives through collective struggle for social change. It is fundamentally a question of 'ideology', of interpreting social activity through the prism of class interest. To many this smacks of 'indoctrination', of distorting the 'truth' to the advantage of those with political power. And it *is*, if it is thought (believed) that 'facts' can be defined unambiguously, and are ideologically neutral: the 'real world' not being defined by intellectual parameters, but being 'obvious'.

For Fidel Castro, 'reality' is not so self-evident: 'Do not allow anyone to believe anything that he does not understand. That is the way fanatics are made and dogmatic, fanatical minds developed . . . We are going to educate, teach to think, teach to analyse and understand' (Castro 1972: 451, my translation). Experience, the 'appearance', has to be understood, interpreted, to make explicit the relations of social power and domination, the 'essence', which are implicit in the process of development. It is a question of 'consciousness': of knowing whose side you are on.

Consciousness is a product of 'praxis', reflecting experience. The principal obstacle is force of habit: prejudices, ideas and customs, which are part and parcel of the extant status quo, which are culturally instilled and inculcated, legitimating an inequitable social order. The culturally defined 'parameters of the real world' bias people's perceptions of experience, leading towards the passive acceptance of a political order contrary to their class interest. The powerless are frustrated from fulfilling their potentials. The culture justifies inequality, based on beliefs in human nature which sanction privilege.

> Class struggle takes place within and against cultural, ideological, state, and other imaginary and real structures ... Social theory at its best defines the modern crisis not only in terms of market relations and productive forces and relationships, but also and more importantly in terms of popular interpretations of these categories, including dominant cultural symbols, lived ideologies, political illusions, family relations, and so on.
>
> (O'Connor 1987: 9, 10)

Consciousness and ideology, through which people understand their existence, have been an explicit policy dimension of the Cuban revolution:

> once the weapons were secure in the hands of the people, it was necessary to wage a great battle in the field of ideology, in the field of politics. It was necessary to dismantle bourgeois culture, at the end of the military struggle the enemy still possessed extremely powerful weapons: those of ideology and political custom.
>
> (Castro, speech in 1973, quoted in Harnecker 1979: xvi)

In July 1960 the Fuerzas Armadas Revolucionarias (FAR, the Revolutionary Armed Forces) and the Dirección Nacional de las Milicias (the National Directorate of Militias) began to promote education sessions in work-centres to raise awareness (see Medin 1990: 8). The Literacy Campaign of 1961 was utilized as a vehicle to raise the consciousness of the disadvantaged. And people have been mobilized through the 'mass organizations', not only for military purposes, but also for education, art, production, etc., with 'years' being designated as the Year of Agrarian Reform (1960), the Year of Education (1961) and so on to galvanize people's consciousness to achieve specific collective objectives.

In the mass and social organizations, our revolution has a powerful and inex-
haustible flow of political and revolutionary energy. They are the link between
the party and the masses ... They constitute the great school that develops the
consciousness of the millions and millions of workers, men and women, old
people, young people and children.

(Castro 1976: 155, my translation)

People are unique 'individuals', albeit *social* individuals, with distinct
values, attitudes, intuitions, skills, talents and expertise. They will differ in
their ability and willingness to participate in the organization of society in
general, and production in particular. Hence there is a need for alternative,
participatory, avenues, to help to realize people's different and changing
creative potentials. 'There have arisen in the world as many interpretations
and applications of socialism as there have been historical circumstances,
cultures and countries. No two socialisms are the same' (Castro 1991a: 11,
my translation).

With the triumph of the revolution there was no unified political movement to take power. Indeed, there was a 'confidence in a popular outburst,
enthusiasm and faith that Batista's power could be liquidated by a quick
uprising combined with spontaneous revolutionary strikes' (Guevara 1960:
509, my translation). But in the armed struggle in the Sierra Maestra, where
in the interaction between peasant and guerrilla a revolutionary consciousness evolved through praxis, it became apparent that the dialectic of
experience and understanding would only develop gradually in the mass of
the Cuban people. Change would not be spontaneous.

In 1959 there were three revolutionary groups, whose total membership
was not more than a few thousand: the 26th July Movement, the Revolutionary Directorate and the Popular Socialist (Communist) Party. In the
subsequent power struggle, Fidel Castro emerged as the undisputed leader,
and the three parties were merged into a unified structure, the Organiza-
ciones Revolutionarias Integradas (ORI, the Integrated Revolutionary
Organizations), which was formed to organize the new government and the
means of production. The early 1960s were difficult: the exodus of professional and technical personnel when the need for expertise was crucial
was in full swing, coupled to the US inspired economic blockade and an
'intuitive' response to the task of social, political and economic organization. With the lack of trained cadres, spontaneous initiatives prevailed over
rational planning, and the business of government, in particular the legislative, executive and judicial functions, was concentrated in the hands of
Castro and a small circle of intellectuals. There was no clear separation of
the functions of the party, the army and the administration. The 1960s were
characterized by voluntarism and idealism, with 'the Party devoting itself
mostly to administrative duties ... the Party had to run everything' (Casal
1976: 24).

Sectarian infighting in the ORI led to the trial in March 1962 of Anibal
Escalante, who favoured 'senior Marxist militants' being in control of

political and economic institutions. However, this was interpreted by the 'Fidelistas' as an incipient patronage-dispensing machine, limiting participation, and a more open integration of the Cuban people into government was envisaged. When the new Partido Comunista de Cuba (PCC, the Communist Party of Cuba) was forged in 1965, with an initial membership of 50,000, the emphasis was upon 'exemplary workers' as cadres, chosen by their work colleagues. But the PCC, which following Leninist ideology was conceived of as the 'vanguard' of the revolution, was weak. Being relatively small, with limited popular participation, the cadres often lacked expertise: in 1975, 20 per cent of party members had not attained sixth grade education, 9 per cent had received intermediate–higher education and 4 per cent had been educated to university level (see Azicri 1980: 327). With chaotic internal organization and coordination between the different departments and sectors within the PCC, it could not fulfil its intended 'leading role' in the communist development of Cuba (see LeoGrande 1980). And at this stage of the revolution it was not apparent that the political practice of 'democratic centralism', which underlies the concept of the 'vanguard party', and was enshrined under article 66 of the 1976 constitution (see below), would militate against extending political participation as people's social potentials evolved.

However, there were some initiatives to organize local government. After the victory of the revolution, commissions were set up to oversee local government, being replaced in 1961 by a more formal municipal structure: the Juntas de Coordinación, Ejecución y Inspección (JUCEI) (see Dilla *et al.*, 1993: 28). The JUCEI were a form of council, composed of representatives from local organizations. These were replaced in 1966 by Poder Local (Local Power), intended to decentralize administration and local government, although still presided over by the PCC.

Of course, for subjective preference theorists the Cuban authorities 'ignore[d] many basic economic *laws*' (Mesa-Lago 1981a: 11, emphasis added). But, as Rodríguez points out, because

> the interrelationship between political, economic and social aspects of the Revolution is not examined, Cubanologists [such as Carmel Mesa-Lago] fail to sustain the thesis that socialist development in Cuba lacks an appropriate economic basis.
>
> (Rodríguez 1988: 101)

With failure of the ten million ton *zafra* in 1970, an over-ambitious goal that, despite huge efforts by the Cuban people to concentrate effort in the cutting of sugar cane, resulted in severe dislocation of the economy, there was a re-evaluation of economic coordination in particular, and the organization of government in general, institutionalizing socialism. Economic shortcomings and the failings of planning were essentially interpreted as limitations on the degree of economic and political participation. It was not so much the failure of the 1970 *zafra* to meet the planned production target that *caused* the post-1970 institutionalization of the Cuban revolution. The need to integrate people into the revolution, so that revolutionary objectives reflected people's needs through their participation, was already an ideological principle of the revolution. And the 1970 *zafra* was the *catalyst* through which the development of socialism in Cuba, as a process, was advanced (see Azicri 1980: 315).

The failure of the 1970 *zafra* was recognized as a consequence of over-centralized economic management, which could not be left to the Council of Ministers. With the nationalization of economic activity, and the key role of the state in the provision of the social services and welfare, it became

> impossible ... to direct and co-ordinate this entire apparatus. It is necessary to create a political structure capable of tying together the different sectors of social production ... The revolutionary process itself has demonstrated the short-comings of the bureaucratic method.
>
> (Fidel Castro in 1970, quoted in Harnecker 1979: xxvi–xxvii)

There was an attempt to move away from the voluntaristic, arbitrary decision-making processes of the 1960s, and to move towards formal avenues to organize and decentralize decision-making, particularly economic coordination. As an effect of the US economic embargo, the Soviet Union replaced the USA as the main trading partner. In 1972 Cuba joined the Communist bloc trading organization, the CAME: and in 1973 the SDPE system of national planning was introduced, although it was not until 1980 that it covered the major part of the economy. The SDPE was modelled on the reforms to the planning system in Russia in the mid-1960s (see Ellman 1971). The planning system was intended to decentralize economic decision-making to the enterprise, which was expected to realize a surplus of sales receipts over production costs.

In an attempt to reconcile the economic objectives of enterprises with the wider political priorities of Cuban society in general, and the social needs of Cubans in particular, Poder Popular was introduced as a participative counterweight to the 'economism' of the SDPE. Sixteen years of provisional revolutionary government, under which the Council of Ministers exercised almost unlimited executive and legislative powers, came to an end with the 1976 constitution. The socialist character of the polity was formalized, legitimizing the Cuban revolution. A nationwide discussion of the draft constitution, through a myriad of meetings of the mass organizations, collective legal offices (*bufetes colectivos*), in workplaces and informal settings, allowed people's comments and recommendations to modify the final draft, which was debated at the First Party Congress in April 1975, and subsequently approved by a national referendum.

The new constitution formalized popular participation in the political process, and on 2 December 1976 the Assemblea Nacional de Poder Popular (the National Assembly of People's Power) was called into session. State functions were decentralized to the Organs of Poder Popular (OPP). The twelve chapters and 141 articles of the constitution, according to Blas Roca, president of the National Assembly of OPP ensured a 'new society under the direction of the working class' (quoted in Azicri 1980: 323). The state was formally distinct from the party.

Necessarily, these revisions to political practice went hand in hand with a revision of the legal system. 'It was not until the early 1970s that the leadership began to elaborate a judicial basis for the revolution which would both reflect its principles and direct the evolution of socialism in Cuba' (Evenson 1994: 2). This judicial review has been itself an evolutionary process, which apart from the changes in the 1976 Constitution, which had been preceded in 1973 by a Code of Criminal Procedure, has seen the enactment of a new criminal code in 1987. And even in the midst of the austerity of the Special Period,

> Cuba is moving toward very progressive reforms of its criminal procedure and continues to modernize its judicial system . . . Although a revolution is a process, not an event, Cuba has attempted to design and implement a new legal order in less than two decades. The complex task of managing a socialist economy and mediating the social contradictions that have emerged in the process of building socialism has produced a permanent state of reassessment and reform in Cuba.
>
> (Evenson 1994: 5, 16)

However, within the OPP, since the party had the 'leading role', 'party potential to intrude into other institutional domains . . . [remains] a danger which, if allowed to run unchecked, may very well hinder the overall drive for the institutionalization of the state' (Azicri 1980: 328). The nationwide adoption of administrative assemblies of the OPP, at national, provincial and municipal levels in 1976, followed experiments in 1974 and 1975 in Matanzas province, where provincial and municipal assemblies operated. This pilot project was evaluated and finally approved at the First Party Congress in 1975.

Inevitably there have been difficulties in the working of Poder Popular, problems of administrative inexpertise, and the failure to synchronize the planning of resources, exacerbating existing shortages, has fermented a degree of disillusionment in the efficacy of participation. But this is recognized as part of the process of progress and development. 'The delegates of Popular Power . . . did not have any experience . . . [and] it will only be with time . . . that they [will] learn the full extent of their responsibilities' (Editora Política 1979: 5, 11, my translation). The subsequent evolution of the socialist process of popular participation has led to constitutional change modifying the operation of OPP, to differentiate further the party from the state. Originally, the 1976 constitution stipulated direct elections, every two and a half years, for delegates to municipal OPP, that level of Poder Popular concerned with providing 'economic, cultural, educational and recreational services' (article 102 of the 1976 Constitution, cited in Azicri 1980: 331) at the municipal level. Provincial delegates were elected indirectly by their municipal counterparts for a similar term. The municipal delegates also elected deputies to the National Assembly of Poder Popular.

The Rectification Campaign of 1986, consequent upon the experience of the SDPE as a system of economic coordination, which manifestly elevated the economic priorities of individual enterprises above the social needs and political objectives of the population, sought to put 'politics back in command'. The 1970 *zafra* was the catalyst that sparked the institutionalization of the revolution and the 1976 constitution, which was 'a first step to be modified subsequently as experience highlighted the need for furthur institutional change to improve the democratic efficiency of these structures' (Dilla *et al.*, 1993: 34, my translation). Similarly, the 'fiscal crisis' and the spiralling foreign debt of the mid-1980s (see Eckstein 1990: 73–7), reflecting the operation of the SDPE, prompted the 1986 campaign to 'rectify errors and negative tendencies', the Rectification Campaign, leading to the Fourth Party Congress in 1991.

> It would be wrong to see these changes [put in train by the Rectification Campaign] as basically issues of economic administration . . . the basic challenge of rectification was the problem of popular participation, the problems of which have been *less significant than the advances in socialist democracy*.
>
> (Dilla *et al.*, 1993: 142, 36, my translation, emphasis added)

In a similar manner to the preparation for the First Party Congress of 1975, which paved the way to the 1976 constitution, between May and November 1990, about three and a half million citizens took part in over 800,000 meetings and assemblies to discuss the issues and themes of the 1991 Fourth Congress of the Communist Party of Cuba (see Madan *et al.*, 1993: 1; see also Politburo of the Central Committee 1991). The subsequent debates at the Congress led to the Constitution Reform Law, a product of the National Assembly of People's Power session of July 1992, which modified 76 of the original 141 articles of the 1976 constitution.

> We had to reconcile the concept of a single party with this idea that the people should nominate and the people should elect [delegates to the OPP]. We had to make it work in practice, because what was known to exist in the world when there wasn't a single party was a multiplicity of parties, and this was the only known procedure for carrying out elections. So we had to create something new, something more just, more equitable, more democratic, more pure, because our main concern was to preserve the purity of our electoral process and prevent any politicking or corruption from filtering in . . . [In our system delegates] . . . don't have to be rich, they don't have to be landowners, or great industrialists, or multi-millionaires. They don't need money, they don't need anything except decency and civic worth . . . We wanted to avoid politicking at all costs, we wanted to have a fair, really fair, process in which a person's worth, a person's personal history, a person's qualities would be the deciding factor.
>
> (Madan *et al.*, 1993: 6–7, 29)

The resulting system of national, provincial, municipal, district and constituency electoral commissions made up of representatives from the mass movements is intended to ensure that 'the grass roots delegates are nominated without any intervention of the Party' (Madan *et al.*, 1993: 15).

Consejos populares (local councils), composed of local government delegates and representatives of key local enterprises, were formed to give more decision-making power on how to manage austerity to the local community during the Special Period. A new form of workplace assembly called *parlemento obreros* (workers' parliament) was also established, in which individuals could discuss and decide how to operate and organize their workplace. Again, the shortages and constraints of the Special Period mean that participation is ever more about managing day-to-day work processes of living and working. These two organizations, together with the trade unions, the OPP and the CDRs, are also consulted on major economic issues, the deliberations being fed back to the leadership. And ten new standing committees have been formed in the National Assembly to provide continuous communication with local government.

In December 1992, more than 7,000,000 voters (around 90 per cent of the electorate) voted in secret ballot, in 13,865 constituencies, for delegates to 169 municipal assemblies. In February 1993, almost the entire electorate voted for deputies to the National Assembly of People's Power, and for provincial OPP delegates (see Madan *et al.*, 1993: 15), and 88.5 per cent voted for the recommended straight ticket (see Pérez-Stable 1993: 52–7). Even the regime's leading dissident, Elizardo Sánchez, accepts that about 80 per cent of the electorate broadly supported the government (see Lambie 1997: 41).

In the December elections, reportedly some 30 per cent of votes cast were invalid, which has been interpreted by observers critical of Cuban socialism as an expression of civil disobedience in a totalitarian state. But people do not have to vote, and even if this is an accurate interpretation of voting behaviour, 'valid' voting still exceeds the record in elections in the UK and the USA; and that is not interpreted as a manifestation of political and civil discontent.

The voting was observed by over 100 journalists from 21 different countries, and vote counting was held in public in each polling station. As Nicolás Riós, a journalist with the Miami based magazine *Contrapunto*, observed: 'The counting of votes was impeccable. It was open and public, and since over 120,000 people were involved in 30,000 polling stations, the results could not be tampered with' (Riós 1993: 113, my translation).

Just as social policy and need have evolved, so has the Cuban constitution. 'The constitution in a socialist society is not just history which has taken place, but it is history in the making' (Dórticos Torrido 1980: 6, my translation). The revolution is a 'process'.

THE COMMITMENT TO EQUALITY

For there to be a 'true' democracy the exploitation of man by man has to be ended. I am absolutely convinced that while there exist enormous inequalities between people it is not possible to have a democracy.

(Castro, quoted in Muñiz 1993: 1, my translation)

Fidel Castro asks (see Muñiz 1993: 23–5): where a small minority has immense fortunes, with the consequent economic control that this implies, how can people democratically organize themselves to share power and responsibility?

For abstract labour theorists, 'freedom' is only fully possible when people can 'choose' how to fulfil their own creative potentials. 'In fact, the realm of freedom actually begins only where labour which is determined by necessity and mundane considerations ceases; thus in the very nature of things it lies beyond the sphere of actual material production' (Marx 1972a: 820). With economic development, human wants multiply, but so do the forces of production with which to satisfy these needs. People have to engage in production to provide the material basis of life. And after survival is assured, then they can fulfil less 'mundane', creative needs. People exist only in society, and higher living standards, widening the scope for satisfying their creative potentials, are achieved by rising productive efficiency, implying greater discrimination within economic activity and increasing economic specialization. Development is a question of superior social cooperation within an extended technical division of labour.

There is a distinct logic to production based upon commodity exchange, where market exchange sets the priorites for the utilization of economic resources within a division of labour.

We saw in Chapter 4 that, within the abstract labour theory of value, the logic of commodity exchange is based on a dialectic between the qualitative (use value) and the quantitative (exchange value) dimensions of value, and, to value individual 'concrete' labour as social 'abstract' labour, production is necessarily geared towards producing surplus value. The receipt of surplus value as profit explains the competitive dynamic in the allocation of resources to alternative lines of production.

The operation of the law of value of commodity exchange eventually sets in train (quantitative) economic crises, the tendency for the rate of profit to fall, which have (qualitative) social effects: the powerless and disadvantaged suffering declining living standards, as labour power is devalued with the increase in the rate of exploitation, as a response to a rising organic composition of capital.

For the abstract labour theory of value, the qualitative (use value) and quantitative (exchange value) dimensions of commodity exchange are the dialectic of social change: the direction and pace of development reflecting people's 'class consciousness'. The subjective preference theory of value emphasizes only the qualitative, the *subjective* preferences of consumers in the maximization of individual utility. And the cost-of-production theory of value, in considering the technical efficiency of production, addresses the quantitative aspect of commodity exchange, the *technical* utilization of economic resources.

The abstract labour theory of value is a dialectic of the subjective preference and cost-of-production theories of value: of consumption and production in relations of commodity exchange.

It is the socialist project to allow individuals as far as possible to fulfil their social potentials, and avoid the conflict and struggle, uncertainty and frustration which are part and parcel of societies founded on commodity exchange.

Hence, the necessary relation between consumption and the productive utilization of the natural environment should be purposefully, rationally organized, reflecting the quantitative and qualitative dimensions of exchange, and regulated to minimize the time spent on 'necessary' work. Market 'forces', according to which production is orientated to realizing an economic surplus rather than satisfying social need, should not be the basis of economic organization. 'Beyond it [necessary work] begins the development of human energy which is an end in itself, the true realm of freedom' (Marx 1972a: 820).

Hence, labour has to be technically organized to produce as efficiently as possible, and the fruits of social production, which is *all* production, should be equally distributed to consumers. *Every* person has changing, creative potentials and needs, which develop as people become conscious of themselves. 'The Cuban Constitution recognizes both political and civil as well as economic, social and cultural rights ... such as the right to work, to social security, to medical care, to education and access to sports and culture' (Evenson 1994: 22). This political structure is not conceived of as a timeless socialist dogma: 'socialist ideas are based on solidarity between people, brotherhood, equality and justice between men, and these ideas assume different forms reflecting different circumstances in different countries' (Castro 1991d: 12, my translation). Castro echoes Marx: 'Men make their own history, but they do not do it just as they please, they do not make it under circumstances chosen by themselves, but circumstances directly encountered' (Marx 1950: 225).

The objective of working towards economic equality to some observers implies repression. In the austerity of the Special Period there has been a partial derestriction of private enterprise in Cuba: for instance, in the case of the *paladares*, private restaurants. These have to be 'family-run', not employing additional labour, to avoid the unaviodable exploitation of wage labour in commodity exchange (where labour power is the commodity). Second, they have to be small – a maximum of twelve seats – to limit the size of individual earnings and growing economic inequality, and hence to maintain the ideological basis of the process of socialist development.

Following the partial, 'liberalization' of private enterprise, a personal income tax has been introduced for the self-employed. The aim is to ensure that the self-employed contribute to the maintenance of the extensive welfare state in Cuba, from which they will continue to benefit. Second, the system is intended to be progressive in the attempt to work towards equality. However, 'Many small businessmen do not declare their full earnings. Even so ... a fifth of Cuba's 168,000 licensed self-employed are in arrears ... Many take the simple way out, not even registering their business' (*Economist* 1997: 62). However, ONAT, the Oficina Nacional de Adminstración Tributaria (the National Tax Adminstration Office) reported that in January and February 1997 over 245,000 taxpayers filed their tax declaration on their annual income for the first time. Given that for more than 32 years there has been an almost total absence of tax collection, the degree of taxpayers' awareness was encouraging (see Lavastida 1997).

Regulations to limit the size of enterprises, to insist on family labour and to tax earnings progressively are a logical consequence of seeing human activity as a product of rational, creative, social human beings: the abstract labour theory of value. If, however, markets are understood to be mechanisms through which independent individuals maximize utility, then the appropriate development policy is to provide incentives to encourage individual enterprise. Anything less is contrary to human nature, and can only be imposed through varying degrees of repression. Hence, the article from the *Economist* quoted above is very critical of attempts to regulate self-employment. 'Fidel Castro has allowed the first tender shoots of free enterprise into his marxist Eden, but when they start to flourish he wishes he had not' (*Economist* 1997: 62). But then the moral and ideological bias of the *Economist* should not surprise us.

Similarly, by emphasizing collective social rights and obligations, Cuba and Castro, which are often treated as synonymous, are accused of violating individual human rights, such as the right to free enterprise. To this, Fidel Castro replies:

> How many hundreds of thousands of lives have been saved by our health programmes ... children in our country without exception receive education, what has been the benefit ... how many women have been saved from prostitution, how many people have been saved from drugs, how many people have found employment and avoided beggary.
>
> (Castro 1991d: 50, my translation)

Castro is proud that

> there has never been a student demonstration, or a workers' meeting broken up with water cannon or tear gas, with rubber bullets and all those other devices they have invented to repress people, because here the ones who have the weapons and defend the Revolution are the workers themselves, the students, the campesinos, the people.
>
> (Castro 1997: 8)

There are different *concepts* of democracy, even though the word is the same. In terms of 'orthodox' representative and pluralist interpretations of democratic participation, the Cuban process of socialist development is inexplicable. For instance, Tatu Vanhanen, asserting that it 'belongs to the nature of democratic government to take care of the many, to serve their interests in the endless struggle for survival in this world of scarcity' (Vanhanen 1997: 4), concludes that Cuba has been 'non-democratic' since the early 1960s. And we can expect that there will be 'democratization' because of 'structural imbalances'. The imbalance is between the index of power resources (IPR) and the index of democratization. That is, Cuba has a degree of equality (IPR) – reflecting the index of occupational diversification, indicative of a level of socio-economic development; the index of knowledge distribution, suggestive of the level of education and the distribution of 'intellectual power'; and the index of distribution of economic power resources, measuring the concentration and distribution of the control of the means of production – compatible with a 'democratic system', as measured by the competition and participation of political parties in elections.

Competing political parties are the 'measure' of democracy, because it 'is an *inevitable* consequence . . . that all those who have power tend to use it for their own advantage . . . because power is concentrated in the hands of a few in an autocracy, it is also used to serve the interest of a few' (Vanhanen 1997: 4, emphasis added). And Cuba is defined as an 'autocracy': QED.

The whole analysis is quantitative, comparing the IPR with election performance, because quantitative indicators 'require subjective [and therefore biased] judgements as little as possible' (Vanhanen 1997: 34). The fact that there is a subjective bias in *choosing* which variable to measure and compare is totally ignored, the analysis being justified by a reference to Karl Popper's 'positivist' theory of science (Vanhanen 1997: 3). But this is little more than an uncritical, axiomatic, assertion. As we have seen in Chapter 4, philosophies of science are also ideologies of knowledge, justifying partial approaches to understanding as 'neutral science', assuming as 'common sense' a particular view of human nature. And these ideologies of knowledge ultimately legitimize a particular political and social order. The characterization of Cuba as 'autocratic' is nowhere discussed or justified; nor is the assertion that 'democratic' governments necessarily 'take care of the many', or that electoral competition is a sufficient condition to ensure democratic 'participation'.

Democracy in Cuba presupposes people's equal ability to participate, implying that economic power is not concentrated in society, and a political constitution that as far as possible is not orientated towards preserving the power of a political elite. Crucially, people cannot be 'empowered' to participate: by definition, people can only empower themselves. If they have to be empowered then they are powerless.

To work democracy . . . has to be a way of life . . . Citizenship is a lot more than voting ... Democracy is never fully in place. It is always in flux, a work in progress. Democracy is dynamic. It evolves in response to the creative actions of citizens.

(Lappé and Du Bois 1994: 14–15)

The political party can only facilitate such a progressive change, and over the past forty years there have been a number of changes in the Constitution intended to remove obstacles to political participation in the process of socialist development:

> socialist democracy mandates the elimination of class divisions between the exploiter and the exploited ... Liberty for one means oppression for the other ... [and] requires not only the destruction of the capitalist class ... The struggle against [cultural and ideological] deformations of the past is a long-term project, not one to be accomplished overnight with the defeat of the capitalist state.
>
> (Evenson 1994: 24)

In fact, the 'struggle against the cultural deformations' to participation is endless. In the process of socialist development, society must *continuously* adapt to people's changing creative potentials.

THE CONTRADICTIONS OF MARKET SOCIALISM

We saw in Chapter 6 that Julio Carranza Valdés *et al.*, recognizing the need for Cuba to trade in the world market consequent upon the collapse of the CAME, formulated an 'alternative, socialist, economic model', designed to increase economic 'efficiency' without 'threatening the achievements of the revolution'. Such a compromise would be achieved through a 'decentralized market economy', though with a 'high level of state participation'. The state would make the 'strategic' economic decisions, within which 'state and private enterprises alike would operate according to a market dynamic that would demand a high level of efficiency and profit'.

Recognizing that competition would generate economic inequality, wealth and income would have to be redistributed to avoid 'extremes of wealth and poverty'. And 'strategic subsidies' would be granted to socially important, though loss-making, enterprises.

In the previous section, we saw that the abstract labour theory of value understands market prices to be an expression of the exchange value of commodities, reflecting the relative value of commodities. A value that exists *only* in the act of exchange, where the individual, concrete labour of producers, is abstractly valued according to social demand and the possibilities of social supply of the commodity.

Values are not consciously determined, ultimately reflecting the value of labour time used to appropriate the natural environment by producers to satisfy the needs of consumers. The market for goods is based upon the market for, and value of, the labour power used in production. The market is essentially a process in which individual concrete labour is valued as social abstract labour.

> The very necessity of first transforming individual products ... into exchange value ... [to] demonstrate their social power ... [means] that production is not directly social ... social production is not subsumed under individuals ... *There can be nothing more ... absurd than to postulate the control by the united individuals of their total production, on the basis of exchange value.*
>
> (Marx 1973a: 158–9, emphasis added)

Why is the social control of production on the basis of exchange value 'absurd'? The implication is that 'market socialism' is a contradiction in terms. Why?

Carranza Valdés *et al.* rationalize the market regulation of production by individual profit incentives, with an effective welfare state to satisfy social needs, by conceiving of value in *quantitative* terms. It is a simple accounting exercise: the rich and efficient subsidize the poor and inefficient, according to political judgements. And if the value of production merely reflects the utilization of natural resources, including labour *time*, then this conclusion is theoretically coherent, and the policy conclusions are realistic. Such are the preconceptions that underlie cost-of-production theory of value.

For the abstract labour theory of value, value is a *social relation*: simultaneously qualitative *and* quantitative. It is not labour *time* that is valued but labour *power*. Labour power is the ability to work, to produce commodities, and is a commodity itself. Labour power, the abstract value of the concrete labour time that is worked, will vary with the social demand and social supply of the commodity that is produced. It will also vary with the labourers' control of the means of production, their power within society. This power will define the intensity of the exploitation of labour within the labour process, and hence the value of the commodity 'labour power'. With the development of an economy founded upon commodity exchange, there is a qualitative change in the value of the quantitative measure of labour time worked by wage labour, a value that varies with exploitation. Labour 'time' is devalued: the same 'quantitative' amount of labour time is (qualitatively) worth less as exploitation intensifies. And exploitation is a consequence of power, of the control of the means of production: a dimension which cannot be addressed in any quantitative notion of value.

The same (concrete) labour time can be (abstractly) valued very differently. Hence, for Marx, labour power is catagorized as *variable* capital, unlike means of production, which are produced inputs into the production process and already have a 'value', i.e. are *constant* capital. In the production process capitalists have to recoup this value or go bankrupt.

We saw in Chapter 4 that it is the competitive dynamic of the capitalist mode of production that leads to the changing organic composition of capital, explaining the tendency for the rate of profit to fall, followed by increased labour exploitation, and implying economic crises. The inability to sell commodities at a price high enough to be sufficiently profitable, the problem of 'realizing value', explains the falling growth rates in the OECD economies in the 1970s, after nearly two decades of prosperity.

Because value is a social relation, qualitative changes in the social relations of production, the relation between 'capital' and 'labour', impact on the quantitative expression of value as exchange value, manifested as price. As a consequence of the ebb and flow of the class struggle between capital and labour, there have been four 'long waves' of capitalist accumulation. Times of relative prosperity have been followed by crises of accumulation, as the rising organic composition of capital makes accumulation dependent on increased exploitation. The halcyon days of economic prosperity in the two decades up to 1970, with historically high economic growth, low inflation and low unemployment, were more than an economic phenomenon: they were reflective of the productive relations between capital and labour. In the *economic* trends of the world economy, there was no hint of the impending economic recession, and economists at the United Nations could confidently write in 1972: 'there is no special reason to doubt that the underlying trends in growth in the early and middle 1970s will continue much as in the 1960s' (United Nations 1972: 125).

In the *quantitative* trends there were no suggestions of world economic prosperity suffering declining fortunes. The changes have been *qualitative*. The commodity relationship between 'capital' and 'labour', which is expressed in the *abstract* valuation of *concrete* labour time, reflected in the exchange value of labour power, on a world scale has changed. The *same* (concrete) labour time actually worked is worth less, and living standards have declined.

CUBAN DEVELOPMENT STRATEGY

What are the implications for Cuba?

Development requires economic specialization and trade, but is there an alternative to the market and the forging of ever stronger competitive pressures within Cuba, leading to impoverishment, unemployment and declining welfare provision, as a consequence of commodity exchange on the world market?

The only alternative is an explicitly socialist development strategy: the allocation of economic resources to satisfy *need* rather than to realize a *profit*. Here, economic management is through the participation of the producers, organized in democratic bodies of self-administration, satisfying social needs reflecting democratic participation. This will be dismissed by sceptics as hopelessly idealistic. But remember, participation is a *process* that evolves with social experience. People become ever more aware of the potentials of *social*, productive organization. People change: 'all history is nothing but a continuous transformation of human nature' (Marx 1936: 124).

Socialism is not a 'system' of social organization, but a 'process' of social evolution. People become ever more free to fulfil their potentials as the 'mundane' aspects of production are reduced to a minimum. A society is 'socialist' in as far as there is change to reflect people's changing creative potentials. Because people are unique, this can only be a reflection of their participation in social organization.

It is necessary to have *faith* in people:

> all human beings are in a fundamental sense philosophers and intellectuals in that they are thinking creative social beings who can readily participate in the world-historical process of building a new culture. To the extent that everyone has beliefs, ideas, feelings, aesthetics as they participate in an evolving social and cultural order, to the extent that everyone exercises a certain impact on their surroundings, everyone is a potential theorist, a bearer of consciousness.
>
> (Boggs 1976: 125)

The only policy proposals compatible with socialist development are for economists to maintain the fiscal balance between state income and expenditure, and the foreign exchange balance of payments. Within these parameters it should encourage and allow people themselves to expand progressively the scope of their participation in the economic regulation of social existence.

As argued above, socialism is a process rather than a system, a process premised on 'faith' in people as creative, social beings, and in which people progressively improve their life chances to fulfil their changing potentials. There are *always*, in every society, 'constraints' resulting in frustration. But in a socialist society, such frustrations are understood to be a symptom of inappropriate and inadequate social participation.

> Perhaps one of the most important aspects of the Cuban case is the consistently flexible and self-critical position that has permitted *errors to be corrected* and lessons to be learned ... the present process of rectification can be viewed as part of the historical task of searching for the best way to socialism in Cuba.
>
> (Garcia 1993: 103–4, emphasis added)

> We Sandinistas learned from Cuba because the revolution has an incredible capacity to correct its own mistakes.
>
> (Doris Tijerina, Nicaraguan Congresswoman, 1995: 43)

Social and economic life has to be compared to *previous* experience, *not* to some 'idealized' model of a 'socialist' utopia. As we saw in Chapter 2, the revolutionary regime in 1959, compared to the experience of Batista regime, for the vast majority of Cubans marked a quantum leap in their being better able to fulfil their potentials. However, state management of the economy was an unknown quantity, and the 1960s, particularly the second half of the decade, was characterized by inefficiency and productivity decline, with Guevara's hoped for emergence of the socialist 'new man'.

After the failed 1970 ten million ton *zafra*, structured decision-making and rational economic management were central to state economic control.

Cuba joined CAME and by the end of the decade the SDPE was in place. As a counter-weight to the elitist, authoritarian implications of 'democratic centralism', Poder Popular was adopted by 1977. However, central planning, membership of the CAME and the party bureaucracy restricted the room for manoeuvre of the Organs of Popular Power and people's participation. And when, in 1986, the economy was in such bad shape that a halt was called to amortization payments, and the servicing of international, hard currency debt, the Campaign of Rectification of Errors and Negative Tendencies was instigated, to redress the political balance in favour of socialist development.

While the control of the economy was centralized, removing the 'market socialism' elements of the SDPE, responsibility at the micro level was decentralized.

> The most serious error of economic policy put in practice between 1976 and 1985 [the SDPE] was undoubtedly its reliance upon economic mechanisms to resolve all the problems faced by a new society, ignoring the role assigned to *political* factors in the construction of socialism.
>
> (Castro 1987a: 13, emphasis added)

The problem with the SDPE was that, within an overall planned strategy, economic decision-making was decentralized to the enterprise. The interests of enterprises to meet targets, norms, and make an economic surplus, took precedence over the more general social interest.

> [We] began [in the mid-1970s] to use economic planning and management methods copied from the European socialist experience... After 10 or 11 years... so many deformations and deviations occurred that I had to stop ... and constantly remember Che and his ... rejection of those methods of socialist construction.
>
> (Castro, quoted in Borge 1993: 49)

New procedures have been adopted in the planning process (see JUCE-PLAN 1988). The number of commodities subject to planning, and the number of directive indicators to enterprises have been reduced. The system of 'material balances' has been decentralized (see Zimbalist 1993: 127). There have also been a number of initiatives intended to promote flexibility, local autonomy and worker participation. For instance, the system of 'continuous planning', introduced in 1988, allows for initiative at the enterprise level in the drawing up of production plans. Targets are based on the experience of the previous year and expectations for future performance. This appears to have been relatively successful, although there are problems of coordination between enterprises, though not as serious as the difficulties encountered under the SDPE.

As well as the introduction of 'continuous planning', there was a return to minibrigades which had disappeared under the SDPE, and an emphasis on labour contingents:

contingents ... were a new experience in construction and scored some spectacular results: they doubled, tripled and even quadrupled productivity ... We began completing projects. In the past [under the SDPE], they hadn't been finished.

(Castro, quoted in Borge 1993: 109)

There was considerable investment in dams, canals and irrigation systems, particularly in the sugar industry, the building of child-care centres, poly-clinics, housing, etc. (see Borge 1993: 111–12). But before the alternative could be established, the Special Period in Time of Peace, consequent on the collapse of the Soviet Union, was announced. Economic development policy, inevitably, was geared to addressing immediate problems, and was based on survival programmes and plans in the event of nothing coming into the country, drawn up many years earlier after the US invasion of Grenada. But it is the 1986 Rectification Campaign that will chart Cuba's future development strategy, not short-term reactions to the Special Period.

Economic problems are being addressed in a socialist context: financial discipline combined with political participation.

Socialism is ... a process of successive upheavals not only in the economy, politics and ideology, but in conscious and organized action. It is a process premised on unleashing the *power of the people*, who learn how to change themselves along with their circumstances. Revolutions within the revolution demand creativity and unity with respect to principles and organization and broad and *growing* participation. In other words, they must become a gigantic school through which people learn to direct social processes, *Socialism is not constructed spontaneously, nor is it something that can be bestowed.*

(Heredia 1993: 64, emphasis added)

There is a new economic and social context to people's political participa-tion. First, the parameters of participation will have to be managed by economists; second, the recent economic reforms have spawned a new class of managers in the operation of Cuban/foreign capital joint ventures. The collapse of Soviet-style authoritarian socialism has promoted a vigorous debate within Cuba as to the meaning of socialism – for instance, see the debate by Carranza Valdés *et al.* on 'market socialism' in Chapter 6 – a process that requires a greater degree of public discussion, especially in the press, which tends to follow the party line rather than encouraging critical discussion.

However, within the managed economic parameters of state expenditure/income, and the foreign exchange balance of payments, there are an increasing number of participative economic initiatives. For instance, the Plan Alimentario (the Food Plan) is a 'knowledge-intensive' strategy based on local knowledge (see Rosset and Benjamin 1994a: 28). Bio-fertilizers and bio-pesticides are being promoted, animal traction substituting for tractors, with local communities more intimately involved with the production process in a Low Input Sustainable Agriculture Programme (LISAP).

Since 1989, Cuba has fully accepted the policy to promote a new science of agriculture [LISAP]. From 1989–1992, they moved substantially to implement this policy at the levels of the research station, the extension services, and the farm producers ... *it is an achievement worth noting by students of politics and public administration.*

(Rosset and Benjamin 1994a: 34, 73, emphasis added)

To this end, planning and a process of participation have been central to Cuba surviving and continuing to develop after the collapse of the Soviet bloc and the resultant Special Period.

Few countries in the world could face the external shocks that have buffeted Cuba since 1989 without mass starvation ... [the] caloric intake has not dropped more than 30% ... and ... other health indicators remain good. This we believe, is a tribute to Cuba's planning and organization. And without a planned economy, it is unlikely that new agro-ecological research results could be implemented so rapidly.

(Rosset and Benjamin 1994b: 95)

In the construction industry under the SDPE, projects were not built in an integrated way. Different sectors and enterprises would only address their own targets, deadlines and budgets. The housing sector would contract enterprises to build houses, and similarly for water, sewage, etc. With the problems of bureaucratic coordination and enterprises having their own interests, there were cases where towns were built without streets, water supply or schools. The Rectification Campaign has seen the application of specialized construction 'contingents', who assign resources and work on a project in its entirety: for instance, building a whole town.

There are also participative strategies in urban renewal programmes in Havana (see Izquierdo 1996). Old Havana (Habana Vieja) is very run down, and a new programme between ministries, municipal Poder Popular and individuals is designed to mobilize people to renovate their own areas. In the first example (in early 1996), resources have been channelled through the Ministry of Basic Industries to a municipal organ of Poder Popular, to be distributed to residents within a certain area, and the residents organize themselves to renovate their environment. This is a pilot scheme, and it is intended that other ministries will 'adopt' different areas of Habana Vieja in similar schemes.

Ultimately, a socialist development strategy for Cuba, while being founded upon a coherent socialist economic strategy, managing the state fiscal budget and the international balance of trade, implies a reactivation and extension of political participation through Poder Popular. Socialist participation, and the extension of freedom, is contingent upon an economic surplus, allowing a diminution of 'labour determined by expediency and external necessity'. The Special Period in Time of Peace, with the emphasis on austerity and sharing shortages, is not a context conducive to socialist development. But, given the rationale of the Rectification Campaign to reassert the 'political' over the 'economic', as the economy picks up (despite of the economic blockade), increasingly there will be opportunities to extend the process of socialist development, which is fundamentally a *political* question, although based upon a socialist economic strategy.

CHAPTER 8

CUBAN DEVELOPMENT: THE FUTURE

PARAMETERS AND INTERPRETATIONS

Chapter 4 identified the various intellectual parameters which structure alternative interpretations of the Cuban development experience. That experience was described in Chapters 2 and 3. Chapter 1 addressed the Cuban 'predicament', and Chapters 5, 6 and 7 applied the analysis of Chapter 4 to specify the policy strategy alternatives to address 'dire straits' in Cuba. This chapter will attempt to evaluate what the future might hold for Cuba.

It is not a question of whether or not the conclusions of competing analyses are 'right' or 'wrong'. Each can potentially provide logical analyses which coherently interpret the 'facts', legitimating a policy strategy to address the problems. But each perspective starts from a set of assumptions (beliefs) about human motivation: axioms and assertions about *why* people behave in particular ways.

These 'unexamined and unexpressed' assumptions provide a rationale to the analysis of human behaviour, giving credence and plausibility to the recommended policy strategy, suggesting why it might reasonably be expected to achieve the stated objective.

> Every theory of society implies a theory of what it is to be human. Every theorist carries out the same fiction, apparently deducing the nature of society from an *a priori* consideration of the innate nature of human beings, whilst inducing the necessary assumptions from the end to be realised.
>
> (Rose *et al.*, 1984: 240)

Assumptions about human behaviour suggest how society *ought* to be organized, and what *should* be the priorities of development; legitimating a policy prescription as a moral aphorism. The ideological and political bias of the analysis is presented as the 'only' alternative, a bias which is justified by a philosophy of science and an ideology of knowledge.

> Explanations in society are not simply scientific responses to a problem. They are weapons in a fight, the basis for praise or blame. It is for this reason that social science can contribute least where the social and political significance of the problem is greatest. The study of economics [and development] has its 'black holes', but they are not the blindness of economists [and development theorists]

so much as the blindness of the social order. For blindness serves its function too, protecting and defending a status quo.

(Harris 1983: 5)

The impartial, neutral analysis is a chimera: a windmill of the 'scientific' intellectual mind. It is not the issue to identify *the* correct theory, but to understand the differences *between* theories and the ideological and political implications of the associated policy strategies. The more analysts understand competing explanations, the more the strengths, weaknesses and essential political interests of the perspective within which they are working will become apparent. Academic rigour demands a comparative study, addressing the issues of concern from the point of view of each perspective: reviewing the literature across the whole intellectual spectrum, and explaining *why* different theorists emphasize particular events, processes and data to arrive at partial conclusions. The social and political consequences of following the recommended policy strategy will then become explicit. Only then can the reader choose which analysis to accept, and consequently where he or she stands in the perennial power struggle which is social existence.

In Chapter 4, it was argued that in the analysis of social phenomena, and hence development processes, 'bias' is inevitable and unavoidable. It is not that analysts 'distort' reality to fit their theoretical procrustean bed, but that they view the world *through* their assumed theoretical perspective. The analysis presents a view of social experience from a particular vantage point. It is the task of the intellectual to ask: what must the 'real' world be like if it appears in the various guises to theorists working in different perspectives?

The real world exists *only* in theory. It cannot be directly observed, but is discovered through observation. Having theoretically constructed an image of the real world, based upon the various explanations and experiences of that world, will not change a person's experience of the *actual* world, or the intuitive perceptions of that world which people inevitably construct if they are to be able to organize their daily existence.

The world will *still* be viewed from within partial intellectual parameters, rationalized by the beliefs in human nature through which human behaviour is understood.

The entrepreneur, the owner of productive forces, will still be concerned to realize a profit, and will attempt to adapt to the ebb and flow of market forces within a short-term time frame. Rationalized by academics as enterprising individuals addressing the subjective preferences of consumers – the theory of utility maximization – this becomes a moral dictum once individuals are conceived of as independent beings. The purpose of life becomes the satisfaction of biologically endowed, subjective preferences, reflecting innate tastes and talents. It is the purpose of government to create an environment of individual 'free' choice.

At the same time, bureaucrats, planners and managers will try to ensure a stable environment within which rational decision-making can be effective, taking into account the long-term productive life of the forces of production; eschewing the anarchy of the market and any interference by the individual initiative of the actual producers. Rationalized by academics, theoretically, as the need to cooperate to produce within a fragmented, technical division of labour, management control of production, not free individual choice in the sphere of consumption, becomes the emphasis. This also becomes a moral imperative when people are considered to be dependent on society for their very being (intuitions, character, potentials, etc.), and political responsibility is not now geared to free individual consumer choice, but the creation of a managed environment in which people may work together in the common interest to improve the general social and economic condition.

Workers in society, who neither own nor manage the forces of production or their working environment, will still struggle for job security and a better standard of living against the tide of market forces; and they will still try to fulfil themselves creatively through the exercise of their individual intuition and initiative in, and control of, the work process. Theoretically rationalized as the need to live in a society within which everyone is encouraged to contribute according to his or her potential if social conflict is to be avoided, this becomes a moral principle if people are believed to be interdependent, creative, social individuals. Their innate biological potentials are only revealed and evolve through social experience, and political participation is the only way to address the social constraints which frustrate individuals from fulfilling their creative potentials; from fulfilling their human nature.

As more and more experiences are built into the theoretical analysis of the real world, and compared and contrasted, the image of that world will change. There is no way of knowing when the 'theory' of the real world is an accurate depiction of that world. Indeed, as people change through social experience, so do the parameters within which people survive and exist, and the 'real' world changes: change and evolution are inevitable.

The intellectual, then, should try to understand analyses of social experience within the theoretical parameters of that interpretation. However, it is not the norm for theorists to acknowledge their partiality, and even less common for them to undertake a comparative analysis of alternative analyses, so as to highlight intellectual biases. Indeed, some theorists try as hard as possible to prevent their work from being 'contaminated' by exposure to alternative understandings. For instance, Roger Betancourt (1991), in the analysis of the Cuban 'predicament', is prepared to consider only analyses which lie within 'the mainstream paradigm', defined as contributions which assume 'optimizing agents subject to constraints ... [analysing] interactions between agents in terms of displacement from one well defined equilibrium to another' (Betancourt 1991: 8). Put simply, he is interested in considering explanations only from the vantage point of the 'utility maximizing individual': the subjective preference theory of value, with all the ideological and political implications identified in Chapters 4 and 5 above. For Betancourt, the axioms which define his real world are self-evidently true, not requiring justification or proof, and 'mark the stage beyond which one does not seek to explain' (Hahn 1984: 6). Such a lack of understanding and such a closed-minded approach to theoretical explanation inevitably breeds intolerance and bigotry. Theorists cannot make sense of alternative points of view: these analyses can only be dismissed as 'economically irrational' (Eckstein 1990: 73). This is knowing without understanding.

The intellectual becomes an ideologue. The argument is for a particular social order, reflecting the implicit assumptions about human nature which define the intellectual parameters of the analysis, which are not justified: 'ideologies produce distorted communication allowing some concepts to be communicated but blocking and distorting others' (Diesing 1982: 5). Theorists using the same words mean different concepts, and cannot engage in meaningful debate. As argued above, to avoid intellectual bigotry a comparative analysis should be advanced, clearly laying out the ideological implications of alternative analytical perspectives, so that readers can choose where they stand.

This has been the project of this book. But the analysis is only of value if something meaningful can be said about the future: basing an understanding of today on yesterday's experience, in order to draw lessons for tomorrow. Tomorrow was born yesterday.

POLITICS IN COMMAND

The political implications of different policy strategies suggest that we should bear in mind the likelihood of political changes to understand future policy potentials. It was pointed out in Chapter 4 that, although there are essentially three perspectives in social and economic analysis, there are *more than* three 'schools' of thought. Often the debate within a perspective between competing schools of thought is far more vigorous and forceful than debates between perspectives. Neo-liberal 'free marketeers' have far more to say to neo-classical theorists and modernization theorists than they do to structuralists or Keynesians. They talk the same theoretical 'language', in this case defined in terms of the utility maximizing individual: the subjective preference theory of value. Within the restricted intellectual parameters of a shared perspective, they *understand* what each other is saying.

Theorists working within alternative perspectives, speaking a different language, are dismissed as being theoretically incompetent, or not being aware of the 'facts' of the 'real' world. Ultimately, this dismissal might be rationalized as those working within different perspectives being 'ideo-logically' motivated, deliberately distorting the truth. They, of course, are 'neutral' and 'scientific'.

An emphasis on 'free' markets and profit maximization, prioritizing utility maximization by independent individuals who are biologically endowed with a set of tastes and talents, implies a 'conservative' political environment. 'Realistically', people act selfishly: we see it all around us all the time. And the appropriate development strategy is to harness individuals' hedonistic motives to the social good. The profit motive means that the talented and industrious put the rest of us to work, and the benefits 'trickle down' to those of us who are 'entrepreneurially challenged' through market exchange. Such a political environment would be based upon a mechanism of 'representative democracy' (see Lambie 1997: 7–8), within a strong legal context for the protection of individual rights and property, allowing people to pursue their individual interests.

Alternatively, a managed economy (including market socialism) implies a variant of 'social democracy'. Because people are dependent on each other, and human nature is not genetically defined but adapts to the needs of the social system through processes of 'socialization', individuals learn to cooperate within an economic and political environment. The economy is organized to utilize fully economic resources in the common interest: the cost-of-production theory of value. And politics is now a 'pluralist demo-cratic' system. The conflicting interests of technically defined 'interest groups' are reconciled to compromise in the general interest, within polit-ical institutions.

A society in which the economy is oriented to the satisfaction of 'need', rather than profitability or technical efficiency, implies a process of political 'participation'. The parameters of economic participation change as people evolve through social experience: people are now interdependent. Human nature is not now biologically determined or socially adapted, but is a dialectic between people's innate genetic inheritance and their social experi-ence. Economic relations follow the logic of the abstract labour theory of value. Policy strategy is a reflection of a process of socialist development through which people are empowered to fulfil their social potentials.

Development strategy of whichever variant is politically defined.

BEING REALISTIC

The subjective preference theory of value bases the analysis of economic interaction and social development on 'universal facts of experience' (Rob-bins 1984: 99), which suggests that individuals are 'different', they attempt to 'maximize utility' and they prefer to 'choose' between alternatives (see Chapter 4). And individuals should be 'free' to act according to their innate nature in a conservative political environment emphasizing individual freedom.

There is no likelihood that the conservative political option based upon representative democracy will become a reality in Cuba in the foreseeable future. Even some analysts working within this perspective admit that no politician 'is going to win a democratic contest in Cuba running on the abolition of a system that has accomplished so much ... for large segments of the population transition to the market may mean a loss of benefits without any obvious gain' (Angel Centeno 1997: 19, 22).

Added to this, there is no incipient entrepreneurial class waiting in the wings to take control on the advent of the free market. The 1901 Platt Amendment, which gave the USA the right to restrict Cuban sovereignty in foreign affairs, and the 1903 Reciprocity Treaty tied Cuba's trade into a dependent relationship with the US economy (see Pérez 1982: 192–9). The War of Independence against Spain, which ended in 1898, bankrupted the powerful sugar planters, the economic mainstay of Cuba, which, coupled to the Platt Amendment and the Reciprocity Treaty, left the Cuban economy wide open to control by foreign capital, especially by US capital. By the 1920s, the only economic opportunities open to the Cuban middle class were 'merchanting and rentier activities, employment with a foreign company or working in politics and public administration' (Lambie 1997: 16). The Cuban economy had been virtually 'confiscated' by the USA (see Blackburn 1963).

> [We] made politics our only industry and administrative fraud the only course open to wealth for our compatriots ... This political industry ... is stronger than the sugar industry, which is no longer ours; more lucrative than the railroads which are managed by foreigners; safer than the banks, than maritime transportation and commercial trade, which also do not belong to us.
>
> (De Carrión, quoted in Pérez 1982: 215)

Politics and the public sector were by far the largest employer and became extremely corrupt: 'every government activity was milked, the lottery, the school lunch programme, driver's licences, parking meters, teacher's certificates. The police routinely extorted millions in protection money from Havana merchants' (Padula 1974: 38).

BEING PRAGMATIC

A conservative 'realistic' scenario is not very 'plausible'. But the 'pragmatic' option of a managed economy, based upon a pluralist democracy organized along social democratic lines, is more of a possibility:

> in Cuba there is the emergence of a potentially hegemonic technocratic bloc, who have privileged access to the world market. This bloc has the capacity to appeal to a wide section of the population, including the traditional bureaucracy, the

self-employed, salaried workers in the most dynamic sectors of the economy, and intellectuals.

(Dilla 1996a: 30, my translation)

We have seen in Chapters 6 and 7 that the potential for managing development and the economy in the general interest, to maintain certain standards of social welfare in the context of a mixed economy, will be compromised by the need to ensure the profitability of enterprises. Since the mid-1960s this has been the experience in all the market-based, mixed economy, social democracies. As a strategy, this is only coherent if value is understood to be a 'quantitative' phenomenon. But if we are to explain the post Second World War experience of pursuing a general social interest through economic management, and failing, then we have to address the abstract labour theory of value: a dialectic between the subjective preference and cost-of-production theories of value.

However, this theoretical debate is too 'esoteric' to encourage political support and enthusiasm directly. In as far as this strategy becomes 'hegemonic', it will do so because it rationalizes the experience of powerful economic interests in Cuba: a rationalization that can be politically presented as a coherent, 'common sense', interpretation of the experience of Cuban development. Hence, it may well become politically important in defining Cuban development strategy.

BEING IDEALISTIC WITHOUT BEING NAÏVE

The subjective preference theory of value addresses individuals' behaviour as it actually is, which does not require explanation, it simply *is*; hence the reference to 'realism'. On the other hand, the cost-of-production theory of value situates activity in the context of a system, which can be better managed with the evolution of technology to achieve higher living standards. The emphasis is not on what *is* but on what *can be*; hence the reference to 'pragmatism'.

The abstract labour theory of value, interpreting change as a result of people's changing intuitions, awareness and consciousness, itself an effect of social experience, tries to identify the *potentials* for development with changed relations between people, rather than what is, or can be, within existing social relations. Development strategy is then a question of how these potentials may be realized, in the context of a power structure which will try to preserve the social status quo to the advantage of the dominant elite. Hence it is a question of being idealistic about achieving the 'good' society, but not being naïve about the difficulties of extending people's freedom through participation.

Notwithstanding the evolution of political and economic participation in Cuba over the past 38 years, the context in 1997 has changed, as have the potentials. The exigencies of the world market have to be reconciled to the principles of the revolution. The issue is often couched in terms of the 'state' versus the 'market'.

However, it is not a question of the state versus the market. To consider the issue in these terms is to situate the argument within the intellectual parameters of the subjective preference theory of value (the market) and the cost-of-production theory of value (the state): and this tends to be the terms of reference of the debate within Cuba – witness the market socialism proposals of Carranza Valdés *et al.* detailed in Chapter 6. It is rather a question of how the market and the state are integrated: the dialectic of the abstract labour theory of value.

How is participation to be effected so as to benefit from the decentralized decision-making of the market, with producers being able to respond to individual needs as indicated by prices, but still *enhance* participation in the achievement of social, economic objectives? 'Three actors are at the centre of this scenario: the state, the market and the *community*' (Dilla 1996a: 10, emphasis added, my translation).

Just as in 1970 (the commitment to the SDPE), 1974 (the beginning of Poder Popular) and 1986 (the Rectification Campaign), we are at a turning point in the evolution of the Cuban revolution: the process of socialist development in face of the austerity of (world) market forces and the economic blockade, and the collapse of CAME and the Eastern European 'socialist' states. In this context, how can the community be increasingly politically autonomous and democratic, 'an objective of popular participation since 1959' (Dilla 1996a: 20, my translation)?

Achieving enterprise profitability, social order and the satisfaction of collective needs within which individuals have the freedom to fulfil their social potentials is part of a process of social and cultural change: socialist development. They can only coexist where labour is empowered by being skilled and creative, participating in the organization and purpose of production. This would be denied if Cuba becomes a docile source of cheap labour to be exploited by foreign investment: the strategy suggested by the theory of 'comparative advantage', touched on in Chapter 5 where national development strategy becomes a by-product of the fluctuation of international prices. Over a longer term this would also be the effect of the technocratic management of the economy through some variant of 'market socialism': the direction of economic activity to maintain a 'mixed' economy, by ensuring the profitability of private enterprise and the income of a funtionless class of rentiers. Inevitably, the socialist ideals of the revolution will be compromised by the logic of 'commodity exchange'.

There has never been an example of an economy not organized according to market imperatives, with decentralized political institutions, in which non-state property is predominant. This is the changing and challenging *process* of democracy in Cuba.

A socialist development strategy, while being founded on a coherent economic strategy – the management of the fiscal budget and international balance of payments – implies extending participation through the institutions of Poder Popular. Socialist participation, the extension of 'freedom', is contingent upon an economic surplus, allowing a diminution of 'labour determined by expediency and external necessity'. The Special Period in Time of Peace, with the emphasis on shared shortages and austerity, is not a context conducive to socialist development. Planning collapsed in 1991, when economic decisions had to be based on available resources which were in short supply, leaving no basis for participation in economic decision-making. But given the rationale of the Rectification Campaign, to assert the political over the economic as the economy picks up (despite the economic blockade) – see the end of Chapter 3 – increasingly there will be the opportunity to extend the process of socialist development. This is a *political* imperative based on a socialist economic strategy.

THE CONTRADICTIONS OF YESTERDAY SET TODAY'S AGENDA FOR TOMORROW

The centralized control of the economy under the SDPE in the 1970s – the organization of labour according to restricted technical efficiency criteria along autocratic, hierarchical management lines – while an advance over previous forms of social and economic control, has left a paternalistic legacy, a legacy which the Rectification Campaign is intended to address. However, despite the emphases of the Campaign, it appears that there is still a dominance of vertical, hierarchical economic relations over horizontal, participative economic relations. The newspaper *Trabajadores* (*Workers*), published by the Confederation of Cuban Workers (the Cuban trade union confederation), could report on 2 November 1988 that 'the planning of the Cuban economy has been characterized by a tendency to bureaucracy and formalism' (my translation): 'politics and administration in Cuba has been very centralized which has limited the power of base institutions ... on occasion being reduced to institutions for mobilizing support and implementing decisions taken at the centre' (Dilla 1996b: 141, 142).

In a 1992 survey of 158 workers in three enterprises in Santa Cruz del Norte, 70 per cent thought participation was insufficient, 48 per cent saw 'workers' assemblies of production' as irrelevant and 61 per cent thought the unions had been disempowered and did not have a meaningful role to play (see Dilla 1996a: 27). But there have been changes in the structure of economic decision-making (see Monreal and Rúa 1994) which may have the potential for enhanced participation, the most significant of which have been the Unidades Básicas de Producción Cooperativa (UBPCs), the most radical structural change in Cuban agriculture since the agrarian reform laws of 1959 and 1963. Large-scale farm enterprises owned and operated by the state began to be dismantled, with the intention of more efficiently utilizing available resources, fostering labour intensive production and import substitution (the drive towards food sustainability) and augmenting labour productivity through greater participation and improved incentives.

Before 1993, state-controlled agriculture, which applied to about 80 per cent of arable land, was organized into: non-sugar cane large-scale state farms, Granjas de Pueblo (GdelP, people's farms), controlled by the Ministerio de la Agricultura (the Ministry of Agriculture); and sugar cane growing, mill-plantation complexes, Complejos Agro-Industriales (CAI, agro-industrial complexes), administered by the Ministerio de Azúcar (the Ministry of Sugar).

On 1 September 1993 the Buró Político del Partido Comunista Cubano (the Political Executive Committee of the Communist Party) announced the policy of the formation of UBPCs. The UBPCs are modelled on the Cooperativas de Producción Agropecuaria (CPAs, agricultural production cooperatives), the formation of which has been fostered among private farmers since 1977. These are voluntary unions, where independent peasants combine their landholdings into one farm to reap economies of scale. At the end of 1996 there were 1160 CPAs (see Carriazo Moreno 1997: 7). The UBPCs differ from the CPAs in that the former do not 'own' the land, it being leased in perpetuity from the state.

The large state farms, the GdelPs and the CAIs, were to be devolved into smaller (although the average size is still about 1000 hectares), more autonomous enterprises: the UBPCs.

> The creation of the UBPCs neither ended large-scale nor strengthened small-scale farming. What it did do was reverse the historic tendency of the post-revolutionary Cuban state to assume direct administrative control over an ever greater share of the nation's agricultural resources and to manage them in ever larger enterprises. This was most obvious in the sugar industry where centralized state controls reached a peak with the integration of the agricultural and industrial operations in CAIs after 1980.
>
> (Pollitt 1997: 191)

The UBPCs began to replace large state farms at the end of September 1993 (see Ministerio de Azúcar 1993). 'By the beginning of the 1993/4 sugar harvest, some 90 per cent of CAI administered cane land and a somewhat smaller percentage of state farm land [GdelP] had been transformed into UBPCs' (Pollitt 1997: 189). By the end of 1994 they accounted for about 42 per cent of the arable area of Cuba (CPAs accounting for about 10 per cent).

The UBPCs are part worker cooperative and part collective farm, mainly composed of ex-GdelP and ex-CAI workers. Part of the remit of the UBPCs, especially the sugar cane producing UBPCs, is to extend food production, both arable and livestock, to work towards greater self-sufficiency in food production, and food production is relatively labour-intensive. Production has also become more labour-intensive because, with the collapse of the import capacity of the Cuban economy in the Special Period, more labour and animal power has to compensate for the lack of fuel and spare parts for machinery, and fertilizers and herbicides for land husbandry. Consequently there has been a labour recruitment drive, and initially the labour is contract labourers, who may be accepted as full members of the UBPC after a probationary period.

Incentives to attract labour and improve productivity and efficiency include the following. With regard to food security, the declining quality and uncertain reliability of the supply of food has been the most acutely felt dimension of falling living standards in the Special Period, and being able to obtain food at prices often lower than food sold within the subsidized state retail distribution system is important. Relative wages have been increased in the agricultural sector to make it a more attractive option and to try to stem rural–urban migration. A fraction of the UBPC profits is distributed to members as dividends to try to link self-management to performance, but since many UBPCs operate at a financial loss (in 1995, 77 per cent of sugar producers and 50 per cent of non-sugar producers recorded a loss; see Pollitt 1997: 205), this is not a strong incentive over the short term. Infrastructure failure – power cuts, water shortages, transport disruption, etc. – are far less common. There is access to building materials for home improvement, and to pharmaceutical products, boots and workwear.

UBPCs are intended to be autonomous, self-managing and self-financing, with the members approving and electing the UBPC administrators. Although the UBPC does not 'own' the land, being a leaseholder, the production is UBPC property, productive inputs are paid for, state credit is available for investment and the UBPC manages its own bank account. However, the UBPCs were not defined within a clear political perspective, being intended to increase productivity through greater participation by the workforce in decisions and management (see Pérez Rojas and Torres Vila 1996). 'The only reference to politics in the legislation setting up UBPCs is the requirement to execute state policy' (Pérez Rojas and Torres Vila 1996: 173, my translation).

Sugar cane has to be sold to the state, although any surplus of food produced over and above state procurement targets can be sold through the free agricultural markets initiated on 1 October 1994. Agricultural production earmarked for the state goes to supply hospitals, schools, social centres and work centres, and to provide the subsidized rations which guarantee minimum food entitlement to the population as a whole. The freely marketed surplus accounts for about 19 per cent of production (see Carriazo Moreno 1997: 13). 'This structural change [the emergence of UBPCs] was a response to the economic crisis and not a response to demands by agricultural workers' (Pérez Rojas and Torres Vila 1996: 169, my translation).

There is a question mark over the autonomy and independence of UBPCs. The commitment to self-management is qualified by the Ministerios del Azúcar and de la Agricultura, which define production objectives in the national interest, including setting the price paid for the output. As such, the UBPC is a hybrid between a state enterprise and an independent cooperative, which has created an awareness from below that workers' freedom and control are qualified. Often workers are not fully informed or consulted by management in the operation and activity of the cooperative, which has led to resentment. Typically, those who became the administrators of UBPCs had previously been the managers of the field operations of state farms (CAIs and GdelPs)

> These appointments required to be, and typically were, ratified by the UBPC assemblies but it was hardly surprising that the frequent complaints thereafter that some managers continued to manage in the same old way, with too much 'tutelage' and too little creative participation.
>
> (Pollitt 1997: 206)

Mainly because the primary activity of sugar producing UBPCs was to supply state-owned sugar factories, and the state sets the procurement price, most analysis of the operation and effect of participation, and the degree of enterprise autonomy, has focused on the non-cane sector (see Carriazo Moreno 1995). Apart from the lack of management expertise with participative forms of organization and administration, tight controls by supply and purchasing agencies left little leeway for participative and creative management, although participative initiatives undoubtedly helped to cope with shortages, evolving husbandry and cultivation practices, and finding alternatives to a deteriorating stock of machinery and equipment.

However, a movement '"from below" can be perceived, with members of UBPCs resisting excessive control on one side, and demanding more autonomy on the other' (Pérez Rojas and Torres Vila 1996: 182, my translation). There is a potential for participation to evolve, based upon the Asamblea General (General Assembly) of the UBPC, to which all members belong. The Assembly has to approve formally production and investment plans, the choice of administrators, the organization of work, procedures for the distribution of the product (wage levels and incentives), disciplinary procedures, etc. This is a potential which is increasingly being realized by workers.

There is a lack of detailed, institutionalized regulations and controls, specifying the rights and obligations of UBPC members, which tends to reinforce the application and operation of existing forms of administration and management. A national conference on farming cooperatives highlighted 'the lack of autonomy in management matters ... [as a] key issue' (see *Cuba Business* December 1995: 3). Moreover, 'Generally the interviews with workers were very positive about expanding their role in participation within UBPCs' (Pérez Rojas and Torres Vila 1996: 179, my translation).

People cannot be empowered; they empower themselves as a reaction to frustrations in fulfilling their social potentials. It seems that such a process of empowerment is at work within the UBPCs. For this to be extended to the economy, the government has to facilitate people's empowerment through the development of a general network of horizontal links between enterprises, which must evolve as an antidote to vertical relations of planning, and commercial decision-making necessarily being independent of social priorities. It is certain that private and mixed (private/state) enterprises will be an important feature of the Cuban economy, and the horizontal political links between enterprises and the community are essential to avoid the fragmentation of political and economic space required for participation. Links have to be established between the trade unions, community representatives (CDRs), different sectors of society (FMC, ANAP, etc.) and professions (journalists, teachers, etc.). And here the strong tradition of involvement of the mass organizations since 1959 has produced capable local leaders and organization. But to achieve a 'genuine political pluralism of negotiation and compromise' (Dilla 1996a: 35, my translation) will be a process of experimentation to see what works best in the new social and economic context.

Empowerment is not a *policy* but a *process*.

SOCIALIST CHANGE

Change and development in every society are the product of a struggle over power and influence in the direction of social and economic affairs between competing interests, ultimately reflecting the evolution of human nature through social experience. A socialist society, while defending the class interest of the proletariat in the face of possible exploitation through commodity exchange, is sufficiently flexible to adapt to people's evolving needs and potentials. And while the outcome of this reflects consciousness, awareness and intuition, and hence is unpredictable, the external environment within which such change will take place is less threatening to Cuban socialism.

For nearly 40 years anti-socialist critics have been predicting the imminent collapse of socialist Cuba. 'No one thought Cuba would survive American interference and aggression. Today no one doubts it' (*Contrapunto* 1997: 5, my translation). The revolution has gained popularity and political ground within Cuba, and since the US presidential elections the militant anti-Castro Cuban-American political lobby, organized around the Fundación Nacional Cubano Americano (National Cuban-American Foundation), is increasingly marginalized, with more moderate critics coming to the fore pushing for meaningful relations with Cuba. And it has been suggested that the declining credibility of the militant, right-wing, Miami-based Cuban-Americans reflects at least in part how they have been implicated in a string of politically corrupt actions.

These Cubans, many of whom were Batista supporters and lived high on the hog while that crook ran the country, seem not to have slept a wink since they grabbed their assets [in 1959] and headed for Florida.

And, since 1960, they have insisted on pulling us [the United States of America] into their madness. Why is it that in *every* incident of national torment that has deflated our country for the past three decades – the Kennedy assassination, Watergate, Iran–Contra, our drug abuse epidemic – the lists goes on and on – we find that the Cuban exiles are always present and involved? . . . Ninety percent of these exiles are white, while the majority of Cubans – 62 percent – are black or of mixed race. The whites knew they couldn't stay in Cuba because they had no support from the people. So they came here, expecting us to fight their fight for them. And, like morons, we have.

(Moore 1997: 177, 179)

The risk of a military confrontation with the USA is diminished with the international condemnation of the Helms–Burton Act, which has obliged President Clinton to suspend Title Three of the Act. This title would have allowed American citizens to sue foreigners in American courts for any business transacted on, with, or through, US property confiscated by the Cuban government. Again, the catalyst leading to the tightening of the blockade was the anti-Castro Cuban-American political lobby.

'Brothers to the Rescue' [is] an exile group that for the past few years has been flying missions over Cuba, buzzing Cuban sites, dropping leaflets, and generally trying to intimidate the Cuban government. In February 1996, Castro was apparently fed up with this harassment, and after the twenty-fifth incident in the past twenty months of the Brothers violating Cuban airspace, he ordered that two of their planes be shot down.

Even though Brothers to the Rescue was violating US law by flying into Cuban airspace (a fact the FAA acknowledges), the Clinton administration again went to the exile trough and instantly got a bill passed to tighten the embargo against Cuba. This embargo has brought the wrath of the rest of the world against us – the UN General Assembly voted 117 to 3 to 'condemn' the United States for the economic violence against Cuba

(Moore 1997: 181)

The reception of Fidel Castro at the Ibero-American summit meeting in Chile, and the FAO meeting in Rome, both in 1996, indicated growing international sympathy for the Cuba. And there has been an improvement of relations between the Vatican and Cuba.

The Cuban economy is growing despite the blockade, and foreign capital is playing an increasing role, although it is important that the regulation of foreign investment has built-in safeguards over the terms of employment, and the rights of employee participation through trades unions which are independent of both the enterprise and the state.

Cuba has opened commercial relations with over 3000 foreign firms from 98 countries, is served by 33 airlines from 17 countries and has diplomatic relations with some 150 countries, and this despite the North American economic blockade.

(Carriazo Moreno n.d.: 6, my translation)

When the whole spectrum of experience is considered, the potential for future development is not quite as bleak as the 'predicament' detailed in Chapter 1 suggests. 'The balance for people without their heads in the sand is favourable to Cuba, despite the obstacles yet to be overcome' (*Contrapunto* 1997: 8, my translation).

THE LONG TERM

Although the privations of the Special Period have not delivered the end of Cuban socialism – the apocalyptic vision of the pro-'free' market observers of the Cuban experience – long-term development policy, partly identified by the priorities of the Rectification Campaign, has to be carefully thought through. Addressing the market in general, and offering incentives to foreign capital in particular, were necessary stop-gaps in the face of the collapse of the CAME. But they cannot be the basis of a socialist development strategy.

Given Cuba's unique historical and political circumstances, the island may be able to integrate an essentially internal development imperative, defined by the revolution, with long-term development priorities which will shape global development strategy into the next millennium. Throughout this book we have plotted the course of Cuban development strategy as a reconciliation between the ideals of the revolution and the exigencies of the world economy: this process is set to continue.

Environmental constraints on increasingly 'globalized' economic development have placed a premium on 'sustainability' (on the definition of 'sustainable development', see Cole 1994a). Increasingly, development strategy must take account of the social consequences, of the environmental effects, of improving living standards. A cultural change is required, restructuring the way society interacts with the natural environment, and necessitating an educated population able to manage a large-scale investment programme for a sustainable future. The objective must be to bring permanent, widely distributed benefits for the people as a whole, while preserving further potential gains for the future. Policy cannot be a product of short-term economic expediency, of opting for the short-term conversion of natural resources into a financial return: a long-term development strategy is required, which pays attention to the diversity of ecosystems and societies.

Such a development culture implies decentralization and community participation through which people's rights and duties will be politically defined. Innovative, sustainable technologies and ideas must be the product of human creativity, suggesting that education is a priority.

Increasingly, on a global scale, wealth will be measured by the health and confidence of people, as well as income.

In recent times there has been considerable debate about the effects of unregulated capital accumulation on the environment. These debates have been under the general rubric of 'sustainable development' (see Cole 1994a). However, despite highly publicized world 'summits' on environmental destruction, there has been precious little effective policy response. The dynamic of environmental degradation, capital accumulation and associated market competition, making productive activity and the use of the environment a by-product of the anarchy of the forces of 'supply and demand', has not been addressed. Thus, Cuba is in a unique position purposively to take note of the environmental dimension of development policy. The economic dynamic of Cuban society is not yet driven by the short-term, financial expediency of productive activity as a reflection of international consumer demand: the world market.

Sustainable development options could be, and in some areas already are, the focus of Cuban development strategy. In industrial development, with an emphasis on knowledge-intensive, high value added industries such as biotechnology, pharmaceuticals and medical equipment, the trend is not towards an economic strategy based on short-term, market expediency. While tourism is being actively promoted, the emphasis is increasingly on 'eco-tourism'. This consists of tourist operations which serve more affluent markets and have minimal environmental impact, and contribute significantly to the local economy. *Granma International* on 20 May 1997 reported on an expanding programme of eco-tourism, and how the profits from the promotion of international camping are being used to provide facilities for the enjoyment of Cuban families. In agriculture there is a commitment to a low input sustainable agricultural programme. And in community development future emphases should be upon communities' participation in identifying their own resource base, potentials and constraints. In this regard, the experience of the mass movements provides a firm basis for such a strategy.

One thing is clear: Cuba cannot return to the conditions prevalent in earlier times. Change is inevitable. However, there has to be caution in the adoption of alternative forms of economic integration. There is always the danger of commercial pressures based on economic and technical considerations overriding Cuba's longer-term interests in sustainability and social justice; of the power of the world market, exercised through 'commodity exchange', achieving what the US blockade could not. It is often argued that when the embargo is lifted, US capital will flood in and stimulate economic growth and efficiency. But the current advantages offered to investors in tourism, an educated and skilled workforce, and viable exports would not be likely to last. Cuba would be forced to compete for investment with low-wage economies such as Haiti and Vietnam; adopting by default a 'comparative advantage' development strategy, increasingly becoming a low-wage, low productivity economy and society, as the exigencies of commodity exchange dominate over the rational, participative imperatives of socialist development.

Further, an effect of an economy and a society based upon commodity exchange is that power becomes concentrated in unelected and unaccountable international agencies and institutions (such as the International Monetary Fund and the World Bank) committed to accumulation rather than social justice. And 'development' becomes a question of extending individual consumer choice, and is not orientated towards people better fulfilling their social potentials.

The option of the managed economy and market socialism, with the state maintaining control of key sectors of the economy and guaranteeing a minimum standard of living, but with private enterprise and initiative being a stimulant to increase producer efficiency and consumer choice, is less and less a viable option. With the 'globalization' of economies, the interests of the investor, as nation states compete ever more vigorously to attract foreign capital to provide the employment which market competition has destroyed, take precedence. And the powers and controls open to the 'managing' state diminish. 'The market is too powerful a mechanism to incorporate as a docile tool of socialist construction' (Dilla *et al.*, 1993: 25, my translation).

> The more Cuba enters the international economy, and the more dependent it becomes on international markets to rebuild its economy, the more control that these markets actors will have on the nature of Cuban development. As these actors tend to harbor an underlying bias against socialist economic designs, and they have a fairly narrow (and short term) conception of what constitutes 'healthy economic fundamentals', this market control will be in sharp contrast to the ambitions of Cuba's current policy makers.
>
> (Moses 1996: 14)

The market still has to be addressed. Even though exchange may be *coordinated* by prices (not *regulated* by prices determined by market forces – the law of value of commodity exchange – and therefore not based on profitability as the criterion for production and resource allocation), this has to be in the context of extended political participation. The continued development of political empowerment cannot be a *policy*, but has to be facilitated by the authorities encouraging initiatives by people to extend control over their lives, to empower themselves. This process seems to be in train in the UBPCs, and economists have to manage the fiscal budget and the international balance of payments to provide the economic 'space' in which such political initiatives might progress and evolve.

> Although the above strategy implies high levels of decentralization and the extension of substantial democratic powers to the local level, its success would depend on a carefully designed central planning system, which would be capable of setting and supporting clear national priorities, while at the same time

encouraging popular decision making at the local level, where the state would
play an essentially enabling role.

(Lambie 1997: 47)

The economic embargo, constraining as it is, is *not* the most important issue
in the Cuban development debate.

Any policy initiative to adapt to the world market, or to the operations of
foreign capital, must be rigorously studied and analysed, highlighting the
possible encroaching and constraining effects of 'commodity exchange', in
a similar way to that in which the option of 'market socialism' was
discussed in Chapters 6 and 7. Such a review process might be carried out
by a team of economists and theorists drawn from various ministries, the
Centre for the Study of the World Economy, the university sector, the
National Bank, various research institutes, the institutions of mass participation, the trade unions, etc. This would put economic and development
policy initiatives in the public domain, becoming the basis for political
discussion, argument and dissent.

The process of Cuban socialist development must be based on increasing
participation, which can only be meaningful in an environment of open and
principled debate. In so far as market prices and commercial relations
regulate and organize productive activity, whether that activity be by
small-scale Cuban entrepreneurs, or large-scale transnational corporations
(perhaps in conjunction with the state), people's participation will inevitably be usurped by the logic of commodity exchange. As we saw in Chapter
7, once the social organization of production is relegated to a by-product of
the exigencies of capital accumulation, the logic of commodity exchange,
citizens' power becomes subordinate to consumer choice, denying the mass
of individuals the opportunity to fulfil their *social* potentials. Efficiency in
the market *can only* be conceived of as *profitability*, which has to be the
consequence of exploitation of labour power (see Chapter 4, 'The citizen as
economic dynamic'). Exploitation is not the preserve of anti-social, grasping
capitalists. If the economy is organized along the lines of commodity
exchange – it matters not who the employer is, the 'free enterprise' private
entrepreneur or the paternalistic 'socialist' state – the production of surplus
value becomes the purpose of economic activity.

Every person is a unique, *social*, individual. And socialist development is
the process of fulfilling people's social potentials. But only people *themselves*
know what these potentials might be, and with social experience creative
potentials *change*. Hence, socialist development can only be conceived of as
a *process* of participation in the organization of social and economic life.

This book has detailed the unique revolutionary heritage of the Cuban
development process. With the collapse of the CAME and the Soviet Union,
the island is at another critical juncture in the process of socialist development, where the ideals of the revolution have to be reconciled to the
exigencies of a changed, and increasingly hostile, world economic environ-

ment. There is an 'internal–external' *dialectic*. Choices *can* be made on how Cuban society will be integrated with the world market. The future is *not* determined by forces beyond the control of Cubans. The ethical principles of the revolution can be integrated with emerging progressive forces which are increasingly critical of, and resistant to the destructive, anti-social consequences of a global development directed by the priorities of capital accumulation: the environmental movement; the demand for work within a world which is increasingly unemployed; the reaction against wealth and privilege among impoverishment; the call for effective health care, education provision, adequate housing, etc.

Cuba is the best placed country in the world to *choose* such a development option. The alternative is the immiserizing effect of commodity exchange and market forces.

REFERENCES

AAWH (1997) *The Impact of the US Embargo on Health and Nutrition in Cuba*. American Association for World Health, Washington, DC.

Acosta, J. (1973) 'Cuba, de la neocolonia a la construción del socialismo', *Economía y Desarrollo*, 19.

Agency for International Development (1990) *The Democracy Initiative*. State Department, Washington, DC.

Angel Centeno, M. (1997) 'Cuba's search for alternatives', in Angel Centeno and Font *op. cit.*

Angel Centeno, M. and Font, M. (eds) (1997) *Toward a New Cuba? Legacies of a Revolution*. Rienner, Boulder, CO.

Anoceto, L. (1997) 'An encouraging year', *Granma International*, 8 January.

Antonio Mella, J. (1975) *Documentos y Articulos*. Editorial Ciencias Sociales, Habana.

ASCE (1991) *Cuba in Transition*. Papers and proceedings of the first annual meeting of the Association for the Study of the Cuban Economy, Florida International University, Miami.

Azicri, M. (1980a) 'The institutionalization of the Cuban state', *Journal of International Studies and World Affairs*, 22(3).

Azicri, M. (1980b) 'An introduction to Cuban socialist law', *Review of Socialist Law*, 6(2).

Azicri, M. (1988) *Cuba: Politics, Economics and Society*. Pinter, London.

Banco Nacional de Cuba (1986) *Informe Económico*, March.

Barraclough, S. (1996) *Protecting Cuban Social Programmes during Economic Crisis*. Draft Report, United Nations Research Institute for Social Development, Ottawa.

Bauer, P. (1976) *Dissent on Development*. Weidenfeld and Nicolson, London.

Bell, D. and Kristol, I. (eds) (1981) *The Crisis in Economic Theory*. Basic Books, New York.

Bengelsdorf, C. (1976) 'A large school of government', *Cuba Review*, 6.

Bengelsdorf, C. (1994) *The Problem of Democracy in Cuba*. Oxford University Press, Oxford.

Bengelsdorf, C. (1995) 'Response to Edelstein (1995)', *Latin American Perspectives*, 22(4).

Benjamin, M., Collins, J. and Scott, M. (1994) *No Free Lunch: Food and Revolution in Cuba Today*. Grove Press, New York.

Bergson, A. (1987) 'Comparative productivity in the USSR, Eastern Europe and the West', *American Economic Review*, 77(3).

Bergson, A. (1989) *Planning Performance in Socialist Economies: The USSR and Eastern Europe*. Unwin, London.

Betancourt, R. (1991) 'The New Institutional Economics and the study of the

Cuban economy', in ASCE *op. cit.*

Bettleheim, C. (1975a) 'Forms and methods of socialist planning and the level of development of the productive forces', in Bettleheim 1975b, *op. cit.*

Bettleheim, C. (1975b) *Transition to Socialist Economy.* Harvester, Brighton.

Binns, P. and González, M. (1980), 'Cuba, Castro and socialism', *International Socialism* 2(8).

Bishop, M. (1984) 'In nobody's backyard', a broadcast on 13 April 1979, in Searle, *op. cit.*

Blackburn, R. (1963) 'Prologue to the Cuban revolution', *New Left Review*, 21.

Blanco, J. and Benjamin, M. (1994) *Talking about Revolution.* Ocean Press, Melbourne.

Boggs, C. (1976) *Gramsci's Marxism.* Pluto Press, London.

Booth, D. (ed.) (1994) *Rethinking Social Development.* Longman, London.

Borge, T. (1993) *Face to Face with Fidel Castro.* Ocean Press, Melbourne.

Bratt, R. (ed.) (1986) *Critical Perspectives on Housing.* Temple University Press, Philadelphia.

Braun, D. (1991) *The Rich Get Richer: The Rise of Income Inequality in the United States and the World.* Nelson-Hall, Chicago.

Brenner, P. and Kornbluh, P. (1995) 'Clinton's Cuba calculus', in NACLA *op. cit.*

Brenner, P., LeoGrande, W., Rich, D. and Siegel, D. (eds) (1989) *The Cuba Reader: The Making of a Revolutionary Society.* Grove Press, New York.

Brundenius, C. (1984) *Revolutionary Cuba: The Challenge of Growth with Equity.* Westview Press, Boulder CO.

Brunner, C. (1977) *Cuban Sugar Policy from 1963 to 1970.* Pittsburgh University Press, Pittsburgh.

Brus, W. (1972) *The Market in a Socialist Economy.* Routledge and Kegan Paul, London.

Bulmer-Thomas, V. (ed.) (1996a) *The New Economic Model in Latin America and Its Impact on Income Distribution and Poverty.* Macmillan, London.

Bulmer-Thomas, V. (1996b), 'Introduction', in Bulmer-Thomas, 1996a, *op. cit.*

Calderon, M. R. (1995) 'Life in the Special Period', in NACLA, *op. cit.*

Caldwell, B. (1982) *Beyond Positivism: Economic Methodology in the Twentieth Century.* George Allen and Unwin, London.

Cannon, T. (1981) *Revolutionary Cuba.* Editorial Jose Marti, Habana.

Cardoso, E. and Helwege, A. (1992) *Cuba after Communism.* MIT Press, Cambridge, MA.

Carnota, O. (1974) 'La profesión de administrador', *Economía y Desarrollo*, 23.

Carranza, J. (1995) 'Rethinking the revolution', *NACLA Report on the Americas*, 29(2).

Carranza Valdés, J. (1992) 'Cuba: los retos de la economía', *Cuadernos de Nuestra America*, 9(19).

Carranza Valdés, J., Gutiérrez Urdaneta, L. and Monreal González, P. (1995) *CUBA: la Restructuracion de la Economia*. Editoral de Ciencias Sociales, Habana.

Carriazo Moreno, G. (1995) 'El proceso de transformación económica en Cuba y las pequeños y medianas empresas. El ejemplo de las UBPC', *Economía Cubana: Boletin Informativo*, 23 (September–October).

Carriazo Moreno, G. (n.d.) *Cambios en la Economia Cubana*. CIEM, La Habana.

Carriazo Moreno, G. (1997) *Cambios Estructurales en la Agricultura Cubano: La Cooperativación*, mimeo.

Carrobello, C. (1990) 'What do people think of their power?', *Bohemia*, July.

Casal, L. (1976) 'Cuban Communist Party: the best among the good', *Cuba Review*, 6.

Castañeda, J. (1993) *Utopia Unarmed: The Latin American Left after the Cold War*. Random House, New York.

Castells, M. (1980) *The Economic Crisis and American Society*. Princeton University Press, Princeton, NJ.

Castro, F. (1967) *History Will Absolve Me*. Jonathan Cape, London.

Castro, F. (1969), 'We will never build a communist consciousness with a dollar sign in the minds and hearts of men', in Kenner and Petras *op. cit.*

Castro, F. (1972) *La Revolución Cubana 1953–1962*. Editorial ERA, Mexico City.

Castro, F. (1976) *Balance de la Revolución: discursos en el Primer Congreso*. Ediciones de Cultura Popular, Mexico City.

Castro, F. (1985) *This Must be an Economic War of All the People*. Editorial de Ciencias Sociales, La Habana.

Castro, F. (1986a) 'Let the spirit of militancy be the main thing we get out of this [3rd CRD] congress', *Granma Weekly Review*, 5 October.

Castro, F. (1986b) 'Main report to the 3rd Congress of the Communist Party of Cuba', *Granma International*, 16 February.

Castro, F. (1986c) 'Speech to the 3rd Congress of Committees for the Defense of the Revolution', *Granma International*, 12 October.

Castro, F. (1987a) 'Discurso Pronunciado en la Clausulá de V Congresso de la Unión de Jovenes Comunistas, La Habana 17 de Abril de 1987', *Cuba Socialista*, 17.

Castro, F. (1987b) 'A historic moment: two speeches by Castro', *New International*, 6.

Castro, F. (1989a) *Granma International*, 18 December.

Castro, F. (1989b) *In Defense of Socialism: Four Speeches on the 30th Anniversary of the Revolution*. Pathfinder, New York.

Castro, F. (1991a) 'The only situation in which we would have no future would be if we lost our homeland, the revolution and socialism', in G. Reed 1992, *op. cit.*

Castro, F. (1991b) 'Destiny has turned us into standard bearers', closing speech of the 4th Congress of the Communist Party of Cuba, 14 October 1991, in G. Reed, 1992, *op. cit.*

Castro, F. (1991c) 'Remarks to the 5th Congress of the National System of Agricultural and Forestry Technicans, 1991', in Rosset and Benjamin, 1994a, *op. cit.*

Castro, F. (1991d) *Presente y Futuro de Cuba*, interview for the Mexican magazine *Siempre!* Oficina de Publicaciones de Consejo de Estado, La Habana.

Castro, F. (1992) *Granma International*, 15 November.

Castro, F. (1995) 'Presentation to the National Assembly of People's Power', *Granma International*, 26 December.

Castro, F. (1997), 'Speech to the closing session of the Pedagogy 97 Congress, Havana, 7 February', *Granma International*, 26 February.

Castro, M. (1997) 'Transition and the ideology of exile', in Angel Centeno and Font, *op. cit.*

Castro, R. (1983) 'Three speeches against bureaucracy', in Taber *op. cit.*

Center for Cuban Studies (eds) (1976) *Constitution of the Republic of Cuba.* Center for Cuban Studies, New York.

Centro de Estudios Sobre America (eds) (1993) *The Cuban Revolution in the 1990s.* Westview Press, Boulder, CO.

CEPAL (Comisión Económica para América Latina y el Caribe) (1978) *Apreciaciones sobre el Estilo de Desarrollo y sobre las Principales Políticas Sociales en Cuba.* CEPAL, La Habana.

Chenery, H. and Srinivasan, T. (eds) (1989) *Handbook of Development Economics.* North Holland, Amsterdam.

Chew, S. and Denemark, R. (eds) (1996) *The Underdevelopment of Development.* Sage, London.

Chomsky, N. (1996) *Power and Prospects.* Pluto Press, London.

Clague, C. (ed.) (1992) *Journey towards Market Reform.* Cambridge University Press, Cambridge.

Clague, C. and Rausser, G. (eds) (1992) *The Emergence of Market Economies in Eastern Europe.* Blackwell, Oxford.

Clarke, S. (1994) *Marx's Theory of Crisis.* Macmillan, London.

CNS (1989) *Balance de las tareas para el perfeccionamiento del sistema de dirección de la economía: febrero 1988–enero 1989.* Comisión del SDE, La Habana.

Cole, K. (1993) *The Intellectual Parameters of the Real World*, School of Development Studies Discussion Paper No. 234. University of East Anglia, Norwich.

Cole, K. (1994a) 'Ideologies of sustainable development', in Cole, 1994b, *op. cit.*

Cole, K. (ed.) (1994b) *Sustainable Development for a Democratic South Africa.* Earthscan, London.

Cole, K. (1995) *Understanding Economics*. Pluto Press, London.

Cole, K., Cameron, J. and Edwards, C. (1983) *Why Economists Disagree*. Longman, London (2nd edn 1991).

Cole, K. and Yaxley, I. (1991) *The Dialectics of Socialism*, School of Development Studies Discussion Paper No. 220. University of East Anglia, Norwich.

Contrapunto (1997) 'Cuba: AÑO 39', *Contrapunto*, 8(2).

CRI (eds) (1993) *Transition in Cuba: New Challenges for US Policy*. Cuban Research Institute, Florida International University, Miami.

Dalton, T. (1993) *Everything within the Revolution*. Westview Press, Boulder, CO.

D'Angelo Hernández, O. (1977) 'Algunos aspectos sociales de la gestión de empresas', *Economía y Desarrollo*, 44.

de la Osa, J. (1997) '7.9: in the top 20', *Granma International*, 15 January.

de Velasco, L. (1993) 'Socialismo y mercado', *Papeles de la FIM*, 1.

del Aguila, J. (1994) *Cuba: Dilemmas of a Revolution*. Westview Press, Boulder, CO.

Deere, C. (1992) *Socialism in One Island: Cuba's National Food Programme and its Prospects for Food Security*, Working Paper, Institute of Social Studies, The Hague.

Deere, C. and Meurs, M. (1992) 'Markets, markets everywhere? Understanding the Cuban anomaly', *World Development*, 20(6).

Desai, M. (1982) 'Homilies to a Victorian sage: a review article on Peter Bauer', *Third World Quarterly*, 4(2).

Diaz, A. (1991) 'Presentación del informe sobre el Programa Alimentario', *Granma*, 26 February.

Diesing, P. (1982) *Science and Ideology in the Policy Sciences*. Aldine, New York.

Dilla, H. (1996a), 'Comunidad, participación y socialismo: reinterpretando el dilema cubano', in Dilla 1996c, *op. cit.*

Dilla, H. (1996b) 'Los municipos cubanos y los retos del futuro', in Dilla 1996c, *op. cit.*

Dilla, H. (ed.) (1996c) *La Participación en Cuba y los Retos del Futuro*. Centro de Estudios sobre América, La Habana.

Dilla, H., González, G. and Vincentelli, A. (1993) *Participacion Popular y Desarrollo en los Municipios Cubanos*. Centro de Estudios sobre América, La Habana.

Domínguez, J. (1978) *Cuba, Order and Revolution*. Belknap Press, Cambridge, MA.

Dórticos Torrido, O. (1980) 'Discurso pronunciado en el acto central por el V Anversario de la Constitución de la Republica', *Revista Cubana de Derecho*, 16.

Dragsted, A. (ed.) (1976) *Value: Studies by Marx*. New Park, London.

Dyker, D. (1976) *The Soviet Economy*. Crosby Lockwood Staples, London.

Eckstein, S. (1980) 'Capitalist constraints on Cuban socialist development', *Comparative Politics*, April.

Eckstein, S. (1990) 'The rectification of errors or the errors of the Rectification Process in Cuba', *Cuban Studies*, 20.

Eckstein, S. (1994) *Back from the Future*. Princeton University Press, Princeton, NJ.

Eckstein, S. (1995) 'Response to Edelstein (1995)', *Latin American Perspectives*, 22(4).

Economist (1996) *Heroic Illusions: A Survey of Cuba, Economist*, 6 April, supplement.

Economist (1997) 'Sea food platter, Havana style', *Economist*, 1 March.

Edelstein, J. (1995) 'The future of democracy in Cuba', *Latin American Perspectives*, 22(4).

Editora Politica (1979) *Sobre las Dificultades Objectivos de la Revolución*. Editora Politica, La Habana.

Edwards, S. and Van Wijnbergen, S. (1989) 'Disequilibrium and structural adjustment', in Chenery and Srinivasan, *op. cit.*

EIU (1988) *Cuba Country Report No. 3*. Economist Intelligence Unit, London.

EIU (1991) *Cuba Country Report No. 4*. Economist Intelligence Unit, London.

EIU (1993) *Cuba Country Report No. 5*. Economist Intelligence Unit, London.

Ellman, M. (1971) *Soviet Planning Today*. Cambridge University Press, Cambridge.

Ellman, M. (1989) *Socialist Planning*, 2nd edn. Cambridge University Press, Cambridge.

Engels, F. (1970) *Socialism: Utopian and Scientific*. Progress Publishers, Moscow.

Engels, F. (1977) *Principles of Communism*. Foreign Languages Press, Peking.

Evenson, D. (1994) *Revolution in the Balance: Law and Society in Contemporary Cuba*. Westview Press, Boulder, CO.

Fagen, R. (1972) 'Continuities in Cuban revolutionary politics', *Monthly Review*, 23(11).

Fagen, R. (1989) 'Continuities in Cuban revolutionary politics', in Brenner, LeoGrande, Rich and Siegel, *op. cit.*

Fagen, R., Deere, C. and Coraggio, J. (eds) (1986) *Transition and Development: Problems of Third World Socialism*. Monthly Review Press, New York.

Felipe, E. (1992) 'La ayuda económica de Cuba al Tercer Mundo: evaluación preliminar (1963–1989)', *Boletín de Información Sobre la Economía Cubana*, 1(2).

Fernández, D. (1994) 'Informal politics and the crisis of Cuban socialism', in Schulz, *op. cit.*

Ferreira, F. and Litchfield, J. (1996) 'Inequality and poverty in the lost decade: Brazilian income distribution in the 1980s', in Bulmer-Thomas, 1996a, *op. cit.*

Figueros, M. A. and Vidal, S. P. (1994) 'The Cuban economy in the 1990s: problems and prospects', in Watson, *op. cit.*

Fitzgerald, F. (1989) 'The reform of the Cuban economy, 1976–86', *Journal of Latin American Studies*, 21.

Fitzgerald, F. (1994) *The Cuban Revolution in Crisis*. Monthly Review Press, New York.

Foley, D. (1986) *Understanding Capital*. Harvard University Press, Cambridge, MA.

Foracs, D. (ed.) (1988) *A Gramsci Reader*. Lawrence and Wishart, London.

Fourth Party Congress (1991a) 'Resolution on the country's economic development', in G. Reed, *op. cit.*

Fourth Party Congress (1991b) 'Resolution on foreign policy', in G. Reed, *op. cit.*

Fourth Party Congress (1991c), 'Resolution on improving the organization and functions of People's Power', in G. Reed, *op. cit.*

Fourth Party Congress (1991d), 'Resolution on the programme of the Communist Party of Cuba', in G. Reed, *op. cit.*

Frank, A. (1996) 'The underdevelopment of development', in Chew and Denemark, *op. cit.*

Frank, M. (1993) *Cuba Looks to the Year 2000*. International Publishers, New York.

Franklin, J. (1992) *The Cuban Revolution and the United States: A Chronological History*. Ocean Press, Melbourne.

Freire, P. (1972) *Pedagogy of the Oppresed*. Penguin, Harmondsworth.

Friedman, M. and Friedman, R. (1980) *Free to Choose*. Penguin, Harmondsworth.

Fuller, L. (1987) 'Power at the workplace: the resolution of worker–management conflict in Cuba', *World Development*, 15(1).

Galbraith, J. and Salinger, N. (1981) *Almost Everyone's Guide to Economics*. Penguin, Harmondsworth.

Garcia, J. (1993) 'Cuban economic policy in the process of rectification', in Centro de Estudios Sobre America, *op. cit.*

Gerassi, J. (ed.) (1968) *Venceremos! The Speeches and Writings of Che Guevara*. Simon and Schuster, New York.

Ghai, D. (1986) *Labour and Development in Rural Cuba*. Macmillan, London.

Godley, W. and Cripps, F. (1983) *Macroeconomics*. Fontana, London.

González, A. (1994) 'Necessary adjustments', *Contactos*, June.

Goode, P. (1979) *Karl Korsch*. Macmillan, London.

Green, D. (1995) *Silent Revolution*. Latin America Bureau, London.

Guevara, E. (1960) 'Notas para el estudio de la ideologiá de la revolución Cubana', in Guevara, 1967b, *op. cit.*

Guevara, E. (1967a) *Man and Socialism in Cuba*. Book Institute, Havana.

Guevara, E. (1967b) *Obra Revolucionaria*. Editoral ERA, Mexico City.

Guevara, E. (1996) *Episodes of the Cuban Revolutionary War 1956–58*. Pathfinder Press, New York.

Gunn Clissold, G. (1997) 'Cuban–US relations in the process of transition: possible consequences of covert agendas', in Angel Centeno and Font, *op. cit.*

Hahn, F. (1984) *Equilibrium and Macroeconomics*. MIT Press, Boston.

Halebsky, S. and Kirk, J. (eds) (1985) *Twenty-five Years of Revolution, 1959–84*. Praeger, New York.

Halebsky, S. and Kirk, J. (eds) (1992) *Cuba in Transition: Crisis and Transformation*. Westview Press, Boulder CO.

Hamberg, L. (1986) 'The dynamics of Cuban housing policy' in Bratt, *op. cit.*

Harnecker, M. (1979) *Cuba: Dictatorship or Democracy?* Lawrence Hill, Westport, CT.

Harris, N. (1983) *Of Bread and Guns*. Penguin, Harmondsworth.

Harriss, J., Hunter, J. and Lewis, C. (eds) (1995) *The New Institutional Economics and Third World Development*. Routledge, London.

Hart, R. (1984) 'Introduction', in Searle, *op. cit.*

Harvey, D. (1982) *The Limits to Capital*. Blackwell, Oxford.

Heilbroner, R. and Milberg, W. (1995) *The Crisis of Vision in Modern Economic Thought*. Cambridge University Press, Cambridge.

Heredia, F. (1993) 'Cuban socialism: prospects and challenges', in Centro de Estudios Sobre America, *op. cit.*

Hernández Hernández, J. and Nikolenkov, V. (1985) 'El mechanismo económico del socialismo', *Economía y Desarrollo*, 68.

Hodges, D. (1977) *The Legacy of Che Guevara: A Documentary Study*. Thames and Hudson, London.

Hope, A. and Timmel, S. (1995) *Training for Transformation*. Mambo Press, Gweru, Zimbabwe.

Horowitz, I. (ed.) (1981) *Cuban Communism*, 4th edn. Transaction Books, New Brunswick, NJ.

Hunt, D. (1989) *Economic Theories of Development*. Harvester/Wheatsheaf, London.

IADB (1993) *Socio-economic Reform in Latin America: The Social Agenda Study*. InterAmerican Development Bank, Washington, DC.

Izquierdo, I. (1996) 'REANIMAR el espiritu de la gente', *Granma*, 21 October.

Jeffries, I. (ed.) (1992) *Industrial Reform in Socialist Countries*. Elgar, London.

Jeffries, I. (1996) *A Guide to the Economies in Transition*. Routledge, London.

Jevons, W. (1970) *The Theory of Political Economy*. Penguin, Harmondsworth.

JUCEPLAN (1981) *El Sistema de Direccion y Planificacion de la Economía en las Empresas*. Editorial de Ciencias Sociales, La Habana.

JUCEPLAN (1988) *Decisiones Adoptados Sobre Algunas Elementos del Sistema de Dirección de la Economía*. JUCEPLAN, La Habana.

JUCEPLAN (eds) (1992) *Decisiones Adoptados Sobre Algunos Elementos del Sistema de Dirección de la Economía*. JUCEPLAN, La Habana.

Karol, K. (1970) *Guerillas in Power*. Hill and Wang, New York.

Kennedy, R. (1969) *13 Days: The Cuban Missile Crisis, October 1962*. Pan, London.

Kenner, M. and Petras, J. (eds) (1969) *Fidel Castro Speaks*. Grove Press, New York.

Keynes, J. (1936) *The General Theory of Employment, Interest and Money*. Macmillan, London.

Kim, I. J. and Zacek, J. S. (eds) (1991) *Reform and Transformation in Communist Systems*. Paragon House, New York.

Kuhn, T. (1970) *The Structure of Scientific Revolutions*. University of Chicago Press, Chicago.

Lage, C. (1996) 'The effects of the results of the first half of the year are directed mainly towards the solution of the economy's fundamental problems', *Granma International*, 7 August.

Lal, D. (1983) *The Poverty of Development Economics*. Institute of Economic Affairs, London.

Lambie, G. (1997) *Cuban Local Government: Democracy through Participation or Political Control?* ECPR Conference Workshop, 'Explaining the Character of New Democracies in Latin America', Bern, Switzerland, 27 February to 4 March.

Lambie, G. and Hennessey, A. (eds) (1993) *The Fractured Blockade*. Macmillan, London.

Lancaster, K. (1974) *Introduction to Modern Microeconomics*. Rand McNally, Chicago.

Lane, D. (1996) *The Rise and Fall of State Socialism*. Polity Press, Cambridge.

Lappé, F. and Collins, J. (1977) *Food First: The Myth of Scarcity*. Souvenir Press, London.

Lappé, F. and Du Bois, P. (1994) *The Quickening of America: Rebuilding Our Nation, Remaking Our Lives*. Jossey-Bass, San Francisco.

Lavastida, O. (1997) 'Renewed taxpayers awareness', *Granma International*, 7 May.

Layard, R. and Parker, J. (1996a) 'Whatever the political crisis, economic growth will be fast', *Observer* 29 December.

Layard, R. and Parker, J. (1996b) *The Coming Russian Boom*. Simon and Schuster, London.

Lee, S. (1997) 'We have initiated economic reforms within socialism', *Granma International*, 19 March.

Leiner, M. (1989) 'Cuba's schools: 25 years later', in Brenner, LeoGrande, Rich and Siegel, *op. cit.*

Lenin, V. (1963) *Collected Works Vol. 1*. Progress Publishers, Moscow.

Lenin, V. (1969) *The State and Revolution*. Progress Publishers, Moscow.

Lensink, R. (1996) *Structural Adjustment in Sub-Saharan Africa*. Longman, London.

LeoGrande, W. (1980) 'The Communist Party of Cuba since the First

Congress, Part 2', *Journal of Latin American Studies*, 12(2).

LeoGrande, W. (1989) 'Mass political participation in socialist Cuba', in Brenner, LeoGrande, Rich and Siegel, *op. cit.*

León, F. (1997) 'Socialism and *socialismo*: social actors and economic change', in Angel Centeno and Font, *op. cit.*

Levins, R. (1991) *The Struggle for Ecological Agriculture in Cuba*. Red Balloon Collective, Boston.

Levins, R. and Lewontin, R. (1985) *The Dialectical Biologist*. Harvard University Press, Cambridge, MA.

Lewontin, R. (1982) *Human Diversity*. Scientific American, New York.

Lewontin, R. and Levins, R. (1997) 'Eppúr si muove – chance and necessity', *Capitalism, Nature, Socialism*, 8(1).

Liss, S. (1994) *Fidel! Castro's Political and Social Thought*. Westview Press, Boulder, CO.

Long, N. and Long, A. (eds) (1992) *Battlefields of Knowledge*. Routledge, London.

Lowy, M. (1986) 'Mass organization, party, and state: democracy in the transition to socialism', in Fagen, Deere and Coraggio, *op. cit.*

Lutyens, S. (1992) 'Democracy and socialist Cuba', in Halebsky and Kirk, *op. cit.*

MacDonald, T. (1995) *Hippocrates in Havana*. Bolivar Books, Mexicao City.

MacEwan, A. (1981) *Revolution and Economic Development in Cuba*. St Martin's Press, New York.

McFadyen, D. (1995) 'The Social Repercussions of the Crisis', in NACLA, *op. cit.*

MacGaffey, W. and Barnett, C. (1965) *Twentieth-century Cuba: The Background of the Cuban Revolution*. Doubleday Anchor, New York.

McNally, D. (1993) *Against the Market*. Verso, London.

Madan, N., Zabala, B., Gort, A., Aguierrechu, I. and Águila, A. (1993) *Extraordinary Circumstances Bring People Together*. Editora Política, La Habana.

Magee, B. (1975) *Popper*. Fontana/Collins, London.

Mandel, E. (1975) *Late Capitalism*. Verso, London.

Mandel, E. (1978) *The Second Slump*. Verso, London.

Mandel, E. (1980) *Long Waves of Capitalist Development: The Marxist Interpretation*. Cambridge University Press, Cambridge.

Marx, K. (1936) *The Poverty of Philosophy*. Lawrence and Wishart, London.

Marx, K. (1950) *Marx and Engels Selected Works* (18th Brumaire). Lawrence and Wishart, London.

Marx, K. (1970) *Critique of Hegel's 'Philosophy of Right'*. Cambridge University Press, Cambridge.

Marx, K. (1972a) *Capital Vol, III*. Lawrence and Wishart, London.

Marx, K. (1972b) *Critique of the Gotha Programme*. Foreign Languages Press, Peking.

Marx, K. (1973a) *Grundrisse*. Penguin, Harmondsworth.

Marx, K. (1973b) *The Economic and Philosophic Manuscripts of 1844*. Lawrence and Wishart, London.

Marx, K. (1974) *Capital Vol. I*. Lawrence and Wishart, London.

Marx, K. (1975) *Wages, Price and Profit*. Foreign Languages Press, Peking.

Marx, K. (1976) *A Contribution to the Critique of Political Economy*. Lawrence and Wishart, London.

Mathéy, K. (1989) 'Recent trends in housing policies in Cuba and the revival of the microbrigade movement', *Bulletin of Latin American Research*, 8.

Medin, T. (1990) *Cuba: The Shaping of Revolutionary Consciousness*. Rienner, Boulder, CO.

Mesa-Lago, C. (1981a) *The Economy of Socialist Cuba*. University of New Mexico Press, Alburquerque.

Mesa-Lago, C. (1981b), 'Economics: realism and rationality', in Horowitz, *op. cit.*

Mesa-Lago, C. (1989) 'Cuba's economic counter-reforms (Rectification): causes, policies and effects', *Journal of Communist Studies*, 5(4).

Mesa-Lago, C. (1993a) 'Introduction: Cuba the last communist warrior', in Mesa-Lago, 1993c, *op. cit.*

Mesa-Lago, C. (1993b) 'Cuban economic strategies for confronting the crisis', in Mesa-Lago, 1993c, *op. cit.*

Mesa-Lago, C. (ed.) (1993c) *Cuba: After the Cold War*. University of Pittsburgh Press, Pittsburgh.

Midgely, M. (1978) *Beast and Man*. Harvester, Brighton.

Ministerio de Azúcar (1993) *Documentos Sobre la Creación y Funcionamiento de las Unidades Básicas de Producción Cooperativa*. Dirección Jurídica, Minsterio de Azúcar, La Habana.

Ministry for Foreign Relations (1991) *Efectos del bloqueo economíco sobre el desarrollo economíco y social y en el desfrute de los derechos del pueblo cubano*. Ministry for Foreign Relations, La Habana.

Moggridge, D. (1976) *Keynes*. Fontana/Collins, London.

Molina, G. (1996) 'It was the US government that refused to receive compensation', *Granma International*, 10 July.

Monreal, P. and Rúa, M. (1994) 'Aperatura y Reforma de la Economía Cubana: las transformaciónes institucionales (1990–1993)', *Cuadernos de Nuestra America*, 11(21).

Montaner, C. A. (1985) *Cuba, Castro and the Caribbean*. Transaction Books, New Brunswick, NJ.

Moore, M. (1997) *Downsize This!* Boxtree, London.

Moses, J. (1996) *Financial Strategies and Consequences for Cuba as It Engages in the World Market*. Unpublished mimeo.

Mueller, D. (1991) *Choosing a Constitution in Eastern Europe: Lessons from Public Choice*. Mimeo, University of Maryland.

Muñiz, M. (ed.) (1993) *Elecciones en Cuba*. Ocean Press, Melbourne.

NACLA (1995) *Cuba: Adapting to a Post-Soviet World*. NACLA Report on the Americas, Berkeley, CA.

Nelson, L. (1950) *Rural Cuba*. University of Minnesota Press, Minneapolis.

North, D. (1990) *Institutions, Institutional Change and Economic Performance*. Cambridge University Press, Cambridge.

North, D. (1995) 'The New Institutional Economics and Third World development', in Harriss, Hunter and Lewis, *op. cit.*

Nove, A. (1977) *The Soviet Economic System*. George Allen and Unwin, London

Nove, A. (1983) *The Economics of Feasible Socialism*. Allen and Unwin, London.

Nove, A. (1988) 'Socialism, capitalism and the Soviet experience', *Social Philosophy and Policy*, 6(2).

O'Connor, J. (1984) *Accumulation Crisis*. Blackwell, Oxford.

O'Connor, J. (1987) *The Meaning of Crisis*. Blackwell, Oxford.

O'Shaughnessy, H. (1984) *Grenada: Revolution, Invasion and Aftermath*. Sphere Books, London.

Ollman, B. (1993) *Dialectical Investigations*. Routledge, London.

Padula, A. (1974) 'The fall of the bourgeoisie in Cuba, 1959–1961', unpublished PhD thesis, University of New Mexico.

Pastor, M. Jr (1992) *External Shocks and Adjustment in Contemporary Cuba*, Working Paper. The International & Public Affairs Centre, Occidental College, Los Angeles.

Pastor, M. and Zimbalist, A. (1995) 'Waiting for change: adjustment and reform in Cuba', *World Development*, 23(5).

Pérez, L. (1982) *Cuba: Between Reform and Revolution*. Oxford University Press, Oxford.

Pérez-López, J. (1986) 'The Cuban economy in the 1980s', *Problems of Communism*, 35(5).

Pérez-López, J. (1992) 'Learning from others: economic reform experiences in Eastern Europe, Latin America and China', *Journal of Inter-American Studies and World Affairs*, 34.

Pérez-López, J. (1994a) 'Islands of capitalism in an ocean of socialism', in Pérez-López, 1994b, *op. cit.*

Pérez-López, J. (1994a) *Cuba at a Crossroads*. University Press of Florida, Gainesville.

Pérez-López, J. (1995) *Cuba's Second Economy*. Transaction Publishers, New Brunswick, NJ.

Pérez-López, J. (1997) 'Cuba's second economy and the market transition', in Angel Centeno and Font, *op. cit.*

Pérez-Rojas, N. and Torres Vila, C. (1996) 'UBPC: hacia un nuevo proyecto de participación', in Dilla, 1996c, *op. cit.*

Pérez-Stable, M. (1985) 'Class, organisation and conciencia: the Cuban working class after 1970', in Halebsky and Kirk, *op. cit.*

Pérez-Stable, M. (1993) 'Legislative and electoral dynamics: reforms and options', in CRI, *op. cit.*

Pérez-Stable, M. (1997) 'The invisible crisis: the exhaustion of politics in 1990s Cuba', in Angel Centeno and Font, *op. cit.*

Pérez Villanueva, O. and Marquetti Nodarse, H. (1995) 'La Economía Cubana: actualidad y tendencias', *Economía y Desarrollo*, 1.

Petras, J. and Morley, M. (1992) *Latin America in the Time of Cholera.* Routledge, London.

Pierson, C. (1995) *Socialism after Communism.* Polity Press, Cambridge.

Pilger, J. (1992) *Distant Voices.* Vintage, London.

Planas, J. (1994) 'Political changes and social attitudes in Cuba during the Special Period: implications', in Schulz, *op. cit.*

Politburo of the Central Committee (1991) *Este es el Congreso Más Democrático: resoluciones, principles interventiones y relación de miembros del Buró Político y del Comité Central.* Editora Politica, La Habana.

Pollitt, B. (1997) 'The Cuban sugar economy: collapse, reform and prospects for recovery', *Journal of Latin American Studies*, 29.

Popper, K. (1959) *The Logic of Scientific Inquiry.* Hutchinson, London.

Popper, K. (1962) *The Open Society and its Enemies Vol. 2.* Routledge, London.

Prebisch, R. (1962) 'The economic development of Latin America and its principal problems', *Economic Bulletin of Latin America*, 7(1).

Preston, P. (1996) *Development Theory.* Blackwell, Oxford.

Primer Congreso del Partido Communista de Cuba (1979) *Tesis y Resoluciones.* Editorial de Ciencias Sociales, Havana.

Reed, D. (1992) *Structural Adjustment and the Environment.* Earthscan, London.

Reed, G. (1992) *Island in the Storm.* Ocean Press, Melbourne.

Research Team on the Cuban Economy (1984) *The Most Outstanding Aspects of the Cuban Economy, 1959–83.* University of Havana Economic Sciences Area, Havana.

Ricardo, R. (1994) *Guantánamo: The Bay of Discord.* Ocean Press, Melbourne.

Riós, N. (1993) 'El sistema electoral: ¿farsa o revolución?', in Muñiz, *op. cit.*

Ritter, A. (1990) 'The Cuban economy in the 1990s: external challenges and policy imperatives', *Journal of Inter-American Studies and World Affairs*, 32(3).

Ritter, A. (1992) 'Cuba's socialist economy at thirty: assessments and prospects', in Halebsky and Kirk, *op. cit.*

Ritter, A. (1994) 'Cuban economic strategy and alternative futures', in Pérez-López, 1994b, *op. cit.*

Ritter, A. (1995) 'The dual currency bifurcation of Cuba's economy in the 1990s: causes, consequences and cures', *CEPAL Review*, 57.

Ritter, A. (1997) 'The Cuban economy in the mid-1990s: structural/monetary pathology and public policy', in Angel Centeno and Font, *op. cit.*

Robbins, L. (1984) *An Essay on the Nature and Significance of Economic Science*. Macmillan, London.

Robinson, W. (1996) *Promoting Polyarchy: Globalization, US Intervention and Hegemony*. Cambridge University Press, Cambridge.

Rodríguez, E. (1997) 'New directions for investment', *Granma International*, 26 March.

Rodríguez, J. (1988) 'Cubanology and the provision of basic needs in the Cuban revolution', in Zimbalist, 1988b, *op. cit.*

Rodríguez, J. (1990a) 'Aspectos economícos del processo de rectificación', *Cuba Socialista*, 44.

Rodríguez, J. (1990b) *Estrategia del Desarrollo Económico en Cuba*. Editorial de Ciencias Sociales, La Habana.

Rodríguez, J. (1997) 'Report on 1996 economic results and 1997 economic and social plan, presented to the National Assembly', *Granma International*, 8 January.

Rodríguez, R. (1995) *Ley del Sistema Tributario en Cuba*. Consultaría Jurídica International, Madrid.

Romano, R. and Leiman, M. (1970) *Views on Capitalism*. Glencoe Press, Beverley Hills, CA.

Rose, S. (1984) 'The limits to science', in Rose and Appignanesi, *op. cit.*

Rose, S. and Appignanesi, (eds) (1984) *Science and Beyond*. Blackwell, Oxford.

Rose, S., Kamin, B. and Lewontin, R. (1984) *Not in Our Genes*. Penguin, Harmondsworth.

Rosset, P. and Benjamin, M. (1994a) *The Greening of the Revolution*. Ocean Press, Melbourne.

Rosset, P. and Benjamin, M. (1994b) 'Cuba's nationwide conversion to organic agriculture', *Capitalism, Nature, Socialism*, 5(3).

Rostow, W. (1960) *The Stages of Growth*. Cambridge University Press, Cambridge.

Schulz, D. (ed.) (1994) *Cuba and the Future*. Greenwood Press, Westport, CT.

Schurrman, F. (1993) *Beyond the Impasse: New Directions in Development Theory*. Zed Press, London.

Scott, C. (1996) 'The distributive impact of the new economic model in Chile', in Bulmer-Thomas, 1996a, *op. cit.*

Searle, C. (ed.) (1984) *In Nobody's Backyard: Maurice Bishop's Speeches, 1979–1983*. Zed Books, London.

Seers, D. (1983) *The Political Economy of Nationalism*. Oxford University Press, Oxford.

Shonfield, A. (1965) *Modern Capitalism: The Changing Balance of Public and Private Power*. Oxford University Press, Oxford.

Sigmund, P. (1980) *Multinationals in Latin America: The Politics of Nationalism*. University of Wisconsin Press, Madison.

Silverman, B. (ed.) (1971) *Man and Socialism in Cuba: The Great Debate*. Atheneum, New York.

Smith, C. (1996) *Marx at the Millennium.* Pluto Press, London.

Smith, W. and Zimbalist, A. (1991) 'Reform in Cuba', in Kin and Zacek, *op. cit.*

So, A. (1990) *Social Change and Development.* Sage, London.

Steele, J. (1996a) *Eternal Russia.* Faber, London.

Steele, J. (1996b), 'Russia boom or bust', *Observer*, 29 December.

Stewart, F. (1994) 'Are adjustment policies in Africa consistent with long-run development needs?', in Van Der Geest, *op. cit.*

Stiglitz, J. (1992) 'The design of financial systems for the newly emerging democracies of Eastern Europe', in Clague and Rausser, *op. cit.*

Stiglitz, J. (1993) *Economics.* Norton, New York.

Taber, M. (ed.) (1983) *Fidel Castro's Speeches, Vol. 2: Our Power Is That of the Working People.* Pathfinder Press, New York.

Taber, M. (ed.) (1985) *Fidel Castro Speeches 1984–5: War and Crises in the Americas.* Pathfinder Press, New York.

Tanzi, V. (1993) *Transition to Market: Studies in Fiscal Reform.* International Monetary Fund, Washington, DC.

Therborn, G. (1986) *Why Some People are More Unemployed Than Others.* Verso, London.

Thomas, J. (1996) 'The New Economic Model and labour markets in Latin America', in Bulmer-Thomas, 1996a, *op. cit.*

Thomas, S. (1992) 'Political economy of privatisation: Poland, Hungary and Czechoslovakia', in Clague, *op. cit.*

Tijerina, D. (1995) 'The meaning of Cuba: four personal reflections', *NACLA Report of the Americas*, 29(2).

United Nations (1972) *Economic Survey of Europe in 1971, Part 1: The European Economy from the 1950s to the 1970s.* United Nations, New York.

UNDP (1994) *Human Development Report 1994.* Oxford University Press, Oxford.

Valdéz Gutierrez, G. (1996) *Referentes Conflictuales de la Reforma Cubana.* Mimeo.

Valencia Almeida, M. (1997) 'Seeing angels after the 4th attempt', *Granma International*, 1 January.

Van Der Geest, E. (ed.) (1994) *Negotiating Structural Adjustment in Africa.* James Currey/ Heinemann, London.

Vanhanen, T. (1997) *Prospects of Democracy.* Routledge, London.

Waller, J. (1993) *Cuba: Health of a Nation.* Cuba Solidarity Campaign, London.

Watson, H. (ed.) (1994) *The Caribbean in the Global Political Economy.* Lyn Reiner, Boulder, CO.

Weeks, J. (1981) *Capital and Exploitation.* Arnold, London.

Weeks, J. (1996) 'The manufacturing sector in Latin America and the New International Economic Model', in Bulmer-Thomas, 1996a, *op. cit.*

White, G. (1986) *Cuban Planning in the Mid-1980s: Centralization, Decentralization and Participation.* Mimeo, Development Studies Association Conference Paper.

Wisner, B. (1988) *Power and Need in Africa.* Earthscan, London.

World Bank (1992) *Governance and Development.* World Bank, Washington, DC.

World Bank (1996a) *Poverty Reduction and the World Bank.* World Bank, Washington, DC.

World Bank (1996b) *1996 World Development Report: From Plan to Market.* Oxford University Press, Oxford.

Zeitlin, M. (1970) 'Inside Cuba: workers and revolution', *Ramparts*, March.

Zimbalist, A. (1988a) 'Cuban political economy and cubanology', in Zimbalist, 1988b, *op. cit.*

Zimbalist, A. (ed.) (1988b) *Cuban Political Economy: Controversies in Cubanology.* Westview Press, Boulder, CO.

Zimbalist, A. (1992a) 'Teetering on the brink: Cuba's post-CMEA economic and political crisis', *Journal of Latin American Studies*, 24.

Zimbalist, A. (1992b) 'Industrial reform and the Cuban economy', in Jeffries, *op. cit.*

Zimbalist, A. (1993) 'Perspectives on Cuban development and prospects for the 1990s', in Lambie and Hennessey, *op. cit.*

Zimbalist, A. (1994) 'Treading water: Cuba's economic and political crisis', in Schulz, *op. cit.*

Zimbalist, A. (1996) *The Cuban Economy in the Era of Helms–Burton.* Conference Paper, CIP/IRELA Conference, Barcelona, July.

Zimbalist, A. and Brundenius, C. (1989) *The Cuban Economy: Measurement and Analysis of Economic Performance.* Johns Hopkins University Press, Baltimore, MD.

INDEX